Massimo So
Walter G. Scott
Christel Nussbaumer

# MARKE**THINK**™

How the best brains, entrepreneurs,
and marketing managers have invented new markets,
like Steve Jobs and Nicolas Hayek.

Foreword by
**Philip Kotler
Edward de Bono
Seth Godin**

Copyright © 2015 Creattività srl, Massimo Soriani Bellavista

*All rights reserved. No part of this book may be reproduced or transmitted in any form or by any means without written permission from the author.*

ISBN: 1500714453
ISBN 13: 9781500714451

Markethink™, Meethink™ and Ideabase™ are Trade Mark owned by Creattività srl.

Graphic design by Studio 361° - Brescia - Italy

Cover design by Davide Agostoni

Printed by CreateSpace, an Amazon.com Company

*In memory of Nicolas Hayek, the Swatch founder*
*A great entrepreneur, an incredible marketer,*
*a true visionary, a legend*

*"If I have seen further,*
*it is because I have stood*
*on the shoulders of giants."*
*Isaac Newton*

*A special dedication to four giants and creative minds*
*of worldwide management thinking:*
*Edward de Bono, Philip Kotler, Seth Godin, Fernando Trias de Bes*

# MARKETHINK — TABLE OF CONTENT

Acknowledgments ........................................................................... 9

Forewords by P. Kotler, E. de Bono, S. Godin ............................. 14

Introduction: why Markethink™? The market has changed ......... 17

## Chapter 1
## Markethink Metamodel and Markethinkers .......................... 25
1.1 MarkeThink™: not a new model but a Metamodel ............ 25
    1.1.1 Why a Metamodel? ....................................................... 26
    1.1.2 Marketing Models and authors ..................................... 27

## Chapter 2
## Marketing Models and Authors Back to the basic ................ 31
2.1 Marketing Defined ............................................................. 31
2.2 Marketing Management Models ........................................ 34
2.3 Marketing Management Process ....................................... 36
    2.3.1 Research ........................................................................ 37
    2.3.2 STP: Segmentation, Targeting, and Positioning .......... 45
    2.3.3 Marketing Mix ............................................................... 52
    2.3.4 Implementation and Control ........................................ 60
2.4 Product versus Service Marketing ..................................... 66
    2.4.3 One-to-One and Direct Marketing ............................... 73
    2.4.4 Scientific Marketing and Data Mining ......................... 75
    2.4.5 Channel Distribution and Trade Marketing ................. 77
    2.4.6 Marketing Myopia ......................................................... 79
    2.4.7 Holistic Marketing ......................................................... 83

## Chapter 3
## Markethinkers and Marketing Models: New trend ................ 87
3.1 Innovative Marketing Model .............................................. 87
3.2 Philip Kotler's New Marketing Models .............................. 88
    3.2.1 "Lateral Marketing" with Fernando Trias de Bes ........ 88
    3.2.2 "Chaotics Marketing" with John A. Caslione ............ 106

| | | |
|---|---|---|
| | 3.2.3 "Marketing 3.0" with Hermawan Kartajaya and Iwan Setiawan | 108 |
| | 3.2.4 Winning at Innovation: The A-to-F Model with Fernando Trias de Bes | 111 |
| 3.3 | Seth Godin | 116 |
| | 3.3.1 Permission Marketing | 119 |
| | 3.3.2 "Ideavirus" | 122 |
| 3.4 | Purple Cow | 126 |
| 3.5 | Guerrilla Marketing by Jay Conrad Levinson | 130 |
| 3.6 | Experiential Marketing | 133 |
| 3.7 | Green Marketing | 136 |
| 3.8 | "Buyology" by Martin Lindstrom | 139 |
| 3.9 | "Lovemarks" by Kevin Roberts | 142 |
| | 3.9.1 The Lovemarks graph | 143 |
| | 3.9.2 The Lovemarks Trinity | 144 |
| | 3.9.3 The Tool | 146 |
| | 3.9.4 "Lovemarks by the Numbers" | 146 |
| 3.10 | Sustainable Marketing by Walter G. Scott | 147 |
| | 3.10.1 The Meaning of Sustainable Development | 149 |
| | 3.10.2 The Role of Businesses in Sustainable Development | 151 |
| | 3.10.3 A Model for Sustainable Marketing | 153 |
| 3.11 | Disruption by Jean Marie Dru | 156 |
| | 3.11.1 The Disruptive Process | 156 |
| | 3.11.2 The "Disruption World Bank" | 157 |
| 3.12 | A little about Digital Marketing | 158 |
| | 3.12.1 Web Marketing and Digital Marketing | 159 |
| | 3.12.2 That Future! The best minds of the past twenty years | 161 |
| | 3.12.3 Changing paradigms: Social Marketing | 164 |
| | 3.12.4 What kind of Marketing will we use? | 168 |

## Chapter 4
## Creativity and Innovation Thinking Models ... 173

| | | |
|---|---|---|
| 4.1 | Innovation in Management | 173 |
| | 4.1.1 Joseph Schumpeter - Entrepreneurs and "Creative Destruction" | 174 |

    4.1.2   Peter Drucker - Management Theory and Practice ...................... 176
    4.1.3   Management Innovation by Gary Hamel ............................................ 178

## Chapter 5
## Creativity Models and MarkeThinkers .................................................. 183
5.1  Creativity Management .................................................................................. 183
    5.1.1   Approaches to the Creativity Process .......................................... 184
    5.1.2   Some Creativity Techniques ............................................................. 185
    5.1.3   Creativity Umbrella and Definition ................................................. 186
5.2  "TRIZ" by Genrich Altshuller ........................................................................ 187
    5.2.1   The TRIZ Problem Solving Method ................................................. 188
    5.2.3   The Inventive Process Based on TRIZ ........................................... 190
5.3  "Creativity Templates" by David Mazursky and Jacob Goldenberg ......... 193
    5.3.1   The Templates ........................................................................................ 193
    5.3.2   The Forecasting Matrix ..................................................................... 195
5.4  Edward de Bono The Guru of Creativity: Past, Present, and Future ...... 195
    5.4.1   About Dr. Edward de Bono ................................................................. 195
    5.4.2   Power of Perception ........................................................................... 196
    5.4.3   "Parallel Thinking" and the "Six Thinking Hats" ........................ 198
    5.4.4   Lateral Thinking ................................................................................... 200
    5.4.5   "Sur/petition" ........................................................................................ 202
5.6  Palo Alto School: From Palo Alto to Arezzo ............................................. 204
    5.6.1   Strategic Therapy Model ................................................................... 205
    5.6.2   CTS Arezzo: therapy as research, research as therapy ............. 208
    5.6.3   Introduction to Stratagems:
            Strategic Therapy Advanced techniques ..................................... 209
5.7  "CreActivity" by Massimo Soriani Bellavista ........................................... 210
    5.7.1   CreActivity ............................................................................................ 210

## Chapter 6
## MarkeThinking Styles .......................................................................................... 215
6.1  The Seven (Plus Three) Brains-Pearls of a MarkeThinker:
     10 CommandMents ........................................................................................... 215
6.2  First Commandment - Motivation: "Stay Hungry" ................................... 223

# TABLE OF CONTENT — MARKETHINK

    6.2.2    Second Commandment - Learning ................................................ 224
    6.2.3.   Third Commandment - Communication ....................................... 227
    6.2.4    Fourth Commandment - Creativity ................................................ 229
    6.2.5    Fifth Commandment - Organization .............................................. 233
    6.2.6    Sixth Commandment - Data Analysis and Evaluation ................ 234
    6.2.7    Seventh Commandment – Risk Assessment ............................... 235
    6.2.8    Eighth and Ninth CommandMents -
             Value and Opportunity Evaluation ................................................ 240
    6.2.9    Tenth Commandment - Practical Thinking: ThinkACT ............... 246

## Chapter 7
## MarkeThink as a Process ............................................................................. 251

7.1    MarkeThink as a Process ..................................................................... 251
    7.1.1    The Endless Cycle of MarkeThink ................................................. 251
    7.1.2    State of Mind .................................................................................... 253
    7.1.3    Challenging Oneself ........................................................................ 253
7.2    Think: The Process ............................................................................... 254
    7.2.1    Focus .................................................................................................. 255
    7.2.2    The Lateral Thinking Point of View ............................................... 257
    7.2.3    The MarkeThink Point of View ...................................................... 258
    7.2.4    The Criteria ...................................................................................... 259
    7.2.5    Idea Generation .............................................................................. 260
    7.2.6    Harvesting ........................................................................................ 263
    7.2.7    The "Idea Brokering" Concept ...................................................... 264
    7.2.8    Collecting Ideas ............................................................................... 265
    7.2.9    Evaluation and Selection ................................................................ 268
7.3    Marketing: The Implementation ....................................................... 273
    7.3.1    Feasibility and Prototype ............................................................... 274
    7.3.2    Prototyping ...................................................................................... 280
    7.3.3    Internal Sales ................................................................................... 281
    7.3.4    Become a Lidear ............................................................................. 282
    7.3.5    Sales and Marketing ....................................................................... 283
    7.3.6    Churn ................................................................................................ 286

## Chapter 8
## MarkeThink Tools ........................................................................... 291

8.1 The MarkeThink Tools and the Ideabase ................................... 291

    8.1.1 MarkeThink Tools ............................................................ 291

8.2 Learning from the best MarkeThinkers ...................................... 292

    8.2.1 Tools to enhance your thinking styles -
           The Ten CommandMents ................................................ 295

    8.2.2 Thinking Style Preference Test ...................................... 298

    8.2.3 Meethink: The Tools for Successful and Efficient Meetings ..... 299

    8.2.4 The Ideabase: A MarkeThink Tool ................................. 305

    8.2.5 Benchmarking, "BenchMarkeThink," and the Ideabase ........ 305

8.3 Applications .................................................................................. 311

## Bibliography .................................................................................. 314

# Acknowledgments

I would like to start by thanking Philip Kotler for being a true source of inspiration and for his amazing life's work; it has been a great honor to have had the opportunity, in the past forty years, of taking care of and editing the Italian versions of his books. I would like to thank fellow academics, authors, and professionals who, with their works, have impacted on my life and allowed me a lifetime of success.

A special thanks, of course, goes to the Università Cattolica del Sacro Cuore of Milan, to all its members, and my dear former colleagues. A note of gratitude also goes to all my students; being able to share my passion and knowledge with them, has been extremely fulfilling.

Above all, I thank my wife, for always supporting and stimulating me during this wonderful life spent with her. Thank you to my daughters and nephews; I dedicate this book to them, hoping that their future can be creative and full of accomplishments. But the most important thanks go to my wife, who has inspired me and given me the most beautiful project of my life: my family.

**Professor Walter G. Scott**


My gratitude goes to all the people involved in the project during these many years of work. At this point of a synthesis I might forget to mention important people, to whom I apologize in advance. I will proceed in a "widdig way", hoping to recall the most significant.

First of all, I will start by thanking the "giants" of thought with whom I worked: Professor Edward de Bono, who, supported the project since its inception. I have been collaborating with him since 1996, and I have truly learned many things from him, not only from the things he taught me, but even more by the example he set in the way he put what he taught into practice. My gratitude for him is total. An important thanks and recognition goes to Professor P. Kotler and Professor F. Trias de Bes. In fact, this book comes from a project that we started in 2008, called Lateral Thinking for Marketing and Sales, of which I was the project leader. The project's goal was to integrate the interesting innovations created by Professor Kotler and Professor Fernando Trias de Bes in their book, *Lateral Marketing*, with the advanced methods of lateral thinking and the development of the thought developed by Professor de Bono; the project lasted ten months. During this period, various models were integrated, leading to interesting solutions. The history of innovations is not always linear; on the contrary, sometimes it's lateral. The three great masters had no interest in continuing the project "Lateral Thinking for Marketing and Sales" together, so following their advice, I continued the project alone, changing the name of the project to "MarkeThink." Therefore, I involved and integrated other authors of marketing such as Seth Godin and other authors of creativity and creative thinking like Genrich Altshuller with the TRIZ method; the psychologist of economy and Nobel laureate Daniel Kahneman, with the heuristics of thought; and the contributions about the strategic thinking of my friend Giorgio Nardone, who is defined as the most creative continuer of the thought of Professor Paul Watzlawick. In the second phase of the project, I had the luck to meet my two wonderful coauthors: Professor Walter G. Scott, one of the most important professors of marketing in Italy, and Christel Cavalli Nussbaumer, expert in marketing and communication.

A special thanks goes to Seth Godin; I was lucky enough to meet him in New York during a seminar about the world of start-ups in 2012 and to interview him to insert his insight in this book. Seth Godin is definitely a great creative thinker and a rare example of a "MarkeThinker," rare because he has achieved success in different fields: as marketing manager in the first part of his career; as an entrepreneur when he created and sold his company to Yahoo and now with the creation of Squidoo; and as an author of best-selling books that sold millions of copies; and opening the most watched marketing blog in the world.

A big note of gratitude goes to my dear friend Professor Giorgio Nardone and his great team (Roberta Milanese and Cristina Nardone) with whom I've work for many years; they are a great example of creative thinkers and creators of markets; thanks to Giorgio's skills, he has made a significant contribution in "unlocking-unblocking" managers and entrepreneurs around the world.

I also want to thank the group of de Bono thinking systems. Starting from far, to the ex-president of de Bono Thinking systems, Kathy Meyers for her support at the beginning of my project; to Steve Keay; to the master trainers and members of the de Bono Thinking Systems and the de Bono Global Network, whom I consider my friends: Donna Pace, a great example of a MarkeThinker, to the legendary and spectacular Sunil Gupta, to Stephanie Ceccato, who supported this project and me at every stage of the process; and a big, special thanks to Amanda Mobbs, a creative philosopher with a gentle soul, creative and passionate; to my Dutch friend Mary Lou Leistikow; to Robert Fisher, who will transform the ideas of this book into a big market opportunity; to Iain Chalmers; to Daniela Bartoli. I also thank my other friends from the network of de Bono Thinking Systems, Peter and Linda Low, Andreas Novak, my Romanian friends Catlin and Mihaela, Ian Chalmers, Nicola Tyler and Zander Powel, my Greek friends Spiros Paolinelis and Antony Demetriou, Suzy Mclellan.

Among my friends from the Swiss University Supsi, who have supported me during these years with passion and professionalism, I especially thank Roberto Klaus, friend and true creative innovator in marketing and sales; I want to recognize Ileana Comaschi, with deep esteem, for wanting to "create and help clients and students" with solutions that are always innovative; to the division responsible, Wilma Minoggio, who has created an environment where freedom of experimentation is combined with the respect of the institution's and the mandate's context. Thank you, friends of the Swiss Television Network: Stefano Laffranchini, Augusto

## ACKNOWLEDGMENTS · FOREWORDS — MARKETHINK

Cholet, and Matteo Besomi, who have given me the ability and confidence to do the first seminar in world of MarkeThink applied to the creation of television formats - they are the ones who had the courage to "taste the first oyster."

A special thanks to my Kung Fu Master Lino Paleari and his assistant Luisella. A magical thanks to Francesco Casorati dear friend and truly Markethinker.

Also a special thanks to my business partner of Sole 24 ore (Paola Gambini, Anna Belloni and Arianna Piantanida).

I thank my partners and associates of Creattività; my business partners Marcella Campi and Valentina Serri for the open mind they give in following innovative projects without ever criticizing me and always supporting me; and my ex-colleague Daniela Montagner, who followed me and helped significantly in the first part of this project. A great thanks also to Cristina Dona, Silvia Pasqualini, Anna Faggin Veronica Aloisio, Silvia Aprosio and Zena. To my friends and ex-partners, Fattore Sette, Andrea Paltenghi, Gualtiero Giuliani, and Davide Agostoni. A special thanks goes to Andrea Forghieri for his help and support in the development of the portal of MarkeThink and of the database of marketing innovations.

It is with pleasure that I thank my friend Erika Leonardi, a true guru of service management in Italy, for her innovative teachings in service management, which is of fundamental importance for companies. Thanks also goes to my friend Marco Camisani Calzolari for his spirit of sharing and for his enlightened insight on the field of internet.

A major thanks goes to Professor Franco Giacomazzi, marketing professor, for inviting me to present this project, many years ago, at the *Politecnico* of Milan, when it was still in its embryonic phase. A special thought goes to my friend Carola Goglio, who has always supported me and has always rooted for the success of my projects.

A special thanks also goes to my friend Adriana Quaglia, a very great example of a MarkeThinker, and to Roberto Pozza, my companion in the path of creativity and other innovative projects. All my gratitude also for my ex-partner of Promostudio, Giovanni Vescovo, *who brought Edward de Bono to Italy for the first time* and gave me the opportunity to meet other gurus of management from whom I've learned a lot, among whom are Richard Normann and Professor Renato Tagiuri, my mentor who would have liked this project for sure; Professor Kaplan and Professor Norton, creators of the Balanced Scorecard; Theodore Levitt, whom I met in Boston in 1998, and Michael Spendolini, the guru of benchmarking.

And thanks to the team of HSM - promoter of the World Business Forum Italy, for their help and support: Fernando Tasco, Diego Gil, and Augusta Leante. We thank HSM for their contribution to increase the level and managerial culture in Italy and in the world. To the team of friends who in the last few years have been part of the "innovative days," to Giannandrea Abate, for his contribution in the text about psycholinguistics, to Lorenzo Marini and his marketing strategies and creative communication, about which a book should be written, and to Valter Ciari too.

A very special thanks goes to my father's family. First of all to my grandfather Mario Bellavista, who in the 50es and 60es has been a pioneer in developing marketing strategies in Italy and created one of the largest Italian advertising agencies; to my uncle Paolo, who has been publisher of important business marketing and communication magazines; to my aunt Cristina, business consultant, and her companion Alessandro Faravelli, company president, who have helped me in my business activities. And of course to my father Fabrizio, digital coach and partner of Emotional Marketing, who introduced me to the most innovative world of digital marketing and social networks, and has always encouraged and supported me in my thousand projects with the freshness of a young boy.

And the last thanks go to my family: my wife, Paola, who is always the first to know about my projects and is always my most ardent supporter, and to my daughter, Matilde. I hope that in the future she can use this book to make her dreams come true, and that she will be able to create worlds that are still undiscovered...

*I would like to underline that the MarkeThink project is totally the result of my intellect **and is not connected with either Professor Kotler, Professor Trias de Bes, or Professor Edward de Bono,** even though I owe them a huge intellectual debt and recognize them in many parts of the book.*

**Massimo Soriani Bellavista**

I want to start by thanking Ettore Cavalli, my husband, for his unconditional love, continuous encouragement, constant moral and emotional support, and...for patiently dealing with me during the biggest rollercoaster of my life! Without his support this would have never been such a smooth experience. Thank you for being my pillar; I love you.

Then, of course, an important thank you and immense gratitude go to my parents, Jacques and Lorena Nussbaumer, for their undeniable love and support, but mainly for giving me the tools, the ability, and the confidence to accomplish everything I ever set my mind to. They have given me the ability to be what I am and follow my heart. Thank you! To my dad, or life mentor, thank you for your guidance, support, and total dedication. To my mom, thank you for your creativity and for opening my mind and my vision of the world. Thank you both for believing in me...

*I want to say a huge thank you to* my grandfather, Jean Nussbaumer, in your own way, believing in me and boosting my confidence. You have done so much for me and are a true inspiration.

A special and warm thank you goes to Massimo Soriani Bellavista, my mentor and coauthor; I would have never written this book if it weren't for you. I am so grateful to you for seeing and believing in my potential, and for continuously pushing me to be and become the best that I can be. Thank you for making me part of this *amazing* project, which has immensely enriched my life and fulfilled one of my life dreams. Sei grande!

I would also like to commend the various institutions that were committed to my education: Institut le Rosey in Rolle and Mr. and Mrs. Gudin, International University of Geneva (IUG), Accademia del Lusso and Il Sole 24 Ore in Milan. And, I express my greatest gratitude to my dear professors: Pierre Berubé and Jean-Claude Pesse; William Twin, Eric Willumsen, Donna Catliota, and Winfried Boeing, Glenn O'Neil, Patrice-Anne Nuq, and Darcy Christen; Simona Riva and Valentina Cagnola; Massimiliano Caccamo, Gabriele Fava, Temistocle Bussino, Nicola Fedel, and Alessandra Colonna.

A note of gratitude goes to my past employers for giving me the opportunity to apply my knowledge and learn more, or simply put, for making me see the world as it is: Thomas Von Arx from the UBS; Eric Valdieu, Jennifer Vorbach, Jean Marc Lunel, Helen Molesworth, Vanessa Green, Fabian Guignard, Alexandra Rebholz, Sanda Nyun Han, and Kanchan Nair from Christies; Nicola Eberl, Martina Vascellari, Alice Agnelli, Petra Radimersky, Dario Vecchione, and Alessandra Redaeilli from Jil Sander; and David Engel from Michael Page.

Last but not least a huge thanks goes to my dear friends Wilson Favre-Delerue, Giuseppe De Peppo, Stanislas Blohorn, Alexis T. D. Adamczyk, Shannon Guerrico, Charly Shriro, Emilie Pastor, Tiago von Geissler, Sylvain Kouzoubachian, Angelo de Falco, and Alexandro Keith Nussbaumer (my brother) for advising, supporting, and befriending me and for pushing me to give my best.

Also, a special thank you goes to the universe and my lucky star!

**Christel Nussbaumer**

# Forewords by P. Kotler, E. de Bono, S. Godin

I am greatly impressed with this new and unique marketing book called *MarkeThink*. This book represents a solid and innovative contribution that will help marketers and managers catch up on the most important literature about marketing. It will introduce marketers, managers, consultants, entrepreneurs, and students to the top thinkers in marketing and their contributions.

*MarkeThink* doesn't create a new model of marketing but serves as the creation of a marketing metamodel. It provides an umbrella for integrating new contributions and innovations in marketing that might come from marketers, university professors, consultants, and entrepreneurs.

Much of the *MarkeThink* project will help marketers develop new marketing ideas. *MarkeThink* covers ten thinking styles that are essential to enhance the skills of a marketer. The marketers' creative process is visualized as passing through eight phases. The first four phases represent the actual creative process - focus, creative techniques, collection, and selection of ideas. The other four phases are concerned with the implementation of the creative process - feasibility, internal sales, promotions and sales, and the last phase, "churn," which is the ability to successfully manage the market's response with further adjustments.

I am intrigued with the addition of the "Ideabase" of marketing, which incorporates the 250 most important marketing innovations, categorized by sector (automotive, insurance, etc.), by underlying creative concepts (the lateral thinking concepts), by type of innovation (design, modulation, etc.) and by market level (marketing mix, need, etc.). The manager who is looking for new ideas can use the Ideabase and find inspiration from what other marketers have done. The Ideabase keeps marketers up to date on innovations from around the world related to their field (today there is less time to catch up) and gives the ability to access cross-disciplinary industries and sectors. In fact, the most important marketing innovations are often born in or drawn from other sectors with suitable adaptations to the new situation.

I am sure that the reader will find many treasures in *MarkeThink* that will supercharge their thinking and creativity and lead to new contributions in marketing.

**Philip Kotler**
S. C. Johnson and Son, Distinguished Professor of International Marketing
Kellogg School of Management, Northwestern University

# ACKNOWLEDGMENTS · FOREWORDS

"Thinking" has been, throughout my life, the heart of my work. I strongly believe that any kind of thinking is a skill that can be developed and learned. I have, in fact, taught how to "think" to both children and adults in the field of education as well as in organizations.

All of us are thinkers; nevertheless not all of us are good thinkers. Nowadays, there is a strong need to develop these thinking skills, especially in organizations. In the current time of crisis, many people are realizing that it is more and more important to be able to invent and create the future we are still unable to grasp.

In the last forty years my methods have been taught to over a million people from around the globe. Most participants of my courses are professionals: entrepreneurs, CEO, managers, and employees; and most of them are related to marketing in some way or another, directly or indirectly. The interesting thing is that even people in marketing have some thinking-skills limitations. When we are new at a job, we learn how to manage our tasks; unfortunately, nobody teaches us how to use our thinking skills to improve performance and innovate.

The present book was born from a project that was started years ago by me, Massimo Soriani Bellavista, Professor Philip Kotler, and Professor Fernando Trias de Bes. The project aimed to create tools to improve P. Kotler's and F. Trias de Bes's "Lateral Marketing" model. This project was very intense but unfortunately didn't go through, and a great creative potential to generate useful marketing tools was left untapped. In many entrepreneurship stories, luck helps the audacious people; a beautiful example of this is the real story of the Post-it, which you will find in the book.

Massimo carried on a little part of that innovative project that we had worked on and created a new project, different from the first one. In order to develop and to enrich the new project, he created a team of high-level professionals: Professor Walter Giorgio Scott and Mrs. Christel Cavalli Nussbaumer. Professor W. G. Scott is one of the most important academic Italian marketing teachers as well as one of the greatest admirers of P. Kotler's work. Mrs. Christel Cavalli Nussbaumer, following her studies in marketing and communication, supported and developed the project with her writing and research contributions, as well as the great backstage work that made possible the publication of this book.

I asked Massimo not to include in this book all the techniques I developed throughout the years; they would heavy the publication. Readers will find referrals to my publications if they would like to learn more about creative thinking skills.

This book offers a lot of useful suggestions and insights about creativity in marketing. I suggest you follow them in order to learn how to generate new ideas as well as higher level ones in organizations to renew from within the culture of marketing.

**Edward de Bono**

The authors have delivered a generous, sprawling, powerful textbook of the new marketing. For those in search of a grounded, well-researched primer on where marketing is (and where it's going), *MarkeThink* is a fabulous place to begin.

**Seth Godin**

# Introduction: why Markethink™? The market has changed

*"There is nothing permanent except change." - Heraclitus (450 BC)*

Since its establishment, the marketplace has been confronted with many challenges and innovations and has gone through major changes. These changes have influenced our society, the individual, industries, and so on.

## Today's Market Scenario

In brief, the most important changes that have occurred in the market can be summarized as follows:

In the consumer goods industry there is an increased concentration of distribution within fewer outlets: In the fifties there were a multitude of small, independent retailers. Now more than 80 percent of consumer sales come from supermarkets.

On one hand there has been a reduction in the number of competitors, but on the other hand, there has been an increasing amount of new brands registered. There have been fewer big competitors, but more brands competing for the same existing market (to a point where internal competition as become extremely fierce). This has led to an ever more segmented market, resulting in always smaller, less profitable, and more saturated markets.

The product's life cycle has been drastically reduced. Once, a successful product had an assured life span of approximately ten years. Today, as soon as a new product has penetrated the market, another change in the market is the reduction of the product's life cycle.

Further it costs more to repair than to replace. For example, an electric razor costs less than sixty euros; its repair can cost as much as one hundred euros with a two-week waiting delay, a time period in which you have two choices: you either stop shaving for those two weeks or buy a disposable/manual one. This will automatically lead to an inconvenience and overcost, so you will just buy a new electronic one. It is way more interesting: you have a brand new, ready-to-use electric shaver for less money with less of a hassle.

Digital technology has revolutionized markets, products, and especially services. Think of the book industry with Amazon.com, or the world of online travel sales with Expedia.com.

The number of trademarks and patents is continuously increasing. The Internet three-letter domains are finished. The Patent and Trademark Office has registered thousands of names, making it difficult for those who want to create a new brand name and penetrate the market with it. This fact has impacted heavily on the visibility, the communicative appeal and effectiveness of the message, leading to always smaller ads, delivering a truly differentiated and valued offer.

The amount of product varieties and derivatives available within each product category has massively soared. A relevant example, just enter a supermarket and go to the yogurt aisle; there are more than fifty different varieties (fruit, jars, diet, not yogurt, etc.).

The markets are hyperfragmented. There is a continuous segmentation of the markets and product differentiation, creating an even more "one to one" market strategy approach, consequently decreasing margins due to the cost of supporting a niche strategy.

## Marketing Overview

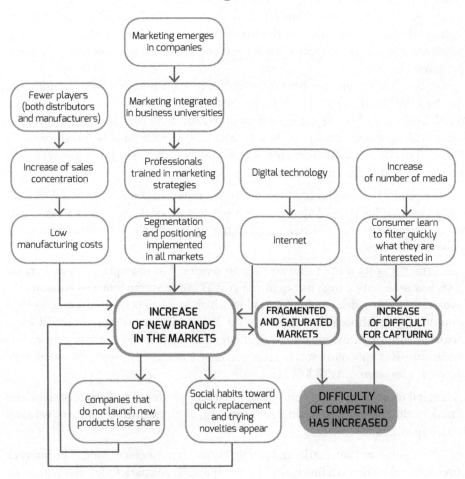

Figure 1: Today - A Marketing Overview by Kotler/Trias de Bes

# INTRODUCTION — MARKETHINK

Advertising saturation is reaching its highest level. Every day a citizen of a large urban area is exposed to an average of two thousand advertising stimuli and communications.

With the continuous increase in the supply of communication channels (more than one hundred television channels, two hundred radio stations, and one thousand magazines, and let's not forget the World Wide Web), it is really becoming difficult to reach one's target audience and gain their interest. Just getting their attention has become a hard task to accomplish.

P. Kotler presents the evolution of marketing as having undergone three key phases: It was initially purely a transactional event. It then shifted to a relationship-based exchange, and then into what we are seeing today, which is an approach based on collaboration. You can see in the figure below what the implications of each phase are.[1]

## The Evolution of Marketing

|  | Transactional Marketing | Relationship Marketing | Collaborative Marketing |
|---|---|---|---|
| Time Frame | 1950s | 1980s | Beyond 2000 |
| View of Value | The company offering in an exchange | The customer relationship in the long run | Co-Created experiences |
| View of Market | Place where value is exchanged | Market is where various offering appear | Market is a forum where value is co-created through dialogue |
| Role of Customer | Passive buyers to be targeted with offerings | Portfolio of relationship to be cultivated | Prosumers-active participants in value co-creation |
| Role of Firm | Define and create value for consumer | Attract, develop and retain profitable customers | Engage customers in defining and co-creating unique value |
| Nature of Customer interaction | Survey customers to elicit needs and solicit feedback | Observe customers and learn adaptively | Active dialogue with customers and communities |

Figure 2: The Three Key Marketing Evolution Phases (P. Kotler)

---

[1] Retrieved from P. Kotler's "Seeking Marketing Resilience and Growth in the Age of Turbulence" presentation, slide 73, during the World Marketing and Sales Forum (HSM) Milan, on June 18, 2009. Published by the Kellogg School of Management, Northwestern University

To give you an even better idea of what the implications are, P. Kotler evidenced in key points what shifts were brought about by the evolution of marketing and its practice. As you can see there are quite a few, showing the radical shift of focus there has been.[2]

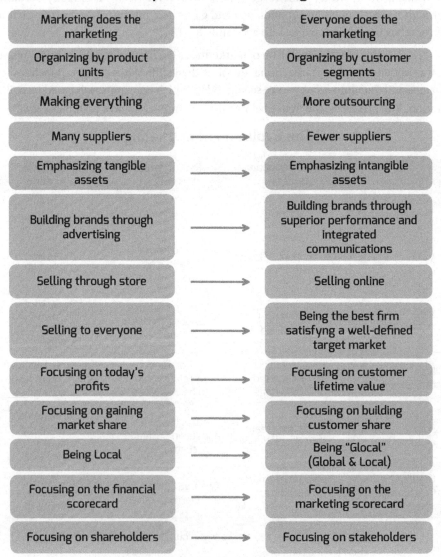

Figure 3: Major Shifts in Marketing (P. Kotler)

---

[2] Retrieved from P. Kotler's "Seeking Marketing Resilience and Growth in the Age of Turbulence" presentation, slide 74, during the World Marketing and Sales Forum (HSM) Milan, on June 18, 2009. Published by the Kellogg School of Management, Northwestern University

# INTRODUCTION — MARKETHINK

You must always remember that the practice of marketing has gone through and will go through many changes, trends, and improvements; some of these are still of highly topical others less so. And, if you consider both management and marketing evolutions, you can clearly see how important it is to innovate and how these shifts have shaped the world we live in; but it also shows us how unstable the market and the environment are, and how we are always in constant evolution and movement, striving for improvement. You can clearly see how, according to P. Kotler, marketing has evolved through the years. Marketing has gone through the following phases, and leaves a question open: What is next?[3]

| THE POSTWAR 1950s | The UNCERTAIN 1980s |
|---|---|
| 1. The Marketing Mix<br>2. Product Life Cycle<br>3. Brand Image<br>4. Market Segmentation<br>5. The Marketing Concept<br>6. The marketing Audit | 1. Marketing Warfare<br>2. Global Marketing<br>3. Local Marketing<br>4. Mega-Marketing<br>5. Direct Marketing<br>6. Customer Relationship Marketing<br>7. Internal Marketing |
| **THE SOARING 1960s** | **THE ONE-TO-ONE 1990s** |
| 1. The four Ps<br>2. Marketing Myopia<br>3. Lifestyle Marketing<br>4. The Broadened Concept of Marketing | 1. Emotional Marketing<br>2. Experiential Marketing<br>3. Internet and e-Business Marketing<br>4. Sponsorship Marketing<br>5. Marketing Ethics |
| **THE TURBOLENT 1970s** | **THE FINANCIALLY – DRIVEN 2000s** |
| 1. Targeting<br>2. Positioning<br>3. Strategic Marketing<br>4. Service Marketing<br>5. Social Marketing<br>6. Societal Marketing<br>7. Macro-Marketing | 1. ROI Marketing<br>2. Brand Equity Marketing<br>3. Customer Equity Marketing<br>4. Social Responsibility Marketing<br>5. Customer Empowerment<br>6. Social Media Marketing<br>7. Tribalism<br>8. Authenticity Marketing<br>9. Co-Creation Marketing |

Figure 4: Marketing Evolution Trends (P. Kotler)

---

[3] Retrieved from P. Kotler's "Seeking Marketing Resilience and Growth in the Age of Turbulence" presentation, slide 74, during the World Marketing and Sales Forum (HSM) Milan, on June 18, 2009. Published by the Kellogg School of Management, Northwestern University

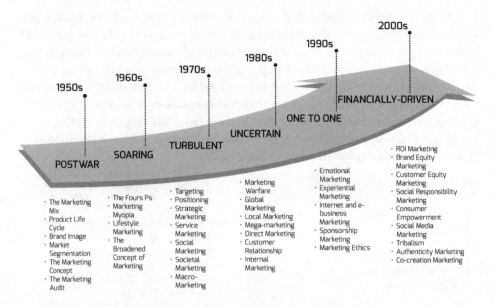

Figure 5: Where are we going next?[4] (P. Kotler)

If the marketing is changed into the objectives, methodologies and tools, innovation has become central to the marketing and for its renewal. In our opinion, there is a strong need for a conceptual and operational model that may innovate this wonderful discipline; this model we called "Markethink" and you'll find it described on the following pages.

---

4   Retrieved from P. Kotler's "Seeking Marketing Resilience and Growth in the Age of Turbulence" presentation, slide 74, during the World Marketing, and Sales Forum (HSM) Milan, on June 18, 2009. Published by the Kellogg School of Management, Northwestern University

# MarkeThink Metamodel

**PART ONE**

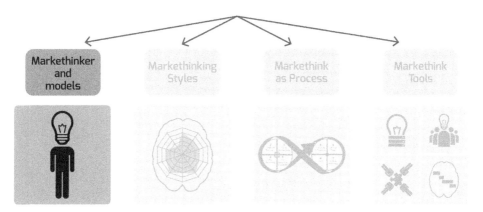

# Chapter 1
# Markethink Metamodel and Markethinkers

## 1.1 MarkeThink™: not a new model but a Metamodel

One of the most interesting concepts developed by G. Hamel is, in our opinion, the concept of "management of management" as a competitive factor. In summary, the competitive factor of a company, in the long run, is not whether a company uses a single innovative management technique, such as Total Quality Management, and makes it the solution to all business problems. What is important is the fact that the company systematically rethinks its management system, contemplating and searching for different, more adapted management models for the company's success and for improvement of performance and results. In our opinion, G. Hamel's approach is very similar to the "double loop learning" concept developed by Argyris and Schon; in other words, it's the concept of "learning to learn". This concept was further developed by MIT professor P. Senge and materialized in his historical book, *The Fifth Discipline*.

What we are attempting to do with our MarkeThink concept is very similar to these concepts, and in particular G. Hamel's "management of management"; we would like our model to become the conceptual umbrella of marketing or "management of marketing management." To enable you to continually rethink the way you do marketing and find ideas, we want to be the catalyst to create a common platform where the existing and most important marketing models and innovations, such as lateral marketing, one-to-one marketing, and permission marketing, to name a few, are taken to a higher level, so they reach their full potential. We want to provide support to both: marketing innovations and companies' successes.

## MARKETHINK — CHAPTER 1

### 1.1.1 Why a Metamodel?

The best way we have found to introduce the concept of metamodel is to use the words of P. Romer, by quoting a passage of his article "Economic Growth"[5]:

> "We do not know what the next major idea about how to support ideas will be. Nor do we know where it will emerge. There are, however, two safe predictions. First, the country that takes the lead in the twenty-first century will be the one that implements an innovation that more effectively supports the production of new ideas in the private sector. Second, new meta-ideas of this kind will be found.
>
> Only a failure of imagination - the same one that leads the man on the street to suppose that everything has already been invented - leads us to believe that all of the relevant institutions have been designed and that all of the policy levers have been found. For social scientists, every bit as much as for physical scientists, there are vast regions to explore and wonderful surprises to discover".

MarkeThink as a step ahead for Marketing: A Metaidea

MarkeThink is not a new trend that wants to impose itself in the minds of entrepreneurs and marketing managers or consultants, but rather it is a process that is intended to be a marketing metaidea. With the concept of a metaidea, we want to focus on a process that supports the development of marketing practices (or any other model for that matter) through the use of the best techniques to enhance one's thinking potential.

The MarkeThink metamodel can be seen through four main lenses:
1. Markethinker and Authors
2. Markethinking Styles
3. Markethink as a Process
4. Markethink Tools

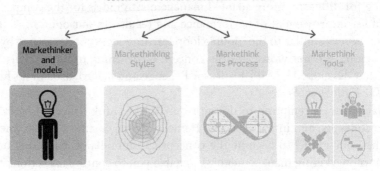

Figure 6: The Four MarkeThink Metamodel Lenses

---

[5] P. Romer, "Economic Growth," in D. R. Henderson's Ed., 1993, *The Fortune Encyclopedia of Economics*. Time Warner Books, New York. You can read the full article at *http://www.stanford.edu/~promer/EconomicGrowth.pdf*

## 1.1.2 Marketing Models and authors

*"It is the theory that tells us where to look." - A. Einstein*

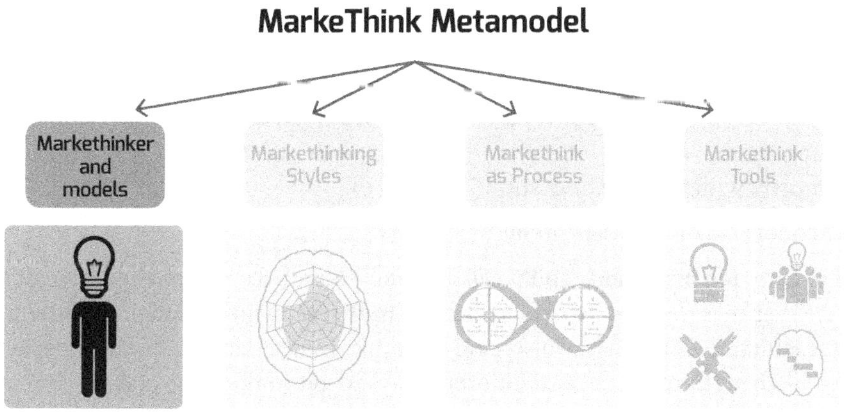

**MarkeThink Metamodel**

Figure 7: Marketing Models and Authors - The First lens of MarkeThink

This section is composed of three main areas:

1. Marketing models and theories
2. Authors, consultants, and entrepreneurs' models
3. Creative and innovative models and authors

### 1.1.2.1 Marketing Models and theories

As we have already mentioned, by revisiting basic marketing, our opinion is that there is a strong need for theoretical and epistemological reflections regarding the various marketing models. We hear, all around and from different sides, that "marketing is dead" but in our opinion this is not true. We believe that the discipline of marketing is in fact more alive than ever; it is only in need of a basic epistemological redefinition that lays down new foundations for its development in the future. We can already see that there are some areas that are approaching marketing in a more "scientific" manner - the whole world of data mining, direct marketing, and marketing research, for example - but, to date, there is no shared scientific model, at the underlying base, that integrates all the major models.

This epistemological confusion, coupled with the strong pragmatic approach of many players in the field of marketing (advertising agencies, marketing directors, etc.) for which the goal is to give concrete and speedy results, has alienated the academic sphere - that prefer models and theory, from the real world of business - that loves pragmatism. As Theodore Levitt said in his book "Marketing Imagination":

"Nothing in business is so remarkable as the conflicting variety of success formula offered by its numerous practitioner and professors. And if, in the case of practitioner, they're not exactly "formulas," there are explanations of "how we did it," implying with firm control over any fleeting tendencies toward modesty that "that's how you ought to do it". Practitioner, filled with pride and money, turn themselves into prescriptive philosophers, filled mostly with hot air. Professor, on the other hand, know better than to deal merely in explanations. We traffic instead in higher goods, like "analysis," "concepts," and "theories." In short, "truth"." Filled with self-importance, we turn ourselves hopefully into wanted advisers, consultants filled mostly with woolly congestion."

Theodore Levitt also said about professors:

"Listen to ten professors, and you'll generally get advice by some multiple of ten. The difference is not that professors believe more firmly in abundance. Rather, besides teaching, professors are also paid to think. Hence, lacking direct experience, each is likely to think up several different ways to get to the same place"

Here you find the words of a great scientist, Kurt Lewin: *"There is nothing more practical than a good theory."*[6] . We consider the theoretical component an imperative to excel in any operational phase.

Authors, Consultants, and Entrepreneurs' Models

> Seth Godin
> Permission Marketing
> STP Philip Kotler Purple cow
> One to One Pepper and Rogers
> Lateral Marketing Theodore Levitt
> Guerrilla Marketing Zig Ziglar
> Marketing Myopia
> Markethink

Figure 8: Authors and Marketing Models

The second area that is linked to models is the one associated with the creators of knowledge in the fields of marketing and marketing management. This area consists of knowledge created by authors (books/articles), the various players operating the market, and the considerable contributions brought by successful consultants and entrepreneurs, who create, in premise, the "operational knowledge of marketing."

In fact, there are areas and industries where the innovations of marketing have been put in place by active market players such as entrepreneurs and consultants; among these is easy to recognize strong actors in the world of technology - the creators of new models, pioneers/entrepreneurs such as Google, Yahoo, Facebook,

---

6   K. Lewin, 1952, *Field Theory in Social Science: Selected Theoretical Papers*, p. 169, Tavistock

Instagram, and others. Last but not least, let us consider P. Kotler's list of pioneers/innovators in marketing - his top thirty marketing visionaries.

## Marketing Visionaries

| Leader | Company | Leader | Company |
|---|---|---|---|
| 1. Anita Roddick | 1. The Body Shop | 16. Richard Branson | 16. Virgin Air |
| 2. Fred Smith | 2. Federal Express | 17. Soichiro Honda | 17. Honda |
| 3. Steve Jobs | 3. Apple Computer | 18. Simon Marks | 18. Marks & Spencer |
| 4. Bill Gates | 4. Microsoft | 19. Luciano Benetton | 19. Benetton |
| 5. Michel Dell | 5. Dell Computer | 20. Charles Lazarus | 20. Toys 'R' Us |
| 6. Ray Kroc | 6. McDonald's | 21. Les Wexner | 21. The Limited |
| 7. Walt Disney | 7. Disney Corporation | 22. Colonel Sanders | 22. Kentucky Fried Chicken |
| 8. Sam Walton | 8. Wal-Mart | 23. Ingvar Kamprad | 23. IKEA |
| 9. Tom Monaghan | 9. Domino's Pizza | 24. Bernie Marcus | 24. Home Depot |
| 10. Akio Morita | 10. Sony | 25. Charles Schwab | 25. Charles Schwab & Co. |
| 11. Nicholas Hayek | 11. Swatch Watch Co. | 26. Herb Kelleher | 26. Souhtwest Airlines |
| 12. John W. Nordstrom | 12. Nordstrom | 27. Paul Orfalea | 27. Kinko's |
| 13. Gilbert Trigano | 13. Club Mediterranee | 28. Jeff Bezos | 28. Amazon |
| 14. Ted Turner | 14. CNN | 29. Jim McCann | 29. 1-800-FLOWERS |
| 15. Frank Perdue | 15. Perdue Chicken | 30. Phil Knight | 30. Nike |

Figure 9: Marketing Visionaries by P. Kotler[7]

Let us also note that out of these thirty, 90 percent are entrepreneurs!

An outstanding author in this field is Peter Frisk, whose book is *Marketing Genius*.[8] Frisk has managed to combine his practical experience as marketing director with very good communication skills, communicating complex concepts in a simple way. Unfortunately we do not have enough space to dedicate to the contributions of Peter Frisk in this book; though as in many other cases, we invite you to read it as soon as possible. In fact, from our point of view, Peter Frisk is a very good example

---

7   Kotler on Marketing, 2001, exhibit 1–3, p. 14
8   *Marketing Genius*, 2006, Capstone Publishing, a John Wiley & Sons company

of a "MarkeThinker." In the lines below we will try to give you a concrete example of what we mean by MarkeThink as a metamodel - take for example an author's marketing model and try to put it in relation to the enhancement of the thinking styles (our ten "commandments").

To better understand, take marketing model, such as one-to-one marketing by D. Peppers and R. Rogers, and, through the process of using their unique IDIC model, identify, differentiate, interact, and customize -and the application of the set of MarkeThink instruments, you will produce a greater quantity and higher quality of ideas for that market.[9] . In fact in this model, presented in D. Peppers and R. Rogers's great book, they propose a brainstorming exercise on how to find sources of customer data within the various databases available or, in other words, a creative phase on how to find valuable information within the data.

In our MarkeThink process, there will always be a phase dedicated to defining the focus (for example, have ideas about "offering the prospect an incentive to volunteer"), an active generation of ideas (a dozen) with a harvesting step, the selection and evaluation of ideas, and last but not least the implementation of the idea, which requires determining its feasibility and developing a prototype, selling it, and evaluating the results, just to start over again. MarkeThink is a process of metaideas for marketing (how to have better ideas, how to create more value and have better implementation, etc.), and it adapts to any existing marketing model.

In summary, MarkeThink is a step ahead for (new) marketing, an accelerator of success.

On the following pages we will present the main models and Marketing authors, knowing that making a choice from hundreds of existing models and thousands of authors around the world is an absolutely impossible undertaking. We know, that the choice we made that it is severely limited and we invite you immediately on www.markethink.guru portal to help report authors and models that we have omitted in this synthetic work and that are worth noting; While the paper version has limitations related to the charges, the portal will have an extended version of hypertext.

---

9   In the 1993 book *The One to One Future* by Don Peppers and Martha Rogers, Ph.D.

# Chapter 2
# Marketing Models and Authors
# Back to the basic

## 2.1 Marketing Defined

*"Marketing is the activity, set of institutions, and processes for creating, communicating, delivering, and exchanging offerings that have value for customers, clients, partners, and society at large." - American Marketing Association*

*P. Drucker defines marketing as "the aim to make 'selling' superfluous. It's to know and understand the customer so well that the product or service fits him and sells itself. Ideally, marketing should result in a customer who is ready to buy. All that should be needed then is to make the product or service available."*

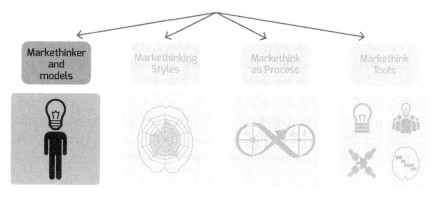

Figure 10: Marketing Models and Author

Let's consider the misleading ideas we often encounter when speaking of marketing. Marketing is *not* the following:

It is not about *sales*. Sales and marketing are both part of commercial activities, but there is an important distinction. Marketing efforts are concerned with establishing the best conditions for the product to be sold. Sales assure that the products are purchased; it profit from and use the tools that the marketing efforts activated and put at their disposal to make the sale.

It is not only about *advertising/publicity*. Advertising is one of the most important aspects of the marketing activities; it is the means to reach marketing goals. Advertising supports marketing functions by determining and creating the most appropriate means to reach the target with the best creative message and communication mix, in order to raise awareness, remain in the consumer's mind, and counterattack the competition's moves.

It is not *public relations*. PR's objective is to maintain the proper amount of information and communication flow concerning the company with the media, the stakeholders, and the shareholders. PR employees manage and establish all company-related communications - important information that the company feels the need to share with the concerned stakeholders. PR is concerned with managing communications about the company; marketing is concerned with managing the company's product communications.

It is not *merchandising*. Merchandising deals with the product's notoriety, appeal, and desirability at the point of sale. It promotes sales at the distribution level by managing the product's exposition and presentation in the assigned space. Merchandising is closely related to marketing. It is responsible for all the aspects related to the management of the product's final phase, when the product is already at the point of sale.

## Ending the War between Sales and Marketing[10]

Sales and Marketing Feud Like Capulets and Montagues

It is a known fact that in many companies sales and marketing are usually conflicting: marketing believes the marketing plan is not properly carried out by sales, and sales blames marketing for setting prices too high and for "being out of touch with what customers want."

In their study, they analyzed the statistics of the relationships in a company and they found out two interesting things. First of all, there are four types of relationships: undefined, defined, aligned, and integrated; they don't have necessarily an

---

10  This is just a small summary of the article by P. Kotler, N. Rackham, and S. Krishnaswamy on ending the conflict that exists between the two functions. We recommend you read the full article for you to get all of its value. You can read the full article at *http://hbr.org/2006/07/ending-the-war-between-sales-and-marketing/ar/*

integrated relationship, this all depends on the needs and the size of the company. Secondly, the friction between these is mainly of an economic or cultural nature; economic, obviously, concerns the allocation of the budget, whereas cultural is more complex "because the two functions attract very different types of people who spend their time in very different ways." In their article they also provide a diagnostics tool to assess the relationship, and propose a series of practical steps to establish a more productive relationship.

To give us a clear vision of the distance that exists between these two functions, the authors shared with us the "Buying Funnel," the interesting exhibit you find below, where we can see how marketing and sales influence customers' purchasing decisions and how the responsibilities are clearly determined.

## The Buying Funnel

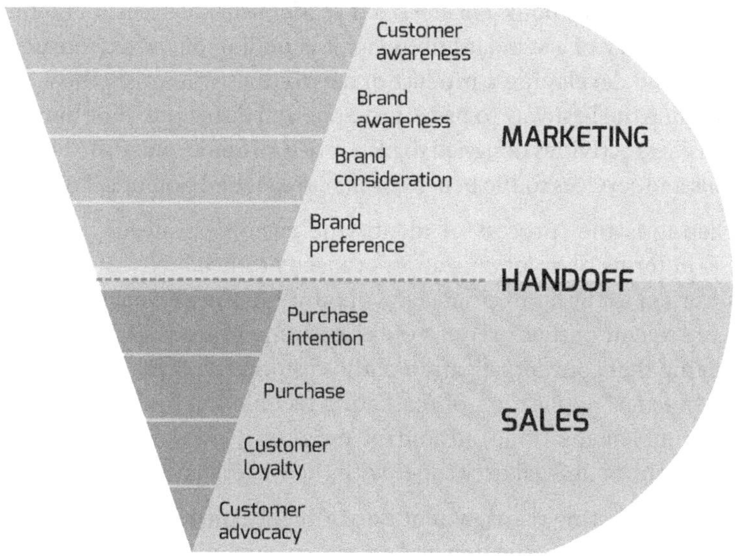

- Customer awareness
- Brand awareness
- Brand consideration
- Brand preference

**MARKETING**

--- **HANDOFF** ---

- Purchase intention
- Purchase
- Customer loyalty
- Customer advocacy

**SALES**

Figure 11: The Buying Funnel *(Harvard Business Review)*

To conclude, the authors "recommend crafting a new relationship between them, one with the right degree of interconnection to tackle your most pressing business challenges."

## 2.2 Marketing Management Models

The American Marketing Association (AMA) defines marketing management as "the process of planning and executing the conception, pricing, promotion and distribution of ideas, goods and services to create exchanges that satisfy individual and organizational needs," and also as "an organizational function and set of processes for creating, communicating and delivering value to customers and for managing customer relationships in ways that benefit the organization and its stakeholders."[11]

According to P. Kotler, "marketing management is the art and science of choosing target markets and getting, keeping and growing customers through creating, communicating and delivering superior customer value"

W. J. Stanton, in his book *Fundamentals of Marketing*, defines marketing as "the creation and delivery of a standard of living: it is finding out what consumers want, then planning and developing a product or service that will satisfy those wants; and then determining the best way to price, promote, and distribute." For him it is "a total system of business activities designed to plan, price, promote and distribute want-satisfying goods and services to the benefit of the present and potential customers."[12]

If marketing is the "process of identifying customers' needs, conceptualizing those needs in terms of an organization's capacity to produce; communicating the conceptualization to the appropriate laws of power in the organization; conceptualizing the consequent output in terms of the customers' needs earlier identified; and communicating that conceptualization of the customer,"[13] then marketing management is the practical application of marketing techniques, tools, and tactics: analysis, planning, implementation, and control, programs, intended to create, build, and maintain mutually beneficial exchanges with the target markets[14],

The role of marketing management is to influence the level, timing, and composition of internal and external demand to achieve organizational goals. Marketing management is the most important discipline of any business management strategy. This is true because it is comprehensive of all the strategic aspects of a business: strategic planning, operations, activities, and processes that lead to reaching the overall organizational objectives and vision for the future by assuring the real delivery of value to the customer. It is all about focusing on satisfying customers through

---

11  Retrieved from *www.marketingpower.com*, the AMA official website dictionary at *http://www.marketingpower.com/_layouts/Dictionary.aspx?dLetter=M*

12  W. J. Stanton in *Fundamentals of Marketing*, 6th ed., 1983, p. 4. McGraw Hill Book Company, Japan

13  Definition provided by Professor Emeritus John A. Howard at Columbia University in 1973. This might be the best and most complete definition of the needs and wants theory. Found in *Marketing Warfare* by A. Ries and J. Trout, p. 2. McGraw-Hill Professional, 2005

14  For more information we recommend you read P. Kotler's book: *Marketing Management: Analysis, Planning, Implementation and Control*

the identification of their needs and wants, and by developing offerings accordingly, to actually satisfy their expectations and requirements. It is important to note that management's goal is to build long-term relationships not only with customers, but with all other interested parties. One has to satisfy the requirements of all stakeholders and deliver value.

Marketing management is the actual process of activating marketing techniques: analyzing, planning, implementing, and controlling the marketing programs. Programs that are designed to create, build, and maintain valuable exchanges with the target market, therefore, direct all efforts toward establishing a mutually beneficial relationship.

These are the core elements of a sound marketing management strategy:
- Understanding your industry's economic structure
- Understanding and knowing, in the best way, who you are and where you want to be
- Scanning the environment to detect threats and opportunities as well as your company's strengths and weaknesses
- Identifying market segments and your targets - ones you can satisfy and deliver value to
- Determining the best marketing strategy for your company and your target market
- Carrying out marketing research, but more important, understanding what lies beneath and how you can compete - attributes, service, features, etc.
- Understanding the competition and their products
- Developing products - create new products that fit your targets by paying attention and listening to them
- Developing marketing strategies by determining the marketing-mix variables, based on previous findings, experience, and social changes
- Determining, elaborating on, and writing the marketing plan
- Monitoring and controlling the results of said plan in order to adjust it as needed

According to H. Davidson, successful marketing management requires profitability, offensiveness, integration, strategies, and effectiveness.[15] P. Kotler sustains that for a marketing strategy to be successful it has to be all about defining its target market carefully and focusing on the right prospects and customers; communicating a unique benefit positioning; and developing the provision of differential values difficult to imitate so as to distinguish the company from competitor so more meaningful in the eyes of the consumer or customer. Marketing consists in carrying out various activities:

1. Organizational analysis - analyzing the internal environment and competences and the external environment. Where are we now?

---

[15] It is known as the POISE framework developed in 2004 by H. Davidson, W. J. Keegan, and E. Arno Brill in their book, *Offensive Marketing: An Action Guide to Gaining Competitive Advantage*, Elsevier Butterworth-Heinemann

2. Setting organizational objectives. Where do we want to be?
3. Establishing the marketing strategy - segmentation, targeting, positioning, and the value proposition. Which way is best?
4. Determining the tactics. How do we get there?
5. Implementing the strategies and the marketing mix. How do we actually get there?
6. Controlling and monitoring. How do we measure results?

In other words, the marketing management concept refers to identifying, choosing, and targeting the appropriate customers, positioning the offer coherently, interacting with customers, controlling the marketing efforts, and performance continuity. It is about integrating, monitoring, and understanding all the marketing variables, and how they are interconnected and interdependent, to achieve the company's objectives. These variables are target markets and segmentation; needs, wants, and demands; beliefs and behavior; product or offering; value satisfaction; exchange and transactions; relationships and networks; marketing channels; supply chain; competition and the environment.

A little insight comes from P. Kotler: "Marketing is a learning game. You make a decision. You watch the results. You learn from the results. Then you make better decisions".

## 2.3 Marketing Management Process

In his book *Kotler on Marketing* (2001, p. 30), P. Kotler gives the five-step formula of the marketing management process:

Figure 12: Marketing Management Process

1. R is *research*, such as market research.
2. STP stands for *segmentation, targeting*, and *positioning* - the strategic aspect of the process.
3. MM is the *marketing mix*, which is the tactical step of the process - what will be done.
4. I for *implementation*, putting things into motion - giving life to the plan.
5. C is for *control* of the marketing programs - outcomes, results, problems, etc.

For marketing programs to be successful, the first step is always *R*, market *research* to identify the different *Ss*, *segments*, which categorize consumers based on their shared values and needs. Once the market has been segmented, it is time to select which one to *target* - what segment can you best satisfy? Then comes *positioning* your product within your target in a way that differentiates it from your competitors. At this point you have made all your strategic decisions and it's time to consider your offering, the tactical aspects of your marketing plan. Last the *marketing mix* decision making, analysis, and definition of the four *p*'s (covered in a later chapter). Now that you have "who" and "what," you have to put it into motion, which is the *implementation* of your marketing mix. The last and fundamental step of any marketing plan is *C, control* of the plan put into motion - to monitor, evaluate, and if necessary modify it to assure you reach marketing and organizational goals.

## 2.3.1 Research

Research is the key to successful marketing-program planning and decision making. P. Kotler says that "research is the starting point for marketing. Without research, a company enters a market like a blind man" (2008, p. 31). It provides marketing managers and top management with accurate, valid, reliable, relevant, and up-to-date information on which to base their decisions. It's the process that produces necessary data and information on key controllable and uncontrollable factors that can affect the outcome of their decisions. This information can be divided into three types according to P. Kotler:

1. Macro environment - demographic, economic, lifestyle, technological, political, and regulatory trends
2. Task environment - consumer, collaborator, and competitor information
3. Company environment - company sales and market share; orders and back orders; costs; and customer profit by customer, product, segment, channel, order size, and all other relevant information (2001, p. 75)

Marketing managers and top management are required to make many complicated tactical and strategic decisions about consumer needs, opportunities, segmentation and target markets, the marketing activities plan, implementation and control, etc. It is a complex task, because they need to take into account the existing interactions between the controllable variables of the marketing mix, the uncontrollable variables and environmental forces, and more importantly, the complexity and volatility of the consumer and his behavior. Management needs to be able to link all the variables together - marketing variables with the environment with the consumer. Therefore research needs to be undertaken in a regular and methodic manner: "ongoing marketing research programs provide information on controllable and noncontrollable factors and consumers; this information enhances the effectiveness of decisions made by marketing managers."[16] Research done poorly will steer you in the wrong direction and increase risks.

Marketing research is a subset of the overall marketing activities and programs

---

16 D.W. Twedt, 1983, "Survey of Marketing Research." Chicago, American Marketing Association

and is primarily done to identify or solve a marketing problem. The whole market research process is composed of two types of focus: overall market research and specific marketing research. These two terms are commonly interchanged, however, "expert practitioners may wish to draw a distinction, in that market research is concerned specifically with markets, while marketing research is concerned specifically with marketing processes."[17].

Marketing research investigates how and why consumers buy, allowing you to draw conclusions on why sales have dropped and how to increase them or similar.

It involves in-depth analysis of how marketing activities affect the consumers. Market research focuses on the target market and its trends and evolutions.

### 2.3.1.1 Market versus Marketing Research

#### Market Research

Market research is "any organized effort to gather information about markets or customers and is a very important component of business strategy."[18] According to the ICC/ESOMAR, market research "includes social and opinion research, and is the systematic gathering and interpretation of information about individuals or organizations using statistical and analytical methods and techniques of the applied social sciences to gain insight or support decision making."[19]

Market research is broader in its scope because it examines all aspects of a business environment, the market, and the consumers. It asks questions about competitors, market structure, government regulations, economic trends, technological advances, and numerous other factors that influence decision making.

Market research involves discovering and learning about a specific market: what it is that people really need, want, and believe, and understanding how they behave to ultimately determine how you are going to market your product in the marketplace. The output is composed of market information: supply and demand, market prices, market segment information - geographic, personality, or use of product differences - and market-trends information.

#### Marketing Research

Marketing research is "the systematic gathering, recording, and analysis of data about issues relating to marketing products and services. The goal of marketing

---

[17] M. McDonald, 2007, *Marketing Plans: How to Prepare Them, How to Use Them*, 6th ed. Oxford, Butterworth-Heinemann

[18] E. McQuarrie, 2005, *The Market Research Toolbox: A Concise Guide for Beginners*, 2nd ed., Sage Publications

[19] ICC/ESOMAR, 2008, "International Code on Market and Social Research" 4th ed. ICC/ESOMAR Amsterdam, the Netherlands. Found at *http://www.esomar.org/uploads/pdf/professional-standards/ICCESOMAR_Code_English_.pdf*

research is to identify and assess how changing elements of the marketing mix impacts customer behavior."[20]

It can also be described as the "systematic and objective identification, collection, analysis, and dissemination of information for the purpose of assisting management in decision making related to the identification and solution of problems and opportunities in marketing."[21]

P. Kotler defines marketing research as "the systematic design, collection, analysis and reporting of data findings relevant to a specific marketing situation facing the company" (2009, p.130).

Marketing research is conducted within marketing, research that companies make to study the target consumers, customers and other companies with technical and marketing programs. They seek to understand and provide the best ways to connect consumers to the product by assessing and analyzing the current direct marketing campaigns, efforts and actions. They put in place activities and decision-making processes for the development of marketing plans and programs, to identify the company's positioning and so on.

Research, whether market or marketing, is carried out for various reasons:

- To understand and gain insight on customers and markets - behaviors, patterns, trends, etc.
- To understand and control marketing programs' effectiveness and learn from experience and gain knowledge
- To get an idea, a picture, of what kinds of new products and services may bring a profit
- To find out if current products and services are meeting your customers' needs and expectations
- To answer a specific question or problem - it may show you that you need to change the offering or it may even indicate whether additional services, benefits, attributes, or features are needed
- To create a sound business and marketing plan, measure the success of your current plan, and find out why it is not working as expected
- To help companies gather information and gain knowledge for the future regarding new products or product lines, opportunities, and also the threats that they may face
- P. Kotler believes that "no company should make big decisions without information about customers, competitors and channels" (2008, p. 97). He further states that "information helps the company learn and fine tune its market targets and marketing programs over time." He views market research as the "foundational element of modern marketing practice" (2008, p. 98).

---

20  Retrieved from *http://en.wikipedia.org/wiki/Marketing_research*
21  N. K. Malhotra, 2004, "Marketing Research: An Applied Orientation" 4th ed., Prentice Hall International

## 2.3.1.2 The Research process

Marketing research is systematic; each procedure must be methodological, well documented, and planned in advance. Note that marketing research should be as objective as possible; the researchers' motto should be "find it and tell it as it is."

The six steps for a successful marketing research outcome according to P. Kotler are as follows:

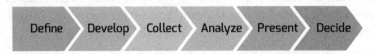

Figure 13: Research - A Step-by-Step Process

1. Define the problem - not too broadly and not too narrowly; set the decision alternatives and determine the research objectives.
2. Develop the research plan and make decisions on data sources, research approaches and instruments, sampling and size, and contact methods.
3. Collect the information, keeping in mind people's resistance to interruption, scanning capabilities and unwillingness to cooperate, and possibly biased or dishonest respondents or interviewers.
4. Analyze the information, and extract findings through data tabulations and frequency distribution.
5. Present the findings that are relevant to the marketing decisions by "translating data into information, insights, and recommendations."[22]
6. Make the decision - weigh the evidence and determine future actions. (2009, p. 131–143)

## 2.3.1.3 Data Sources - Where to Find Needed Data

There are two types of data collection sources available to the market researcher: secondary research, which is general and already available, and primary research, which is unavailable and for a specific purpose.

### Secondary Research

Secondary research is the first step in the process of gathering information; it gives you the starting points and the general picture and saves you time and money. It's concerned with the analysis of readily available, already published data. With secondary data research, you can identify competitors, establish benchmarks, and identify target segments. It is a type of research that costs far less than primary research, but rarely meets the exact needs of the researcher.

---

[22] M. Fielding, May, 2006, "Global Insights: Synovate's Chedore Discusses MR Trends," *Marketing News*, May 15, 2006, pp. 41–42

There are many available sources for getting your hands on the basics of your research program:

- Trade associations, shows, publications, and magazines
- Government agencies and their publications concerning demographics
- Department of Commerce and economic indicators, the International Trade Administration, the chamber of commerce
- Colleges and universities
- Community organizations
- Online resources, databases, search engines, forums, and social networks
- In-house databases and data warehouses
- Periodicals and journals
- Commercial data from marketing research firms such as Nielsen

## Primary Research

Primary research is the execution and compilation of research for a specific, well-determined purpose, for which there is no current and relevant data available. Its goal is to gather data from analyzing current sales, advertising campaigns, and marketing plans, as well as from analyzing the effectiveness of current practices and competitors' actions, and the coherence between the product, the market, and the environment. It is conducted from scratch; the output is original and collected to solve a specific problem or answer key questions and doubts.

Primary research can be undertaken through different approaches. It can be based on questioning - qualitative and quantitative - or based on observation through ethnographic studies or experimental techniques.

## Qualitative

Qualitative methods help you develop and fine-tune your quantitative research methods. They can help define problems and are used to learn about customers' opinions, values, and beliefs. Qualitative research refers to specific research whose results are analyzed through subjective measures, words, and discussion, as opposed to statistical analysis. It provides a deeper insight into the market's opinions. It generally involves smaller groups of individuals being interview in a more intimate manner, it is more expensive to conduct and analyze, and the results are usually extremely subjective. Customers may be asked to provide written responses to a questionnaire or to give an explanation of how a product makes them feel or how their experience with it was.

Qualitative marketing research is generally used for exploratory purposes and is not to be generalized to the whole population;

Exploratory research provides insight into and comprehension of an issue or situation. It is conducted to explore the problems' dimensions, to get some basic idea about the solution at the preliminary stages of research, and to investigate assumptions. It's an unstructured and qualitative approach to research.

Ethnographic studies produce a qualitative output through the observation of social phenomena - interactions, reactions, and actions - as they take place in their natural setting. These observations can be made at one time (cross-sectional) or they can happen over several time periods (longitudinal).

## Quantitative

Quantitative methods employ mathematical and statistical analysis, requiring a large sample size for validity. This quantified data collection usually sheds light on statistically significant differences. The results are as accurate as can be (it all depends on your research plan), objective, and straightforward.

Quantitative data is usually easier to obtain and manage; both phases of the process, getting the data and determining its meaning, are relatively simple. It involves looking at the numbers of people who purchased a given product or asking customers to provide numerical answers, such as rating a product on a scale of one to ten. Getting information whose results can be shown by numbers. Quantitative research is generally used to draw conclusions and test specific hypotheses. It involves a large number of respondents using random sampling techniques so as to generalize from the sample to the population.

Conclusive research has the sole purpose of deriving a conclusion through a search process. The results of the study can be generalized to the entire population. It is essentially a structured and quantitative approach for research and the production of this research is the result of management information systems (MIS).

Experimental techniques in almost artificial environments, where the researcher controls fake factors and manipulates variables, such as laboratories or test markets. The results of these techniques are quantitative in nature.

To collect primary research there are a few available instruments:
- Interviews - by phone or face to face, in-depth one on one
- Surveys - online, by mail, or in store
- Questionnaires - online, by mail, or in store
- Focus groups - gathering a sampling of potential clients or customers to get their direct feedback
- Observations - in store, in home, or in any other environment

There are many marketing research techniques available, each with a determined focus.[23]

---

23 Compiled from Wikipedia's Marketing Research page, found at *http://en.wikipedia.org/wiki/Marketing_research*

# CHAPTER 2  MARKETHINK

| AD Tracking | Concept testing | Copy Testing |
|---|---|---|
| Advertising Research | Brand name testing | Demand Estimation |
| Viral Marketing Research | Marketing Effectiveness and Analytics | Mystery Consumer/ Buyer |
| Segmentation research | Online Panel | Sales Forecasting |
| Brand equity research | Store/ Distribution Audit | Test Marketing |
| Price elasticity testing | Positioning Research | Coolhunting |
| Buyer Decision Process Research | Internet Strategic Intelligence | Customer Satisfaction Audits |
| Brand Association Research | Commercial Eye Tracking Research | Brand Attribute Research |

Figure 14: Focus-Specific Research Techniques, wikipedia

There are other types of research that have a specific finality, such as the following:

- Descriptive research to quantify demand
- Causal research to understand and probe cause-and-effect correlations
- Exploratory research to "shed light on the true nature of the problem and suggest solutions or new ideas." (Kotler, 2009 p. 132)

## Good versus Bad Research Practices

There are, like in most things, good and bad practices in marketing research, and these are the seven good characteristics of effective research (adapted from P. Kotler, 2009 p. 144):

1. Scientific method - it uses the principles of the scientific method: careful observation, formulation of hypothesis, prediction, and testing.
2. Research creativity - at its best, it develops innovative ways to solve a problem
3. Multiple methods - marketing researchers shy away from overreliance on any method and recognize the value of using two to three methods to increase confidence in the results.
4. Interdependence of models and data recognize that data are interrelated from underlying models that guide the type of information sought.
5. Information costs do not go hand in hand with values. The costs are easy to determine, it is difficult to quantify the values.
6. *Healthy* skepticism Marketing researchers show a *healthy skepticism toward glib assumptions made* by *managers* about how a *market works*. They are *alert* to the *problems caused* by "*marketing myths.*"
7. Ethical marketing - the misuse of research can harm or annoy consumers and increase their resentment toward the invasion of their privacy or a disguised sales pitch.

## 2.3.1.4 Tips for Getting Good Research Results

- Give customers an incentive to fill out your questionnaire or to participate in one of your marketing research activities.
- Create simple, short, and straight-to-the-point questionnaires that can be easily understood.
- Don't try to get answers to many questions all at one time - make sure you know what you really need and tackle it little by little.
- Go for open-ended questions that require a more detailed response than just "yes" or "no," and always try to balance quantitative with qualitative research.
- Always pay close attention to your marketing/market research, don't overspend, and make sure that you always have resources available if you need to redo your research if things don't turn out as you expected.
- Interview your employees, especially your sales force is in constant contact with customers and can provide useful in-field insight.
- When conducting interviews or leading focus groups, make sure you record every answer exactly as it came out to ensure the research results are as accurate as possible.
- When asking for participation and collaborations, always create a friendly environment and encourage discussions of your product's strengths and weaknesses, and create a two-way collaborative dialogue.
- Always remember that no research is 100 percent accurate; no research can predict the future with certainty.
- Once you've developed an action plan based on your research and implemented it, make sure you constantly monitor the results through more research.
- Make contingency plans and be prepared to start doing marketing/market research.
- No matter which technique you are using for market research, the goal is to ask a set of questions to get a set of answers to your key questions, and new ideas.

The Five Bad Characteristics of Marketing Research[24]

1. Establishing a *narrow conception* of the research
2. The presence of *an uneven caliber of researchers*, hiring *less competent* researchers or data providers
3. *Poor framing* of the research problem, objectives, and alternatives
4. Getting late and occasionally *erroneous findings*
5. Conflicts due to personality and *presentational differences*

---

[24] Found in P. Kotler, and K. Keller, 2009, *Marketing Management*, 13th ed. p. 143–144. Prentice Hall - Pearson International. Based on R. Grover and M. Vriens, 2006, pp. 3–17, "Trusted Advisor: How It Helps Lay the Foundation for Insight," in *Handbook of Marketing Research*, California, Sage Publications. And, C. Moorman, G. Zaltman, and R. Deshpandé "Relationships between Providers and Users of Market Research: The Dynamic of Trust within and between Organizations," *Journal of Marketing Research* 29, 1992, pp. 314–328.

P. Kotler offers a final word to emphasize the importance of executing a sound and thorough market research program: "It is interesting, however, that top companies like Procter & Gamble (P&G) and General Mills want their brand managers to do fresh research each year to track what customers think of the category and competitive brands. P&G executives actually criticize brand managers who spend too little money on marketing research" (2008, p. 98).

## 2.3.2 STP: Segmentation, Targeting, and Positioning

### 2.3.2.1 Segmentation

*"Market segmentation is a method for achieving maximum market response from limited marketing resources by recognizing differences in the response characteristics of various parts of the market. It is a strategy of divide and conquer that adjust marketing strategy to inherent differences in buyer behaviour." - F. Webster*

According to W. J. Stanton, "market segmentation consists of taking the total heterogeneous market for a product and dividing it into several sub-markets or segments each of which tends to be homogeneous in all significant aspects."[25]

For P. Kotler, "market segmentation is the sub-dividing of a market into homogeneous subsets of costumes, where any subset may conceivably be selected as a market target to be reached with a distinct marketing mix. The power of this concept is that individual sellers may prosper through creatively serving specific market segments whose needs are imperfectly satisfied by the mass market offers" (1972, p. 166).

Segmentation is concerned with classifying people with similar needs, characteristics, values, and/or behaviors into groups - market segments. Dividing the market into smaller heterogeneous segments that can be reached efficiently and profitably with a company's offering.

Because people - consumers - are different, with different attitudes, beliefs, preferences, and so on, a company cannot possibly satisfy all of them with one unique product. This is true especially now, if you consider how saturated and fragmented the market is and how almost every need is being satisfied. Marketers have even made people discover needs that they weren't aware of having. Companies really have to dig deep into consumers' attitudes and behaviors to identify and develop the most adequate market segment profiles to which they can offer a product that goes beyond their basic, and even complex, needs that are already being satisfied. Uncover the hidden segments!

---

25  W. J. Stanton in *Fundamentals of Marketing* 6th ed., 1983, p. 66. McGraw Hill Book Company, Japan.

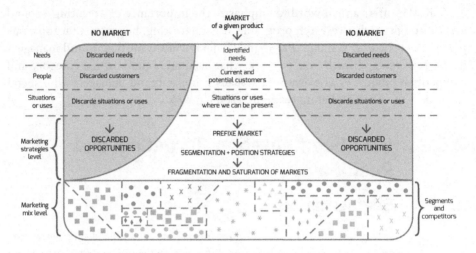

Figure 15: The Marketing Process Scenario, Kotler, Fernando Trias de Bes

## The Objectives of Market Segmentation

According to P. Kotler, "the purpose of market segmentation is to determine differences among buyers which may be consequential in choosing among them or marketing to them" (1972, p. 43).

For E. Pearce, "the purpose of market segmentation is to determine the difference among purchasers which may affect the choice of marketing area or marketing methods."[26]

Segmentation is grouping customers on the basis of a homogeneous characteristic such as habit, behavior, age, income, education, lifestyle, etc. By identifying needs, desires, tastes, priorities, and buying patterns of a specific segment to:

- Determine marketing strategies, targets, and organizational goals
- Become more consumer oriented and customer centered
- Identify the areas where new customer markets can be created or expanded

## Importance of Market Segmentation

According to M. I. Mandell and L. J. Rosenberg, market segmentation benefits marketers and consumers.[27]

- Gains, knowledge of marketing opportunities - give a better vision to locate and compare opportunities
- Enables adoption of the most effective marketing program - by knowing customers' needs, it is easier to formulate and implement different programs for each market

---

26 From J. Ashok, *Principles of Marketing*, 2009–2010, p. 89. New Delhi, India, V.K. Global Publications Pvt, Limited
27 M. I. Mandell and L. J. Rosenberg in their 1981 book, *Marketing*, 2nd ed. Prentice Hall of India

- Allows for the correct allocation of resources by focusing all marketing efforts on the consumer and only targeting selected markets
- Gives a better assessment and understanding of the competition - gives insight to the strengths and weaknesses of competitors to later choose a different strategy, target, etc.
- Gains customer-needs knowledge - allows you to understand consumers' buying behavior and why consumers behave the way they do
- Enables adjustment of the products - modify, adapt, or adjust products or communications based on changes in their taste, needs, etc.
- Creates and delivers effective advertising and communications - different appeals can be formulated for each segment according to their characteristics (selecting correct media and content)
- Enhances the efficiency of marketing efforts - it allows you to offer the correct combination of pricing, promotions, and distribution based on each segment
- Increases sales by satisfying the different demand patterns and adapting the offerings accordingly to satisfy each segment
- Increases the benefits for the consumer - gives the consumer a choice and satisfies their unique needs

Segmentation can be classified into four levels. Mass marketing: the same product for all consumers - Ford is said to have remarked that "any customer can have a car painted any color that he wants as long as it is black"[28]. Second segment: a different product for one or more segments. Third: niche marketing, different products for different subsegments; and last or fourth: micromarketing, segmentation to the extreme - tailoring products, services, and marketing strategies to a local audience (the community) within a larger audience/community.

There are various variables available for segmenting the market that go from very narrow to broader and more complex analysis. Through time and with the evolution and saturation of the marketplace, the marketing function really needs to search, combine, and uncover segments that aren't being satisfied or that can be profitable, or even find new business opportunities.

From 2004 to 2005 Massimo Soriani Bellavista and Roberto Klaus carried out research under the name "Dividi et Impera" (in English, "Divide and Conquer"), on the types of customer segmentation; this project was financed by the Swiss SUPSI and commissioned by Banca del Gottardo.

"Divide and Conquer" is a proposal for a new approach to behavioral segmentation through data mining. Here is an excerpt.

There are many segmentation and positioning strategies and they have different approaches, but really they can be divided into three macrotypes.

---

[28] Remark made by Henry Ford in 1909 about the T Model, published in his 1922 autobiography, *My Life and Work*, Chapter IV, pp. 71–72. Doubleday, Page & Company

1. A priori segmentation - beforehand
2. A posteriori segmentation - in retrospect
3. Mixed or integrated segmentation

## A priori segmentation

A priori segmentation is carried out by those who conduct the analysis. The particularity of this approach is that the variables and criteria for segmentation are defined a priori, before the study even begins. The analysis begins with the global demand, and then proceeds by breaking it up into the subsequent segments whose number, and possibly composition, have already been determined at the time the variables and criteria were chosen. The outcome generally consists of very homogeneous segments that are often not very indicative or innovative in relation to their response to targeted marketing actions and efforts. If you divide your clients into segments based on "geographical" variables, they would all fall under the same classification, providing zero differences and static clusters. In a nutshell, a priori segmentation enables us to (only) see what we want to see and what is already there.

## A posteriori segmentation

A posteriori segmentation, on the other hand, involves creating demand clusters based on similarities inferred from the entire information base that, although apparently selected a priori, does not provide a "discriminatory function" for the various segments. The weight and influence of each variable on the underlying structure of the demand behavior derives from the successive aggregations and combinations made using several techniques, such as neural networks and cluster analysis, to name a few. The technique and technology used belong to the ones used in data mining, where finding the clusters is fast and accurate. To better understand this concept, consider a "psychographics" basis of segmentation, both a priori and a posteriori. The significant difference is given by greater predictability a posteriori approach and the fact that the variables are not the result of a prior decision, which gives room for adjustments.

## Mixed or Integrated Segmentation

In some cases, due to the businesses constraints, you have to proceed with a mixed methodology: a priori on the one side, and then a posteriori within the chosen segment. In some cases this approach to segmentation provides an important methodological contribution and excellent results.

During research they identified more than thirty types of segmentation used in organizations; these are some of them, to be used as a stimulus for further analysis.

| Segmentation by - based on | | |
|---|---|---|
| One to one | Business | Profitability |
| Use | Psychographic | Socio-demographic |
| Behaviour | AuM | Geographic |
| Loyalty | Product based on assortment | Confidentiality |
| Benefits | Actual and potential wealth | Source of wealth/income |
| Phase of the process | Internal resources | Null segment |
| Risk propensity | Profession | Network |
| Consulting need and mandate | Lifestyle | Ethnic, religious and cultural origin |
| Life time value | Motivation and attitude | ... |

Figure 16: Segmentation (Soriani Bellavista / Klaus)

Segmentation is the market analysis and research that determines what the market's opportunities are; it is what leads you to determine who you are going after.

## 2.3.2.2 Targeting

Once you have isolated the market interesting and valuable segments, defined and measurable, you need to decide where to direct your efforts to reach them. This is the process of measuring the segments' attractiveness and selecting which ones to target with your specifically designed marketing programs.

When a company is determining its targeting strategy, it has to base it on the potential business success, considering factors such as the segments' growth potential and profitability, competitive rivalry, environmental and social forces, and the fit of the segment with the company's vision and identity. The use of situational-analysis models can be quite useful at this level, combined with all the previous research.

If you have the correct information through a coherent segmentation strategy and your objectives are clear, determining whom to target will come easily; just assure yourself that what you have to offer them is of value. If you haven't done a proper market segmentation, be careful because targeting the wrong segment, well, it can be fatal! In this case, you target will be not interested and the one that might be doesn't hear from you. For this reason, we suggest to make you sure that the fit exists between you, your offer, and the market segment you are targeting.

### 2.3.2.3 Positioning

*"Positioning is not what you do to a product.*
*Positioning is what you do to the mind of the prospect."* - A. Ries and J. Trout

"The aim of positioning is to locate a specific brand in the minds of consumers so that potential benefits for firm can be maximized. An effective positioning helps a firm in its marketing strategy by elucidating the brand's access, how it helps consumers in attaining specific goals and by explaining that how it will do so in a distinctive manner."[29]

"Marketing positioning refers to a process through which marketers try to establish an image or identity in the minds of their target market in regard to their product, brand or company. It is an act of designing a firm's product and image to attain a significant place in the minds of its target market."[30]

The concept of positioning was first introduced in 1969 by Jack Trout,[31] who in 1981 popularized the term in collaboration with A. Ries in their bestseller, *Positioning - The Battle for Your Mind*.[32] They define it as "an organized system for finding a window in the mind. It's based on the concept that communication can only take place at the right time and under the right circumstances."

Positioning the company's offerings in the market for consumers to know what the benefits of said offer are. P. Kotler defines positioning as "the effort to implant the offerings' key benefit(s) and differentiation in the consumers' minds"

Positioning is the strategy that aims at establishing a determined positioning of the brand and its products in the minds of existing and potential customers. It's placing the product in the right place within the minds of consumers, with the appropriate and desired image, through the execution of well-planned and carefully executed marketing programs. Here you can see a simple example of positioning in the fast food market based on price and quality:

---

[29] J. R. Darling, 2001, "Successful Competitive Positioning: The Key for Entry into the European Consumer Market" in the *European Business Review*, 13 (4), pp. 209–220

[30] M. C. Cant, J. W. Strydom and C. J. Jooste, 2009, "Marketing Management," 5th ed. Juta and Company Ltd.

[31] J. Trout, "Positioning" is a game people play in today's me-too market place. In *Industrial Marketing*, vol.54, no. 6, June, 1969, pp. 51–55.

[32] J. Trout and A. Ries, 1981, *Positioning, The Battle for your Mind*. McGraw-Hill

# CHAPTER 2 — MARKETHINK

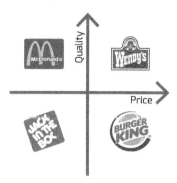

Figure 17: Example of Brand Positioning Matrix

The main goal of a positioning strategy is to plan the product's position in a way that gives you a greater competitive advantage. It is positioning yourself as close as possible to who you are as a company and what your product is really about.

Consumers' perceptions of you, your product, and its attributes define the place you have in their mind, and perception is reality. Don't overdo it. Don't pretend to be what you are not. Don't promise what you cannot deliver. There is no point to pretending to have a high-quality product if you don't! It will only hurt you!

It is important to carefully consider the position you want your product or service to have in the mind of consumers; how they perceive you and your positioning will determine the product's success or failure. It explains the place you hope your offering will occupy in consumers' minds - how they see your product compared to competitors', and what the benefits they associate with it are. It's the process that decides and plans how you want the public to see your product, service, or brand, instead of letting consumers decide on their own. Marketers have to influence and shape consumers' understanding of the concept and their perceptions and attitudes toward the product for it to actually be positioned as intended. It is all about creating value through distinctive appeal - corrects attributes and brand image.

There are a few key guidelines involved in determining one's positioning in the marketplace:

- Identify the business's direct competition and understand how they are positioning their business today. Develop your knowledge on the market, consumers, and society and its evolution.
- Compare your company's positioning to competitors'; identify and develop a distinctive, differentiated and value-based positioning strategy, statement, key messages, customer value propositions, placement, attributes, etc.
- "The most successful positioning occurs with companies that have figured out how to be unique and very difficult to imitate" (Kotler 2003, p. 135).

## 2.3.3 Marketing Mix

Making marketing decisions and establishing the controllable parameters of the marketing mix require detailed tactical decisions. These parameters are product development, pricing statement, distribution contracts, and promotional campaign development.

### 2.3.3.1 Product Mix

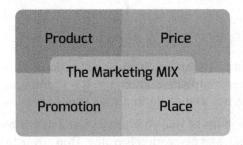

Figure 18: The Four Ps - Elements of the Marketing Mix

> "Marketing mix represents the settings of the firm's marketing decision variables at a particular point in time...the set of controllable variables that the firm can use to influence the buyer's response". - P. Kotler

The marketing mix, according to W. J. Stanton, is "the term used to describe the combination of the four inputs that constitute the core of a company's marketing system - the product, the price structure, the promotional activities, and the placement system."[33]

N. H. Borden, the professor who coined the term "marketing mix" in 1953, defines it as follows: "the marketing mix refers to the apportionment of effort, the combination, the designing and the integration of the elements of marketing into a program or mix which on the basis of an appraisal of the market force will best achieve the objectives of an enterprise at a given time."[34]

In 1960, E. J. McCarthy proposed a classification of this concept into the four p's, which identified and determined the product, the price, the place, and the promotion - the elements on which to base the market offering decisions.[37]

---

[33] Found in the Rai University of New Delhi India MBA Material, Chapter 1, and Lesson 1. "Introduction to Consumer Behavior," p. 2. You can find the full chapter at http://s3.amazonaws.com/ppt-download/consumerbehavior-notes-091031234213-phpapp01.pdf.

[34] During his 1953 presidential address to the American Marketing Association. In "The Concept of Marketing Mix," Journal of Advertising Research Vol. 4, June, 1964, pp. 2–7. He further developed the concept and established that for each P there are twelve managerial policies.

## 2.3.3.2 The Four Ps of the Mix

### The Product

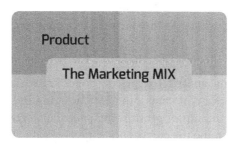

Figure 19: The Four Ps - Product

- Target - consider the four *w*'s: Who? What? When? Where?
- Function - what is it for? What need does it satisfy? What's its functionality and attributes?
- Quality - what level of quality should it have within the market?
- Competitive advantage - what makes it different? What's its unique value proposition?
- Packaging - does it stand out? Is it easy to open and use? Is it ecofriendly? Does it save space? (One can argue that this element should have a voice of its own.)

One can also take into account the design, the product line derivation, and the services associated with the product. Also consider the product as being the brand, or the service.

### The Price

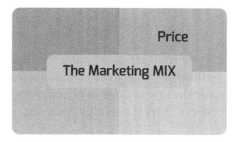

Figure 20: The Four Ps - Price

This is an extremely delicate point because it is strongly dependent on external factors, such as the market demand, competition, and the purchasing power of consumers. It is also a component that determines the product's positioning and the competitive approach and advantage, therefore influencing the product's market share and accordingly the sales volume.

One should always be sure of the following points when establishing the price strategy:

- Have clear and shared marketing objectives with the client.
- Determine, at best, the level of demand.
- Analyze the pricing strategies in your market - competition, similar products, industry.
- Estimate the cost of the unit - production, distribution, communication.

There is an interesting approach to pricing goods known as "yield management," which involves the "process of examining and factoring in consumer behavior to achieve the maximum amount of profit from a perishable good. Consumer behavior is examined to determine the correct price level to make the item enticing to the consumer. The idea is to coordinate timing, price, and consumer buying patterns to achieve the best return. The issue with yield management is that it can often result in unfair pricing for consumers."[35]

Some interesting operational work has been carried out by Hermann Simon and Danilo Zatta's team on how to improve pricing strategies to increase profits and maximize the company's success (for more detail see the bibliography).

## The Place

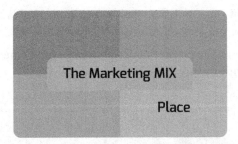

Figure 21: The Four Ps - Place

Where will the product be sold, and how will it get there? The whole logistical process involved in getting the goods from manufacturing to the consumer - at the right place and time, for the lowest costs, is of concern at this level of the mix; distribution, channel members, market coverage, locations, and logistics are all elements to consider.

Specific considerations have to be made when determining the distribution network. The distribution network is the set of interdependent organizations and interconnected systems of sources and destinations the product goes through before reaching the final consumers. The conditions are: the distribution request coverage for that market to achieve the goals; the level control prefix of the product

---

[35] Retrieved from *http://www.investorwords.com/8736/yield_management.html#ixzz2jxOoMUUd*

during transportation and at the point of sale; the total cost of distribution - order processing, the cost of lost business, inventory, human limitations of management; ability for multi-channel gods respond to changing market conditions and due to the evolution. (Can the manufacturer adapt to change?).

It's about understanding and identifying the buyers' behaviors and patterns: how and where do they buy?

## The Promotion

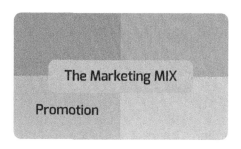

Figure 22: The Four Ps - Promotion

Promotion refers to the integrated communication activities strategically planned to stimulate consumers and push them to buy. It's the design and creation of plans to reach your target market with your message, catch their attention, and get them interested until finally they become actual customers. The communication mix is composed of various means:

- Advertising
- Sales promotions
- Public relations
- Personnel selling - sales force
- Direct marketing

There are many available promotional tactics, but we believe that by using your imagination you can all come up with creative new ways of promoting efficiently and effectively. For example, collecting and mini collecting, gift on/gift in pack, scratch off, and even comarketing.

## Promotion versus Advertising

We believe that people often don't have a clear understanding the difference between the terms "promotions" and "advertising."

Promotion is a brief action applied on a product or service to increase sales by giving an incentive to the consumer. Promotion objectives are to increase sales, boost big-pack sales or usage, invite customers for tryouts, increase purchasing recurrence, and gain loyalty.

- Promotional campaigns have short-term objectives compared to advertising campaigns, but have a more immediate response rate in terms of sales increase and ROI.
- Promotions get the best results when supported by advertising; they are closely linked.
- Promotional activities target both the consumer and the distributor.

Advertising is, on the other hand, the dissemination of a message to get consumer attention and increase awareness and visibility on a determined product through the use of adequate media. Advertising objectives are to attract consumers' attention, maintain their interest, solicit their desire, and induce them to take action - the AIDA model.

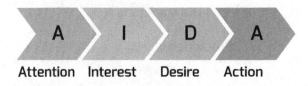

Figure 23: The AIDA Model

### 2.3.3.3 Service Mix

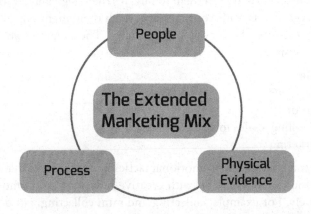

Figure 24: The Extended Marketing Mix [36]

The service marketing mix, proposed by academics B. Booms and M. Bitner in 1981 develop the most effective, coherent, and satisfying service strategy, is composed of a total of seven *p*'s [37]. I recommend that you start implementing these additional three *p*'s in the product marketing mix. The "product" business is becoming more and

---

[36] Marketing strategies and organizational structures for service firms B. Booms, M. Bitner, 1981 in marketing of services, James H. Donnelly and William R. George (eds), American Marketing Association, Chicago, 1981.

[37] Proposed in their "Marketing Strategies and Organizational Structures for Service Firms," which appeared in J. Donnelly and W. George's *Marketing of Services*, American Marketing Association, Chicago, 1981, p. 67

more linked to services, and the future of most commercial exchanges will be more service oriented. Service quality associated with a brand and its products will make the difference in regards to competitors. The others three topic *p*'s are the representation of said service and providing evidence to render the service more tangible. The consideration of these can be a great competitive advantage that can last through time if well applied.

## People

People refers to the ones who manage the front-line interactions, the ones in charge of the exchange's success and responsible for establishing the relationship between companies and customers - it is greatly important to have the appropriate people in the company. People who are properly trained and customer oriented to deliver the service in the most homogenous way possible. Generally, the people in charge of delivering a service should have good interpersonal skills, a good understanding of the service, and knowledge about the products. I also believe it is important to have people already predisposed to helping others and to being of service, people who are open, empathic, and willing to go the extra mile. The "contact" employees are the ones who contribute to the quality of the service and its delivery. Because a service is a live-through moment, positive interaction is essential for establishing a positive exchange and delivering a satisfying service experience. The attitudes and behaviors of the service provider affect and influence the customers' perceptions of said service and the customers' future loyalty. This is extremely important because their perception of value and quality influence their satisfaction level and their purchasing intentions accordingly.

## Processes

Processes are the organizational sequence of activities that help manage and support the service delivery in terms of efficiency and effectiveness - by this we mean the systems that assist "people" in delivering the service (flow of activities, information systems, procedures, mechanisms, administration, networks, supply chains, and so on).

## Physical Evidence

Physical evidence is the proof that supports the existence of the service extension -location, accessibility and visibility, the website, the infrastructure, and the visual impact. It is the environment where the service is delivered and where the interaction takes place, together with all the tangible commodities and the tools that are of support to the service delivery and facilitate the performance. This is quite an important element of the service marketing mix. (Though I would say that it is as important for the product mix and positioning strategy.) By this we mean where and with what mediums the service will be delivered. This is an area easily judged by customers, since they see, feel, and experience it directly. The physical evidence must correspond to the customers' expectations and represent the brand's image. Customers will base their perception of the company not only on how they are served, but on what they see of the service provision - Internet, offices, lobbies, employees' appearance, hygiene, and many other aspects.

In the table below, you can clearly see the difference between a product and a service.

| PRODUCT | SERVICE |
| --- | --- |
| The product is generally concrete | The service is intangible |
| Ownership is transferred when a purchase is made | Ownership is not generally transferred |
| The product can be resold | The product cannot be resold |
| The product can be demonstrated | The product cannot usually be effectively demonstrated (it does not exist before purchase) |
| The product can be stored by sellers and buyers | The product cannot be stored |
| Consumption is preceded by production | Production and consumption generally coincide |
| Production, selling and consumption are locally differentiated | Production, consumption and often the selling are spatially united |
| The product can be transported | The product cannot be transported (though 'producers' often can) |
| The seller produces | The buyer/client takes part directly in the production |
| Indirect contact is possible between company and client | In most cases direct contact is necessary |
| Can be exported | The service cannot not normally be exported, but the service delivery system can |

Figure 25: Product versus Service Industries (R. Normann)

## 2.3.3.4 Recent Approaches to the Mix

When we think of the marketing mix, we automatically remember the well-known four *p*'s, but the complexity of the market is forcing marketers to consider different elements and new perspectives when establishing a service or product strategy. Through time and experiences, these approaches have been proposed:

### Four Cs: The Customer Mix

R. Lauterborn realized that there was a need to understand the consumer. In

1993 he defined a consumer-oriented model to shift from mass marketing to niche marketing [38]. He proposed that before determining the four *p*'s, one should focus first on the consumer by determining the four *c*'s:

- Customer's *value* - not only the product itself. Find out what people want and how they want it before developing it.
- Customer *cost* - cost of ownership, not only the price. The overall cost to satisfy the customer and getting to reach your product.
- Customer *convenience* - product accessibility and purchasing model, not only the place. It's about finding out where they want you and when they want you.
- Customer *communication* - more than the promotion. Communicate with them rather than promote to them.

This implies the need to develop and maintain a relationship based on marketing strategy to develop and modify the four *p*'s correctly and coherently. We need to create a product that is projected with the collaboration of both the consumer and the value's chain to determine the price according to the consumers' perceived value of the product and related services. We need also to create a distribution strategy based on the direct contact with the client, managing the best buying conditions directly; and to deliver a direct and personalized communication in order to establish a real, two-way, multibeneficial dialogue. Considering the four *c*'s can truly help establish loyalty and a long-term relationship.

P. Kotler stated that the four *p*'s represent the seller's vision and thinking, while the four *c*'s represent the buyer's vision and approach. To Kotler, the four *c*'s are a reminder that consumers have power, that they want value for a low cost with a high level of convenience and real communication (2008, pp. 61–62).

## The SIVA Marketing Model

This is yet again a new way of interpreting the four *p*'s; it provides a more customer-driven approach to defining the product/marketing mix.

The SIVA Marketing Model, suggested by C. Dev and D. Schultz in 2005 is a customer-focused marketing approach that provides an alternative to the four *p*'s model. It is a customer-centric model that focuses on how they value and perceive the transaction. [39], This model was proposed to rearticulate the four *p*'s for companies to be able to cope with today's market environment, where the power has shifted from the company to the consumer. The four elements of the SIVA model are as follows:

- *Solution* - the product should became the solution. How appropriate is your solution to the customers' problems or needs? The idea is that the product is driven by the consumers' needs. Marketing no longer defines the markets or dictates

---

[38] Robert F. Lauterborn, Don E. Schultz, and Stanley I. Tannenbaum, 1993, "Integrated Marketing Communications." McGraw Hil

[39] Chekitan S. Dev, and Don E. Schultz, 2005. "Simply SIV" in *Marketing Management Journal*, vol. 14, issue 2, pp. 36–41. American Marketing Association

preferences. It's the consumer who does. Now marketing has to understand the consumer's need, articulate it, and find a solution to it.
- *Information* - the promotion should become now information. Does the customer know about your solution? How? Are they in possession of the adequate information to make a purchasing decision? Share the solution's information and allow them to decide whether it satisfies them or not.
- *Value* - the price is seen as the value. Does the customer understand the transaction's value? Its cost and benefits? What they will gain from it, and what might they have to give up? Pricing strategies are based on the value the product delivers to the customers rather than on the old economic theories.
- *Access* - the place is all about access. Where do the consumers find your solution? How easily can they make the transaction - buy, receive, and see? It is no longer about where to sell and place the goods but about providing the solution when and where the customer wants it.

Now all you have to do is apply these different approaches in your marketing strategies, combine them with the traditional ones and with your own, start getting to know your customers, and offer them what they want, how they want it, and where they want it. You are no longer the driving force; you are being pushed around and dominated by consumers. It's easy, right?

## 2.3.4 Implementation and Control

*"In the majority of cases - we estimate 70 percent - the real problem isn't bad strategy but bad execution." - R. Kaplan and D. Norton*

*"Everyone knows that the implementation of new ideas is more important than the idea itself." - E. de Bono*

*"Strategy is implementation." - L. Gestner, Former CEO of IBM*

Implementing the plan - getting there! And controlling the outcome - ensuring results.

At this point of the process, the marketing plan has been developed and the product has been launched into the market. As we know, the environment is not a static place, and consumers evolve constantly; it is therefore essential to monitor the plan's results and outcomes, as well as the marketing efforts, closely. This allows the company to keep up with the changes and evolutions and take the necessary actions to continue being relevant in this ever-changing environment. The marketing mix can be adjusted to accommodate said changes; opportunities can be caught and problems avoided. The marketing process doesn't end with the implementation phase; it requires continuous monitoring and adaptation to keep satisfying a customer's needs consistently through time and through all the phases of his or her life, of his or her "persona."

## 2.3.4.1 Implementation and Control

Once you have set your strategic and tactical plan, you have to put the plan into motion and develop the actual offering, based on the marketing mix, and put it on the market. Implementing the marketing plan has designing the product or service, pricing it, distributing it, and promoting it. It is the process of allocating the resources, determining who, how, and when things will be done, and actually doing them. It's the plan's execution!

To successfully implement your marketing strategy, all the departments of your company have to be involved and cooperate; they must all work in sync with each other - R&D, purchasing, production, logistics, financial and accounting, human resources, and of course the marketing department. It is management's role to ensure this happens by carrying on key activities:

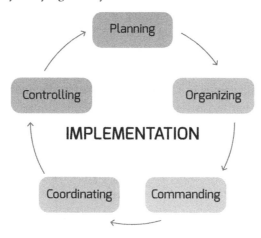

Figure 26: Implementation Activities

Effective implementation is all about managing, measuring, and controlling all marketing activities. The core of a marketing plan's implementation is its execution, the actual process of doing the planned activities. A written plan is useless if not acted on; it requires taking action, managing it, and following up. For implementation to be successful there are a few requirements:

- Focus on the tasks at hand and allocate time to avoid deflection of distraction or objections.
- Maintain effective and efficient coordination of activities and feedback.
- Pay careful attention to details and apparently irrelevant information, results, etc.
- Always be on top of who's doing what, when, and how. Know who is responsible and accountable for carrying out tasks.
- Be active and proactive, don't wait to see what happens, be on top of things, and don't waste time. Strive to continuously move forward.

- Make sure that you overdeliver and underpromise. Promise only what you know you can deliver, and don't deceive.
- Do only what you do best - the rest, outsource it. You cannot do it all, and it's best to allocate your time and resources to where you can truly deliver added value.
- Make people accountable for their successes and failures on assigned tasks.
- Constantly follow up. Check and double-check completion and deadlines; get and give feedback.

Implementing a strategy is all about putting things into motion, executing the strategy, evaluating and monitoring the progress, and making the necessary adjustments and modifications to stay on track.

A strategy is implemented by the means of various programs, procedures, and budgets. It concerns the allocation and organization of the company's resources by taking advantage of the existing synergies between business units and functional areas, and putting into place the necessary organizational changes. Implementation planning includes program planning to establish schedules and deadlines, costs, and technical operations. It integrates directions, resources allocation and availability, and functional, operational, and productive needs and requirements.

A strategy usually comes in the form of a written document that is highly abstract with conceptual terms and priorities. For the implementation purpose, it needs to be interpreted and transformed into detailed plans and guidelines for it to be understood at the functional and operational level of the organization, and also to uncover practical issues that weren't visible at the conceptual level. The translation of the strategy should be done according to the various functional areas, such as marketing, procurement, HR, and into specific compliance and policy.

The key to successful implementation is the evaluation and control of the execution phase, which consists of the following:

- Defining what parameters are to be measured and what the target values to reach for each parameter are
- Performing the measurements
- Making the comparison between the predefined standards and the measured results
- Making the necessary changes and adjustments

## Control Systems

Once the necessary adjustments and modifications have been made, it is important to continue measuring the results and evaluating the "new" strategy. To do this in the most efficient manner, developing and implementing control systems is key. Theses control systems define the standards of performance, measure the actual performance of the strategy, and give the necessary inputs to make the appropriate decisions and actions.

Note that the implementation process is continuous and dynamic: if you change one component or variable, a change, modification, or adaptation in the whole strategy may be required. It is therefore crucial to constantly monitor the environment and the process, and control results frequently to adapt as fast as possible to changes, to avoid problems, and to see opportunities.

The effective implementation of a strategy involves the process of developing policies and executing plans that lead to the real behavioral change necessary to reach various objectives and the overall goals. "The implementation effectiveness is the difference between a project that has simply been completed and one that has been completed and delivers the intended business value. It is the difference between success and failure. Implementation effectiveness is not something you 'do'. It is a way of thinking."[40]

## 2.3.4.2 Governance

Governance is the activity of governing. By this we mean the decision-making power that defines expectations, grants permission and power, verifies performances, and controls of the correct behavior and respect of the best business practice, laws and regulations. It is the glue and process that aims to ensure the company's positive performance and actions, and the delivery of a "worthwhile pattern of good results while avoiding an undesirable pattern of bad circumstances."[41]

An organization should always have two types of governance, one at the corporate level and one at the project level. The corporate one governs the whole organization's actions; the project one governs the projects that have been undertaken by the company.

Figure 27: System Governance Elements

---

40 Retrieved from "Implementation Institute: The Bridge between Strategy and Execution," found at *http://www.implementationinstitute.org/*

41 Retrieved from Wikipedia at *http://en.wikipedia.org/wiki/Governance*

- *Corporate governance* is "a set of processes, customs, policies, laws, and institutions that affect the way people direct, administer, and control corporations. It also includes the relationships among the many players involved in the corporate goals."[42]

## 2.3.4.3 The Marketing Balanced Scorecard

L. Gestner, former CEO of IBM, says that "strategy is implementation." If this is so, we have to move from the declared strategy, which is the written description of it, to the "acted" strategy, the executed strategy. To further sustain the idea that implementation is central to the success of a strategy, R. Kaplan and D. Norton studied many companies and found out that 70 percent of strategy failures are not due to the strategy in itself but due to its execution.[43] To resolve the strategic implementation failure, they developed a set of operational tools merged into one tool: the balanced score.

During an HSM seminar, P. Kotler said that "the chief marketing officer must demonstrate the return on marketing investment" and further recommended "the creation of a marketing scorecard that captures the number of new customers added every year, measures the level of satisfaction of current customers and indicates the brand's health."

"One of the worst mistakes a company can make is to set and review only financial goals to the neglect of other measures of company health and performance" (Kotler 2001, p. 186). P. Kotler suggests that a successful company needs to analyze the company's performance and results through different perspectives, because depending on where you focus, the results might not always be the same. To do this he suggests that you examine your company's performance through three balanced scorecards: the financial, the marketing, and the stakeholders'. For the purpose of this book we will only look at the marketing one.

The marketing scorecard is composed of several marketing indicators such as market share, customer retention and satisfaction, and product and service quality, along with all other relevant marketing indicators. Keeping track of the indicators' results will allow management to put the results into perspective and have clear understanding of them, how they got them, and how each area - strategic or product development - impacts the overall results.

It is a scorecard inspired by the widely used business balanced scorecard, but it focuses on the marketing strategy rather than on the business. It allows you to know exactly where you stand with your marketing strategy and activities and gives a

---

42  Retrieved from Wikipedia at *http://en.wikipedia.org/wiki/Governance*
43  In their 1996 book, *The Balanced Scorecard: Translating Strategy into Action*. Boston, Harvard Business School Press.

clear view on what the return of your marketing efforts are. It helps you to see what is working and what is not, to determine where it is that you need to focus your attention, and to improve the marketing and business results as a whole.

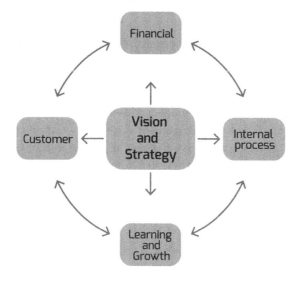

Figure 28: A Balanced Scorecard

The marketing/balanced scorecard is a metrics tool to measure the effects of a marketing plan and to keep track of its execution in order to anticipate and avoid surprises.

"The main point is that senior management should not confine its scrutiny to the financial scorecard. Behind good financial results may lurk some impending marketing weakness" (Kotler 2001, p. 191).

The scorecard is a great tool for managers to use to assess the true effectiveness of the marketing tactics activated. It provides the quantitative justification and data to support the costs and the assigned budget for marketing and its activities and various plans. It enables managers to control and keep track of the key performance indicators.

Good implementation, with good governance and the correct and consistent use of balanced scorecards, is the most effective way for the CEO and the CFO and CMO to determine exactly how the marketing expenditures translate into corporate revenues and how the marketing strategy is translated into operational terms.

The marketplace is changing quickly, and marketers can't keep up if they continue thinking of marketing through the old model. We are experiencing a shift of the marketing paradigm, which is all about changing the focus, moving away from old models, procedures, and concepts. Today's model:

- We are focusing on marketing strategies, rather than using known tactics.
- We build brands with coordinated and integrated marketing strategies through the direct contact established between the brand and the public. It is no longer only about selling through advertising.
- We are focusing on the customer's lifetime value and what a product can bring the customer in time, instead of focusing only on profitable transactions.
- The company is no longer the unit of analysis; we are now analyzing the whole value chain: Are we really meeting our targets' needs? And the company's?
- Segmentation is not only based on geographic or demographic variables, but on behavioral ones such as loyalty, usage, and beliefs.
- The main goal of marketing management was to gain a larger market share, capturing new customers; today it is all about the importance of keeping and satisfying existing customers.
- Performance is now measured not only by financial metrics but by strategic and marketing metrics as well. It's more than just about cash; it's about establishing a valuable exchange that lasts through time. Performance is also clearly related to the value it delivers.
- Before it was all about the shareholder; now it is all about stakeholders. The company has to consider all its audiences and satisfy all of them as well. Remember that the public now has more power than ever; they have a voice, and it is heard.
- The marketing function is now carried by all the areas of a company - everyone does marketing. It's a cross functional process, and the more it's interconnected and transversal, the better the outcome.
- Timing is not the same: Before, developing and implementing a marketing plan was long, slow, and quite static. Today it is fast and active with immediate impact.

## 2.4 Product versus Service Marketing

### 2.4.1 Product Marketing

*"A product is anything that can be offered to a market for attention, acquisition, use or consumption that might satisfy a want or need. It includes physical objects, services, persons, places, organization and ideas." - P. Kotler*

*"A product is a bundle of utilities consisting of various product features and accompanying services." - W. Alderson*

Marketing, as we know, is the integrated process used by companies to get consumers interested and ultimately loyal. It is the process that generates: the strategy to define sales techniques, business communication and development; to establish a customer base, relationship and create value for customers as well as for the business. It is used to identify, keep, and satisfy customers.

# CHAPTER 2 — MARKETHINK

An essential element of marketing management is marketing-mix decision making. These decisions are concerned with creating the best offerings for its target market. The four *p*'s model was established to respond to marketplace evolution and enable companies to develop strategies that responded to the changing needs and behaviors of consumers.

## 2.4.2 Service Marketing

> "Service is an action or an activity which can be offered by a party to another party, which is basically intangible and cannot affect any ownership. Service may be related to tangible product or intangible product." - P. Kotler

Service marketing is what the name suggests: the marketing of services rather than products. It is the marketing of intangibles! How you market and manage your services can have amazing or terrifying consequences on your company and its success.

Let's understand the nature of a service:

- *Absence of ownership* - it is used straightaway or rented for a determined period of time. When you purchase it, you can't own it; you can use it, but it's not yours.
- *Intangible* - it cannot be held or touched. It is more like an experience that impacts perceptions.
- *Inseparable* - services go hand in hand with the provider.
- *Perishable* - it has a determined validity in time and cannot be stored. The service is usually developed and used in sequence.
- *Heterogenic* - no two services can be the same time after time. Services are extremely variable due to the human involvement in their delivery.

Services can and should be seen as part of a spectrum: not all products are pure goods, and so, not all services are 100 percent services. In a restaurant, for example, the waiter is part of the service, and the food is the product. Therefore it is essential to always consider service marketing elements when determining business and marketing strategies. A service can, and should, be associated with the product's overall value. A good product technical care is a service!

These elements of the service mix need to be taken into account in all marketing efforts, since keeping them under control can reduce the gaps between customers' and the organization's expectations and perceptions, as we will see later on.

For B. Steinhoff, "the raw material of services is people. The main material of services is in fact people; nevertheless, there are many other supporting factors from the raw material of services such as advanced tools, clean, secured, comfortable physical environment, accurate, advanced and up to date technology and service."[44]

Managing services is much more complex than managing products; It is ex-

---

[44] B. Steinhoff in his book *The World of Business*, 1979, p. 113. McGraw Hill Book Co.

tremely hard, if not impossible, to reach and then maintain service standardization. There are a lot more external and internal influencing forces and factors to consider and manage, within and outside of the company's control.

Services are an important benefit to consumers only if the experience is positive and rewarding. Because a service originates from personal contact, the exchange between two subjects is essential. The level of satisfaction can determine the way a consumer judges your marketing efforts and your company as a whole. V. Zeithaml, in collaboration with A. Parasuraman and L. Berry, determined in 1988 the first five "key quality services dimensions":[45]

- Reliability, performing the promised service accurately and dependably
- Responsiveness, the profound willingness to help and be of service
- Assurance, the ability of employees to convey trust and confidence
- Empathy, providing individual attentions and caring
- Tangibles, the physical attributes of the company

They later expanded the list and established the "ten determinants of service quality": access, communication, competence, courtesy, reliability, responsiveness, securities, tangibles, and understanding/knowing the customer.[46]

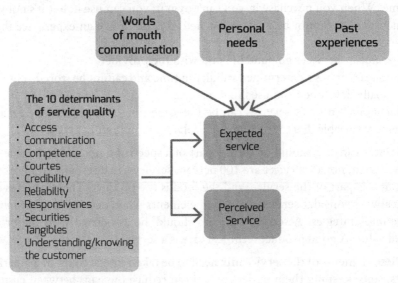

Figure 29: The Ten Determinants of Service Quality.[47]

---

45 In "SERVQUAL: A Multiple Item Scale for Measuring Consumer Perception of Service Quality." *Journal of Retailing* no. 64 Spring, 1988, pp. 12–40
46 A. Parasuraman, V. Zeithaml, L. Berry, 1985: "A Conceptual Model of Service Quality and Its Implications for Future Research." *Journal of Marketing*, vol. 49, pp. 41–50
47 It's a process-analysis methodology proposed by L. Shostack in "How to Design a Service," 1982, *The European Journal of Marketing*, Bradford, vol. 16, issue 1, pp. 49–64

# CHAPTER 2 — MARKETHINK

## James Heskett's Service-Value Profit Chain

This service-profit chain concept was put forward by J. Heskett, E. Sasser, and L. Schlesinger to show the relationship between profitability, customer loyalty, and employee satisfaction, loyalty, and productivity. They proved "that there is a direct financial link between superior service experiences, customer loyalty, and company performance (growth and profits)."[48] These are the main elements of the chain:

- Profitability and revenue growth
- Customer loyalty - companies with profit and growth are characterized by a large number of loyal customers and they are well disposed towards the three Rs: retention, repeat business, and referrals.
- Customer satisfaction - having service designed and delivered to meet targeted customer needs results in satisfied and loyal customers.
- External service value - satisfaction depends on the company's ability to create value for the customer through a well-defined service concept.
- Employee retention - value is created by loyal employees.
- Employee productivity - satisfied and loyal employees are far more productive.
- Employee satisfaction - employee loyalty is driven by employee satisfaction.
- Internal service quality - to engage employees and ensure employee satisfaction, the company has to build up the best possible internal quality through effective workplace design, job design, employee selection and development, employee rewards and recognition, and tools for serving customers.

The authors sustain that management and the organization has to concentrate, mainly, on providing their customers, suppliers, investors, employees, and other stakeholders what they individually need and value in order to create a value-added proposition. Focusing on value and on how it is delivered and paying attention to what it is that each stakeholder needs the most will automatically lead to organizational change, increasing effectiveness and profits. When the organization works on satisfying all its constituencies' needs and delivers what they value, customers will become more responsive to the offerings, employees will be more productive, and the cost of turnover will decrease, and investors will benefit from it with a higher return on investment.

The value-profit chain recognizes the importance of a company's three key stakeholders: the customer, the investor, and its employees. It's a model that stresses the importance of the *interrelationship* among their behaviors.

The following are true:[49]

---

[48] "The Service Profit Chain Theory and Mode" by J. Heskett, E. Sasser, and L. Schlesinger (Harvard University researchers), in their 1997 book, *The Service Profit Chain: How Leading Companies Link Profit and Growth to Loyalty, Sales and Value*, Simon & Schuster

[49] James L. Heskett, Thomas O. Jones, Gary W. Loveman, W. Earl Sasser, and Leonard A. Schelsinger: "Putting the

- Profits and growth are primarily achieved by customer loyalty.
- Customer loyalty is the direct consequence of customer satisfaction.
- Customer satisfaction is mainly influenced by the value of the service customers receive and experience.
- Value is created by satisfied, loyal, committed, and productive employees.
- Employees' satisfaction depends primarily on the quality of the support services and policies available to them in order to deliver the best result to the customer. This refers to the internal quality of the services.

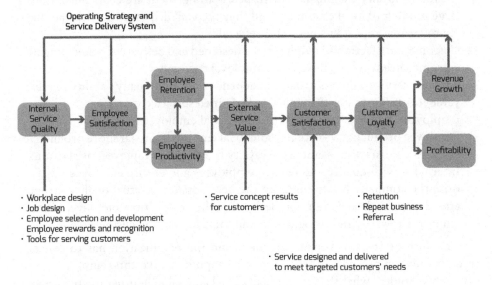

Figure 30: The Service-Profit Chain Flowchart (hbr.org 2008)

## Service Quality Framework by A. Parasuraman, V. Zeithaml, and L. Berry

The service quality framework was developed in 1985 by A. Parasuraman in collaboration with V. Zeithaml and L. Berry to measure the ten aspects of service quality and to measure the effectiveness of the service. It is a tool to measure the gap between customers' expectations and the actual experience - between the expected and the perceived service they received. This is what is called the "customer gap"[50].

The service quality framework and the determination of the customer gap are methods that involve developing an understanding of the perceived service needs

---

Service Profit Chain to Work," *Harvard Business Review*, March–April, 1994, pp. 164–174

[50] In "A Conceptual Model of Service Quality and Its Implications for Future Research," *Journal of Marketing*, vol. 49, pp. 41–50

of customers, comparing it to the best service provider on the market, and analyzing the differences to put forward the existing gaps. These gaps should then be used to improve the quality of service.

The ten aspects of quality service, known as "SERVQUAL" concepts, are reliability, responsiveness, competence, access, courtesy, communication, credibility, security, understanding knowledge of the customer, and tangibles. The SERVQUAL concepts were redefined in the early nineties by A. Parasuraman and his team to a simpler and more user friendly acronym: RATER, which is useful for qualitative exploration and assessing customers' service experiences. RATER stands for reliability, assurance, tangibles, empathy, and responsiveness. These concepts were developed to support the Gap Model put forward by the service quality framework, which is a conceptual model of service quality that indicates that customers' satisfaction and perception toward a service depends on five existing gaps within the consumer-organization relationship and the environment.

SERVQUAL provides a comprehensive and thorough examination of service needs and quality, providing valuable insight on how to improve the overall quality of a service. It provides detailed inputs about the customers' perception of the service and the performance level they perceive.

According to P. Kotler, "there are two ways to get a service reputation: one is to be the best at service; the other is to be worst at service" (2003, p. 168). "In an age of increasing product commoditization, service quality is one of the most promising sources of differentiation and distinction. Giving good service is the essence of practicing a customer orientation" (Kotler 2003, p. 167).

## The Consumer Gap Model

*Gap 1* - the difference between customers' expectations and management perception of customers' expectation

*Gap 2* - the difference between management's perception of customers' expectations and the way this is translated into service quality specifications and designs

*Gap 3* - the difference between standards of service quality and the actual service delivered

*Gap 4* - the difference between the service delivered and the promised service quality

*Gap 5* - the difference between the customer's expected service and perceived service

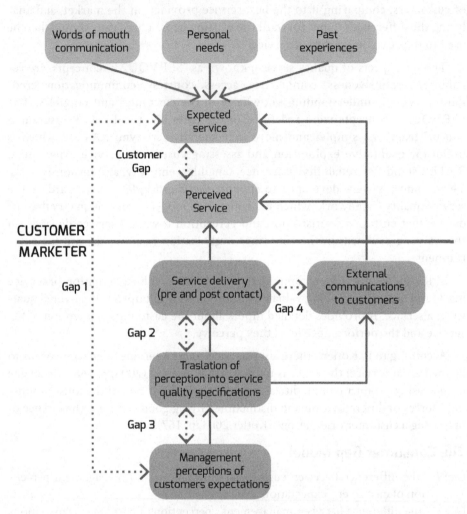

Figure 31: The Integrated Gaps Model of Service Quality[51]

---

51  A. Parasuraman, V. Zeithaml, L. Berry, 1985: "A Conceptual Model of Service Quality and Its Implications for Future Research," *Journal of Marketing*, vol. 49, pp. 41–50

## 2.4.3 One-to-One and Direct Marketing

### 2.4.3.1 One-to-One Marketing by D. Peppers and M. Rogers

One-to-one marketing is a customer-relationship management (CRM) strategy that focuses on personalizing all interactions with customers to establish and nurture customer loyalty. The CRM concept was introduced by D. Peppers and M. Rogers in their 1993 book, *The One to One Future*.[52]

They set forth the concept of managing customers rather than products, differentiating customers and not only the products. They suggest measuring the "share of customers" and not the "share of market" and developing "economies of scope" rather than "economies of scale." This is a marketing strategy that is delivered directly to the specific consumer.

This strategy is based on their "IDIC" methodology which stands for the four stages of One to One marketing,[53]

1. Identify - profiling potential customers: get to know them, collect data about their preferences, habits, and interests, and find out how it is that you can satisfy their needs.
2. Differentiate -distinguishing the customers based on their needs and in terms of lifetime value to the company. Segment them in more restricted and homogeneous groups.
3. Interact - engaging with the customer to learn more about him or her and start working on establishing a relationship. Open a two-way communication flow. What they say can be of great help in the future.
4. Customize - individualizing everything from the product to the communication to the service for the singular customer. Give the customers exactly what they want.

This marketing approach is absolutely not new. Back in the day, the one-to-one marketing approach was widely used by most store owners. They had a restricted reach and served a specific local market, so they were able to pinpoint their offering to each individual customer and run their business accordingly - inventory, merchandise, and even employees.

This approach aims to deliver a product, service, or promotion to each individual customer and to constantly provide a better service or product or both. To do this you need to remember and analyze each individual's preferences, habits, and characteristics. Nowadays, this approach is greatly supported by the Internet, infor-

---
[52] The book's full title is *The One to One Future: Building Relationships One Customer at a Time*.
[53] In an article by Don Peppers, Martha Rogers, and Bob Dorf: "Is Your Company Ready for One-to-One Marketing?" Harvard Business Review, January–February, 1999. You can find the full article at *http://hbr.org/1999/01/is-your-company-ready-for-one-to-one-marketing/ar/1*.

mation technology, and all the existing organizational systems that assist in collecting, sorting, combining, analyzing, and sharing all customer-related information throughout all communications. For example, by obtaining information from customers' shopping bags through fidelity program cards, along with their online navigation habits, a business can deliver a pinpointed offer or promotional plan to each customer that really fits him or her and will most certainly lead to a higher level of satisfaction than just giving the customer a discount on something he or she actually couldn't care less about.

### Personalization versus Differentiation

Personalization is an extreme type of product differentiation. It attempts to make a unique product offering to each single customer. It is not differentiation, because differentiation's focus is to differentiate one's products from the competition's. Personalization is differentiating the product based on the single customer, for each customer.

Amazon.com is the best example of a one-to-one marketing approach applied. Each registered user receives targeted offers and a recommendations list, among other things. When research starts, the results are based on the previous navigation patterns, therefore presenting results in order of probable preference and to fit the customers' tastes, habits, and so on. They simply suggest products that pertain directly to the personal choices of each Amazon.com client. Even the welcome page is composed of only potential-interest content and related novelties.

## 2.4.3.2 Direct Marketing

Direct marketing is direct, unsolicited contact with potential and existing customers with an attempt to increase sales and raise awareness. It is a marketing activity that allows great accuracy in targeting the right customer and those most susceptible and receptive to your message. The main challenge in direct marketing is having an adequate, up-to-date customer database. Without it, all attempts of delivering a positive direct marketing message will fail, because there is no interest and you are not welcome!

This marketing method is useful because it allocates the available resources where most certainly they will have an impact. It produce the desired results and allows for a more accurate measure of the campaign's success in terms of reaching the company's goals and ROI. This type of campaign helps increase sales to existing customers, reestablish past or slowed-down relationships, and/or generate new business.

There are various forms of direct marketing, and each one has specific targets and specific objectives to reach. They must be handled with caution to avoid overwhelming the customers, as we will see in a later chapter in S. Godin's "permission" marketing approach.

- *Direct mail* - this puts all the information needed about the product and/or service, as well as material to take action, directly in the hands of the interested, targeted recipient.
- *Leaflet drops and handouts* - this is a less targeted form of direct marketing. It is useful for products or services that have a universal appeal.
- *Telemarketing* - this is simply contacting the actual or potential customer by phone. This is a form of direct marketing widely used in B2B marketing, because people are more receptive to it, and targeting is usually more relevant. Its main advantages are that it can test the customers' interest and get their feedback immediately, it provides the possibility to directly ask the consumer questions about his or her needs, desires, and preferences, and it allows for the effective explanation of complex messages.
- *E-mail marketing* - this is extremely cheap and can reach thousands of recipients - it's the easiest way to target and reach the exact person sought after. When using this form of direct marketing, don't forget to take into consideration the spam phenomenon; your audience is bombarded daily by such tactics.
- *SMS and text marketing* - this is becoming a widely used technique to speak directly to the end customer. Messages can be personalized or modified and are easy to send to large groups quickly. Mobile phones are always at close reach; the owner usually takes it everywhere he or she goes, allowing you to communicate time-sensitive messages. And, very important, SMS messages are generally always read. Considering that the portable phone is a very personal device, it is a powerful tool for directly delivering personal, time-sensitive, and valued marketing messages.

## 2.4.4 Scientific Marketing and Data Mining

### 2.4.4.1 Scientific Marketing

Scientific marketing is an approach to market research based on the systematic application of analytical testing and statistical methods of gathering and interpreting market information and customer data. It is an approach to marketing that follows a well-defined process capable of collecting and analyzing the right data about the market, about actual, prospective, and potential customers, about competition, and about the industry.

It is a strategic marketing research tool that uses the scientific method to turn inputs into valuable outputs. The scientific method is all about formulating a hypothesis, testing it, and validating the findings in order to confirm the initial hypothesis, reject it, or modify it.

It's the scientific way of collecting, analyzing, and interpreting inputs (data) and processing outputs (information). It is a marketing strategy in that it enables companies to increase the value of marketing inputs and outputs, to establish connections among them, and to establish relationships, in order to offer a more valuable product or service to the right consumers.

## 2.4.4.2 Data Mining

Data mining is the tool that gives true value to the scientific approach of the research: the optimization of the collected data and the combination of it with the organization's existing data.

Data mining, "the extraction of hidden predictive information from large databases," helps companies focus on the most important, relevant, and valuable information in their data warehouses. It's a set of tools able to predict future trends and behaviors, giving businesses the ability to make proactive, knowledge-based decisions. Data mining tools uncover hidden patterns.

### The Scope

Data Mining is a process that requires you to sift through large amounts of material, cleverly probing it to find its value, to establish connections and relationships. It assists in the generation of business opportunities by providing two fundamental capabilities.[54]

An Automated Prediction of Trends and Behaviors, it automates the "process of finding predictive information in large databases"; allowing complex questions that require extensive analysis to be answered directly from the data and its analysis, fast and continuously. For example, a model might predict a person's income based on their education level combined with other demographic factors; you can establish that a person with a bachelor's degree living in a certain neighborhood will probably have an income greater than the average. For example, analyzing data gathered from retail sales can identify apparently unrelated products that are usually purchased together.

### From Raw Data to Usable Information to Precious Knowledge

Data mining refers to the process of analyzing data through different angles, perspectives, and dimensions, and summarizing it all into valuable information that can be used to increase revenue, cut costs, improve customer knowledge or processes, and so on.

It's an analytical tool, a software, which gives the user the ability to analyze data from many different dimensions, to categorize it, and to summarize the established connections and the identified relationships. Technically it's the process of finding correlations or patterns among dozens of fields in large relational databases. It is a

---

54 Retrieved from "An Introduction to Data Mining - Discovering Hidden Value in Your Data Warehouse," by Kurt Thearling at *http://www.thearling.com/text/dmwhite/dmwhite.htm*

process that can transform large quantities of unrelated, disorganized material into classified and organized data into relevant and coherent information, and ultimately support the development of the most valuable asset: knowledge.

### Major Elements of Data Mining

- Extracting (transformation) - transaction of the data onto the data warehouse system
- Storing and managing the data within the multidimensional database system
- Providing data access to business analysts and information technology professionals
- Using application software for the analytical process - it's therefore a more accurate and attainable output
- Presenting the data in useful, ready-to-use formats, such as graphs or tables
- Commonly Used Data Mining Techniques
- *Artificial neural networks* are nonlinear predictive models. These models learn through training and resemble biological neural networks in structure. They are all interconnected and function just as our brain does: one thing triggers another one, which in turn triggers another.
- *Decision trees* are tree-shaped structures that represent sets of decisions. These decisions generate rules for the classification of a data set. There are specific decision-tree methods - an example is the Classification and Regression Trees (CART).
- *Genetic algorithms* are an optimization technique that use processes such as genetic combination, mutation, and natural selection in a design based on the concepts of evolution.
- *Rule induction* is the extraction of useful if-then rules from data based on statistical significance.
- *Data visualization* is the visual interpretation of complex relationships in multidimensional data.
- *Graphic tools* are used to illustrate data relationships.[55]

## 2.4.5 Channel Distribution and Trade Marketing

*"For many companies making the product doesn't cost as much as bringing it to the market." - P. Kotler*

Trade marketing and distribution are elements of the mix that are concerned with increasing the brand's product demand at the wholesaler, retailer, or distributor level, instead of the end-consumer level. The relationship established by these elements assures that product can be pushed and can influence consumer-buying behavior to ensure that they give the right value to it within the competitive scenario.

---

55 Retrieved from "An Introduction to Data Mining - Discovering Hidden Value in Your Data Warehouse," by Kurt Thearling p. 28 at *http://www.thearling.com/text/dmwhite/dmwhite.htm*

L. P. Bucklin wrote that "a channel of distribution comprises a set of institutions which perform all of the activities utilized to move a product and its title from production to consumption."[56]

### 2.4.5.1 Distribution

The distribution chain needs to be considered as a "partner." His role is essential in getting the products to the end consumers; it assure accessibility and availability. But it is also an important source of information; it is in the field and have constant, direct access and contact with the end user and the market as a whole.

A *distribution channel* refers to the established route undertaken by the product to get to the final consumer. The determination of the channels depends on the products' characteristics as well as the overall marketing strategy and objectives.

The phrase *"channels of distribution"* describes the supply chain that helps marketers get to the seller and from there to the final consumer; they are designed to move the product from the company's hands to the consumers'. They consist of all activities and organizations that help assure the exchange is as efficient as possible: handling and shipping, storing, selling, promoting, and displaying. P. Kotler suggests that "whatever the number of market channels a company uses, it must integrate them to achieve an efficient supply system" (2003, p. 54).

Distribution can be considered as direct, when the producer distributes to the consumer; as short, when there is only one intermediary between the producer and the final consumer; or as long, when there is more than one intermediary.

Distribution can also be classified as intensive, when the aim is to distribute the offerings through a wide range of distributors with large stocks of the product on a continual basis; it can be selective, when the products are distributed selectively through multiple channels, and only the desirable resellers have the product in stock; and it can be exclusive, when only a few selected resellers or authorized dealers have the exclusive right to sell the product within a determined territory.

Channel Selection - Creating the Network

There are a few parameters to consider when determining the distribution strategy:
- Characteristics of the market of reference - consumer's location, buying patterns, etc.
- Product characteristics and classification (food goods, soft goods such as clothing, and hard goods such as furniture)
- Sales force organization
- Cost per unit

---

56 In the "Theory of Distribution Channel Structure," University of California, Institute of Business and Economic Research, Berkley, 1966

- Product life cycle: obsolescent or expiration
- Logistics management

### 2.4.5.2 Trade Marketing

"Choosing the right channels, convincing them to carry your merchandise, and getting them to work as a partner, is a major challenge. Too many companies see themselves as selling to distributors instead of selling through them" (Kotler 2003, p. 54).

Trade marketing is an element of the mix essential to the placement and distribution strategy of a product or service, and of value to the success of overall marketing efforts; customers are at the end of a long supply chain, and they usually don't get their goods directly from manufacturers.

Trade marketing refers to all the efforts developed and targeted to the distributors to ensure that they are positioning and promoting your products adequately, especially toward product's competitors. It is all about establishing the right profitable and mutually beneficial relationship with the intermediaries - increasing their demand and gaining competitive advantage. It aims to increase consumer demand and the visibility of the products properly distributed, marketed and promoted by trade players. When defining a trade marketing strategy, the focus is on the fundamentals of sales: distribution, display / visual merchandising, promotions, and price; you can also take into account the supply chain, production, and packaging (size, weight). The elements of the trade mix consist of trade advertising and incentive programs, promotional and merchandising support, special payment terms, and pricing strategies.

Trade marketing involves performing activities to establish a mutually beneficial partnership with the distribution channels to make sure that your products and brand are properly promoted, and involves them to do more for their brand against competitors. This is achieved by marketing products directly to the distributor, implemented with commercial activities and incentives; give them tangible and nontangible benefits for distributing and promoting your brand. Give trade good reasons to carry and push the product on the market, and make them want to be part of your success story.

## 2.4.6 Marketing Myopia

Marketing myopia is a theory introduced by T. Levitt in 1960 that defines a state of mind that restricts one's capability of seeing the market for what it is and what consumers really want and need.[57] Marketing myopia leads to a distorted view of

---

[57] The concept was first discussed in "Marketing Myopia" an article by Theodor Levitt published in the *Best of HBR 1960*, *Harvard Business Review*

the companies and the business operated by them; it usually means that managers have focused essentially on the company's needs, products, and profits, instead of defining itself in terms of their target audience and consumers - what is it that the consumer truly needs and wants and is willing to pay for, as well as the environment and the marketplace.

This shortsightedness is an obstacle to big corporations' continued growth; they fail to see or consider or grasp the opportunities and threats they are facing.

T. Levitt believes that firms are trapped in a dimension because they don't ask a vital question: "What business are we really in?" He strongly believes that "sustained growth depends on how broadly you define your business and how carefully you gauge at your customers' needs."[58] Most organizations rarely reach their full potential, and lead themselves to the fall, mainly due to a shortsighted and self-centered vision.

He advocates that growth is not stopped due to market saturation but is stopped rather due to management failure. Management looks at marketing only through their conceptions, their points of view, and the revenue it will create, instead of looking at it from their consumers' crucial point of view.

## Example

According to T. Levitt, in the July–August 1960 *Harvard Business Review*, the American railroad business didn't stop growing because there was no longer a need for passenger and freight transportation, nor because the industry was in decline; on the contrary, the transportation business was in full florescence. Railroad companies faced huge challenges because they failed to determine the business they were operating in; they were in the railroad business, not in the transportation business (it is clear they belonged to the latter). If they had clearly seen and understood what business they belonged to, they could have remained the top players - they could have expanded their offer, penetrated new markets, and become the competition in the transportation industry. "The reason they defined their industry incorrectly was that they were railroad oriented instead of transportation oriented; they were product oriented instead of costumer oriented."

## An Example of a Nonmyopic Vision

I found this example in S. Godin's book *Purple Cow*, and I think it's a good one to illustrate what marketing myopia is and how a company can gain a competitive advantage from having a 360-degree vision.

Logitech was one of the fastest growing technology companies in America, with products far from the cutting-edge technology found in Silicon Valley. The key to their competitive advantage is that they are not a cutting-edge technology company. Logitech has been really successful because they understood that to have a competi-

---

58  In "Marketing Myopia" by Theodor Levitt, *Best of HBR 1960*. *Harvard Business Review*

tive advantage they needed to focus on some other attribute than technology. They understood that they weren't in the cutting-edge technology business but in the fashion business, the fashion-technology business. Their main goal is not to change the core of the product but to change its style, design, and functionality. They don't bother with innovating chips; competition is there for that. What they work at is creating more fashionable and trendy products that "create a better user experience."[59]

## The Solution

According to Massimo Soriani Bellavista, the solution to having perfect sight and bypassing myopic vision is to look at things the way a chameleon does: with one eye we look at the present toward the same direction, toward the same shared goal, and toward what is happening here and now. With the other we look at the world around us, the environment, trends, people and cultures, and so on.

Look at the outside and what is happening out there. Look for your own satisfaction, to satisfy your curiosity. Dare to be daring, to be creative. Imagine new scenarios, new ways of doing. Keep track of the external changes, what happens in the world, and the various industries and what influence all this can have on you, your projects, and your company. This will allow the company to stay alert to the outside world and aware of the internal world, to be prepared for changes, and to be willing to make the leap. For example, the Google Calendar Schema: every week, half a day has to be dedicated to creativity, innovation, and developing individual ideas and projects.

Figure 32: A Chameleonic Vision (Depositphotos.com)

## Time Line and Inner Eye

Look at the past and present as well as at the future!

In Chinese medicine, diseases are divided into two categories: ones concerning the right side of the body are related to something of the past, and diseases related to the left side are linked to the emotions associated to their belief system; predict what

---

59 Godin, S. 2005: *Purple Cow: Transform Your Business by Being Remarkable*, p. 60

their future holds. Concerning this, we can associate the metaphor with the marketers' sight and range of vision, where one eye should look at marketing issues related to the past and present, while the other one looks, simultaneously, to the future for opportunities, threats, and potential problems. In fact, if we are too involved in tackling only today's or yesterday's problems, we will never be able to seize the opportunities or prevent the problems that tomorrow will bring.

Peter Fisk best-selling author and marketing innovation expert, explains this concept in a different way[60]. In his book, *Genius Marketing*, he states that marketers need to have a more "intelligent" and "imaginative" approach to the future. We will use his words and framework for more clarity.

Genius marketers work in "double time," creating the future while delivering today, making everyday decisions, taking both small and significant actions that have fundamental implications for the short and long term. They connect the competing demands of evolving markets and improving services, they combine the extreme objectives of delivering more sales while building brands for tomorrow, and they do this by aligning a more intelligent and imaginative approach to their marketing.

Based on this, he believes that they "can only achieve this" if they have confidence in where they are going, as well as where they are" (Fisk 2012, p. 420).

In the table below you can see what he means by being more intelligent and imaginative when thinking of what comes next.

| More Intelligent Futures | More Imaginative Futures |
|---|---|
| Insights. We still treat people as averages, and are far from truly understanding them as individuals. | Ideas. Insights are not enough. It is the power of original thought that will differentiate and transform business. |
| Brands. There are few great brands out there that truly reflect and inspire, energize and enable people. | People. Business has not yet found out how to unlock the true emotional force of human beings, inside or outside. |
| Companies. Most companies are still not genuinely customer focused, working outside in for the long term. | Communities. People want to be with people like them, to learn and work, to meet and get the most out of their lives. |

Figure 33: More Futures (*Genius Marketing*)

He gives one more insight on the matter at hand: "Cycles can reveal secrets as to how our world will evolve, short and long cycles that influence our markets. Understanding how the future is likely to evolve will determine how we should act now" (Fisk 2012, p. 421). (For some examples please refer to his book.)

---

60  He is also the founder and leader of GeniusWorks, a brand and business innovation company that works with business leaders to develop and implement more inspired strategies for brands, innovation, and marketing.

### Marketing Hyperopia

Clearly the time and dedication you put toward the future cannot divert your attention from current issues. If you don't manage today, what you see in the future will not be for you. P. Kotler and R. Singh coined the term "marketing hyperopia," by which they mean a "better vision of distant issues than of near ones"[61]; this is clearly the opposite of marketing myopia. In fact, some companies can "see far ahead" but often lose sight of today and the daily activities, investing too much in advance on opportunities the market is not ready for, and leading companies to completely collapse.

So, one eye looks at the present, while the other one looks out at the future, keeping a good eye on priorities.

## 2.4.7 Holistic Marketing

Figure 34: Holistic Marketing Dimensions[62] (P. Kotler)

There is a strong need for marketers to develop a more complete and cohesive approach to marketing and interaction with consumers, which goes beyond the traditional marketing management concepts. The holistic approach to marketing is a "concept based on the development, design, and implementation of marketing programs, processes, and activities that recognizes the breadth and interdependencies"; it recognizes that everything matters, and attempts to "recognize and reconcile the scope and complexities of all the marketing processes" (Kotler 2009, p. 59–60). This more recent and needed approach is based on developing, designing, and imple-

---

61  P. Kotler and R. Singh coined the term in 1981 in: "Marketing Warfare in the 1980s," pp. 30–41. *Journal of Business Strategy 1*, vol.3

62  Elaborated from P. Kotler's scheme in *Marketing Management*, 13th ed., p. 61

menting marketing programs, processes, and activities that value the interdependencies of all functional areas and understands that everything matters. The important components of a holistic marketing approach are as follows:

## Integrated marketing

Integrated marketing "integrates" all marketing activities and programs like creating, communicating, and delivering value. Every functional area of a company should interact directly with the customer and among customers; all the customer-facing processes need to be integrated so the customer sees only one face and hears only one voice when interacting with the company. The design and implementation of a single activity is done by keeping in mind the value of all the other activities to it.

## Internal marketing

Internal marketing ensures that the whole organization adopts the appropriate marketing and customer-oriented principles through training, motivating, and incentivizing employees to care for customers and serve them. Everyone needs to understand and share the marketing strategy and objectives and work together to achieve them. The whole company needs to buy into the marketing plan, be involved, and share the enthusiasm. They need to understand, and be willing to go the extra mile for the company and the plan's success. You can achieve this if you are good at selling and promoting your plan with the whole organization.

## Performance marketing

Performance marketing is "accomplished by focus on the alignment of marketing activities, strategies and metrics with business goals."[63]

Performance marketing is about the measures you take to understand the returns, from a business point of view, brought by your marketing expenditures and activities. It used to be all about market share, margins, and sales, but now, with all the changes society has undergone, there are other things that matter and need to be taken into account. Consider the simple fact that the consumer now matters more than anything; his or her perception is reality. These are things such as your legal and ethical behaviors and your social behavior. Sales, revenues, margins, and ROI will still be taken into consideration, but marketers are going to need to dig deeper. They are going to need to examine the results further to see beyond the numbers and understand the customers' satisfaction level - who they really are, what their real positioning is, and so on. It's about keeping track of your marketing actions and results through special plans developed to measure marketing performance levels. You can create plans to evaluate the overall performance of marketing and also to measure the marketing areas independently, to see where you need to improve, and

---

63  K. Collins, 2007. "Marketing Performance Management Improves Accountability," *Gartner*.

to make sure you maintain high levels of performance. These plans can look to find the percentage of new, lost, and won-back customers and why they belong to each category, and also the customers' perceptions of your products and/or service quality in comparison to competitors'. There are many things you can deliberately look for; just remember to dig deeper in the results and the consumers' answers. For performance marketing plans to be effective, they need to assume three critical roles: data gathering, analysis, and metrics management.

## Relationship marketing

Relationship marketing comprises all the efforts made to establish a deep, enduring, mutually beneficial, and trustworthy relationship with the people involved directly or indirectly with the company's activities. The ultimate goal of this approach is to build and maintain a unique asset known as the "marketing network" of a company, which is composed of all the stakeholders' trust, support, credibility, and positive action. "One of the things of most value to a company is its relationships - with customers, employees, suppliers, distributors, dealers, and retailers. The company's *relationship capital* is the sum of the knowledge, experience, and trust that a company has with its customers, employees, suppliers, and distribution partners. The relationships are often worth more than the physical assets of a company. Relationships determine the future value of the firm" (Kotler 2003, p. 150). "Relationship marketing marks a significant paradigm shift in marketing, a movement from thinking solely in terms of competition and conflict toward thinking in terms of mutual interdependence and cooperation" (Kotler 2003, p. 151).

We should consider a fifth type of marketing approach that focuses on establishing a mutually beneficial relationship through *socially responsibility marketing*, which represents the role the company plays in terms of considering social welfare and concerns for society at large. It is about taking responsibility for the impact their operations have on our society - customers, employees, the community, the environment, and even the future generations - and what they do to make things better. By being socially responsible and designing programs to improve welfare, a company shows concern for the people and the environments where they do business. It's about being more socially responsible for one's actions, being responsive to social concerns, and manifesting support for social causes. Being a socially responsible marketer brings goodwill, sustains branding efforts, and improves public perception. It means doing things in an appropriate and ethical manner to change our society for the best, encouraging change and investing in it.

P. Kotler defines holistic marketing as "the move from a product focus to a customer focus: from selling products to satisfying customers." According to him, this type of marketing calls for the implementation of four processes. The company needs to do the following:

- Enlarge the view they have of their customers' needs and lifestyles. "The company should stop seeing its customers only as customers of its current products and

start visualizing broader ways to serve them and their lifestyles."
- Evaluate the impact of each and all departments' efforts on the customer satisfaction level. "The marketing task is to unify everyone in the company to 'think customer' and deliver the company's brand promise."
- Assess the effects and results created by all the undertaken plans, activities, and actions on the various stakeholder groups. "Holistic marketing calls for partnering with employees, suppliers and distributors to work as a team in order to deliver the best possible value to the target customer."
- Consider the company's industry, its various players, and its evolutions in a broader way. "Many industries are converging, presenting new opportunities and new threats to each industry player." Get out of your myopic vision. (2008, p. 19)

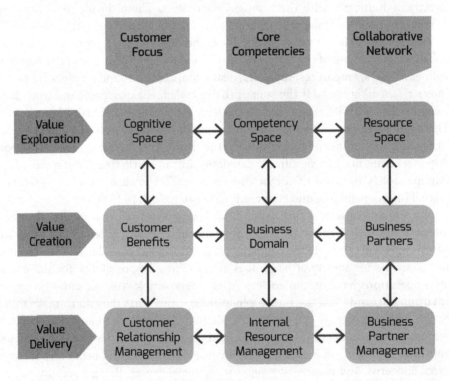

Figure 35: Holistic Marketing Framework (P. Kotler)[64]

---

64  Elaborated on from P. Kotler's scheme in *Marketing Management*, 13th ed., p. 78

# Chapter 3
# Markethinkers and Marketing Models: New trend

## 3.1 Innovative Marketing Model

*"Business and its organization have two and only two basic functions: marketing and innovation. Marketing and innovation produce results: all the rest are costs." - P Drucker*

*"Firms face a dilemma. If they don't innovate, they will die. And if they do innovate - and their innovations are not successful - they may also die. Yet innovation is a safer bet than standing still. The key is to manage innovation better than your competitor. Innovation and imagination must be made into a capability." - P. Kotler*

**MarkeThink Metamodel**

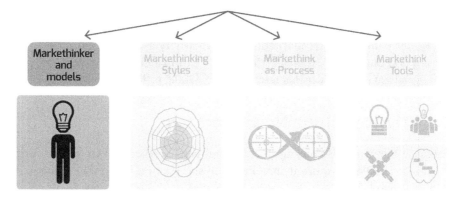

Figure 36: Marketing Models and Author

In the following pages we will present a summary of the most innovative authors and marketing models. Of course, we know that it is a non-exhaustive summary of all the minds and innovative models, we invite you to come to the website www.markethink.guru where you will find a greater number of authors.

## 3.2 Philip Kotler's New Marketing Models

Those who have had the great fortune of meeting Philip Kotler are usually amazed by his great charisma and by his genuine curiosity toward what others have to say with the passion and attention of the eternal learner, but always with a generative and creative approach.

Professor Philip Kotler is a highly praised strategic marketing academic, "hailed by the Management Centre Europe as the world's foremost expert on the strategic practice of marketing and awarded many prizes and recognitions, among them the award from the European Association of Marketing Consultants and Sales Trainers for "marketing excellence."[65], He has also been assigned the title of "leader in marketing thought" by the Academic Members of the AMA.[66] This is a great achievement; in fact, there are few scientific disciplines that allow for its authors to be considered the fundamental pillars of a discipline, as well as the pioneer in his field.

Thanks to the worldwide network of teachers and professors, managers, and professionals of excellence with whom he collaborates, he has been able to stay up to date and always manages to innovate "his" science, the science of marketing, of which he is the father.

### 3.2.1 "Lateral Marketing" with Fernando Trias de Bes

*"Same problem but different solutions."*

P. Kotler defines "lateral marketing" as a creativity approach that differs from vertical marketing. "Vertical" marketing works within a given market; lateral marketing visualizes the product in a new context." (2008, p. 10).

#### 3.2.1.1 The Need for a New Approach

Because our world is constantly changing, because the markets are saturated, and because people are more demanding, the success of a marketing strategy de-

---

65 Retrieved from *http://www.kotlermarketing.com/phil1.shtml*
66 Retrieved from *http://www.kellogg.northwestern.edu/faculty/directory/kotler_philip.aspx*

pends on its originality and on the company's capability of being unique and creative. We need to shift from the traditional marketing concepts to approaches like "lateral" marketing ones. The lateral marketing process, established by P. Kotler and F. Trias de Bes in their 2003 book, *Lateral Marketing: New Techniques for Finding Breakthrough Ideas*, if done correctly, leads to the following:

- The same product but a new use, which is the vertical expansion of a marketing offering
- A new product with new use, which leads to a new market offering or category
- A new product but the same/similar use, which creates a subcategory

Lateral marketing is an operative process that, when applied to existing products or services, generates innovative ones. It helps generate innovative goods that satisfy needs, desires, or targets not yet satisfied. Lateral marketing is a methodic process whose starting point is an existing product or service. Lateral marketing is a very valuable approach to produce innovation and creative new ideas, but it needs to be considered as a complement to vertical marketing. It means breaking down the product's components, attributes, or elements and examining them to find lateral displacement possibilities, to move us out of our comfort zone and the logical sequence of events, patterns, and certitudes.

*The Development of Segmentation and Market Segments: From the Initial Market to the Current Situation.*

- The first brand creates a category.
  A category is the determined selection of concrete needs, specific people, and usage situation in which a product or service can be offered. The market is composed of different categories and subcategories that are related to a complete and closed system of needs, people, and situations associated with the product.

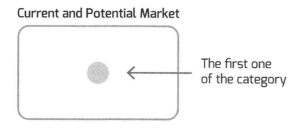

Figure 37: The First Brand Creates the Category

- The first challenger comes in within the same market segment.
  When the first challenger comes in, the concept of positioning comes into play, and the process of "divide and conquer" starts. The term comes from the Latin expression "divide et impera," which was a political and sociological approach where one power would break down a territory into many smaller and more manageable areas to maintain control. In marketing and segmentation, we can

see it as dividing the market into as many small segments as possible, which you'll target specifically with one offer to maintain your leadership, market power, and influential position. They penetrate the same category or subcategory.

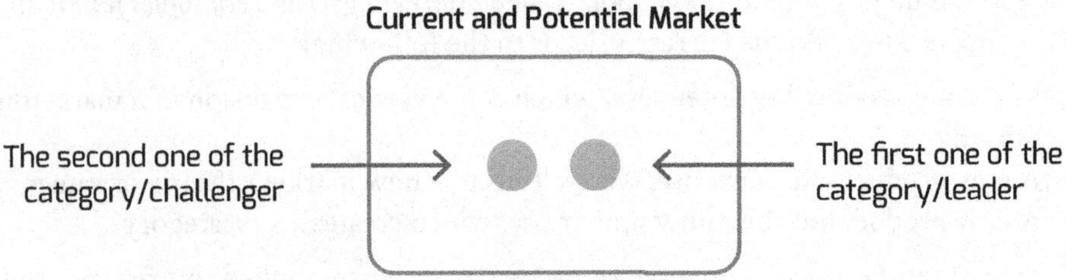

**Current and Potential Market**

The second one of the category/challenger → ● ● ← The first one of the category/leader

Figure 38: Challenged by the Second Brand

- Another player comes in but serves another, untapped segment and becomes the leader. The newcomer opens/creates a new segment within the market. Market fragmentation takes place: the market segmentation increases, and the segments get smaller and less profitable.

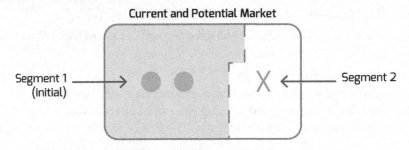

Figure 39: Segmentation Begins

- Competitors and new players, instead of creating and developing new segments, penetrate and invade existing segments, rendering the marketplace ever more saturated.

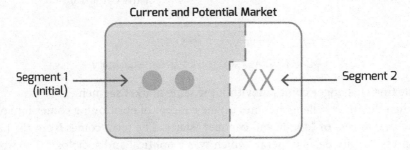

Figure 40: Competitors Start Invading Existing Segment

# CHAPTER 3

# MARKETHINK

- Segmentation has led to the current market situation, which has led to the full fragmentation and saturation of market segments.

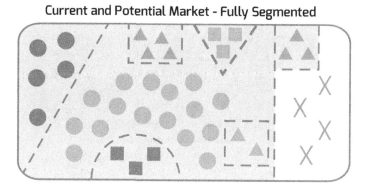

Figure 41: A Fully Segmented Market

In Summary

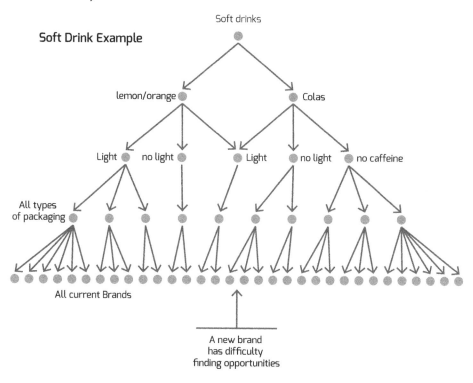

Figure 42: The Soft Drink Industry, A Hyperfragmented Market

## 3.2.1.2 Lateral versus Vertical (Traditional) Marketing

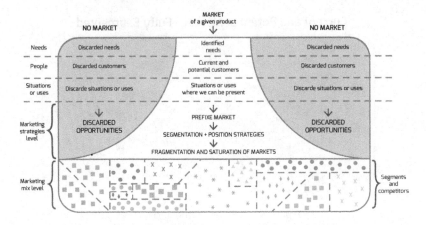

Figure 43: Areas Examined by Lateral versus Vertical Marketing

To understand what makes lateral marketing different from vertical marketing, it's important to have a clear understanding of both approaches in order to compare them and see what advantages each brings. Once again, it is important to remember that without the vertical approach there can't be a lateral approach.

The approach to marketing used today by most marketers is vertical; it's the traditional way. With vertical marketing, marketers continue segmenting existing markets, creating ever more niche markets that are always less profitable. They follow the logical patterns that don't take into account environmental, social, and market changes. It's based on preestablished and rigid rules.

The lateral marketing approach develops new products for much wider markets by creating needs and expanding the existing markets in a transversal way, with a totally innovative and creative approach. The lateral marketing approach puts into discussion an existing product or service, starting from the vertical approach requirements, while developing strategies and products that distort the product and the beliefs about traditional consumption habits and established standards.

The vertical approach looks for the competitive advantage within defined markets. The lateral marketing approach searches for an extension of the market: appraising needs, targets, and situations that were neglected by the vertical definition of the product or service. To gain the competitive advantage, you've got to be the first one.

The lateral process involves an important or radical transformation of the product. In other words, lateral marketing explores and operates in the areas in which vertical marketing is not active, adding the needs, the uses, or the targets previously managed without the appropriate modifications.

# CHAPTER 3 — MARKETHINK

From the operations point of view, vertical marketing proceeds in a sequential way, by means of selection. It is an analytical process that excludes the concepts that don't belong in the potential or existing market definition. It is defined and measurable. Lateral marketing proceeds by the means of creation. The concept of choosing new ideas and applying changes doesn't follow an apparent order. In fact, while in vertical marketing the selection happens by exclusion, lateral marketing takes into account of all the alternatives.

| Appropriate Situations | |
|---|---|
| Vertical Marketing | Lateral Marketing |
| More adequate in markets of recent creation that are in a first stage of development | More adequate for mature markets where growth is zero |
| For developing markets and for making them larger through varieties and through the conversion of potential customers into current customers | For creating markets or categories from scratch, for merging different types of business, for reaching targets we could never reach with our current product, and for finding new uses |
| Under a less risky business philosophy | Under a more risky business philosophy |
| When few resources are available | When there are more resources available or business is ready to invest and wait |
| When a secure, even low, incremental volume needs to be ensured | When we want to reach a high volume of business |
| In order to defend markets, by fragmenting them through the number of brands and, therefore, making markets less attractive for new entrants | To attack markets with a generic competition from outside the arena of direct competitors |
| To innovate stemming from our mission and keeping our business focus | To redefine our mission, and to seek other markets |

Figure 44: Appropriate Situations for Vertical versus Lateral Marketing

## 3.2.1.3 The Process

The authors determined that there are three steps to the process. It is important to keep in mind that this is a process that calls for the use of creative techniques.

Choose your focus! What is it that you are going to focus on to generate a lateral dislocation - an attribute, its design, or its usage? To choose the correct focus point, you need to apply vertical marketing techniques and decide what level to concentrate on:

*Level 1:* The market - need, target or occasion (place, time, and situation).
*Level 2:* The product, analysis of the main attributes - tangible product/services, packaging, brand attributes, and use.

*Level 3:* The remaining elements of the mix - promotions, distribution, place, and communication.

Provoke a lateral displacement to create a gap. The creation of the gap is done by moving laterally through existing and established patterns, by creating interruptions in logical and sequential thinking, and by challenging assumptions and processes. If there is no gap, if there is no disconnection with the existing product, and the lateral marketing approach cannot exist.

To understand the lateral dislocation process, the authors use a simple concept: a flower, which has one main characteristic wilts. If you move laterally from this point and consider the possibility that it never fades, you create a gap. By trying to breach this gap you can come up with great new marketable ideas; in this case they came up with fake flowers and accomplished what was assumed impossible: flowers that never fade! This idea of never-fading flowers has been taken to a higher level: they found a way to preserve real, fading flowers, so that they can be intact through time.

Cancel the gap! You cancel the gap and find an innovative solution by generating new associations, connections, and correlations.

### 3.2.1.4 Creating the Gap

There are six techniques to generate lateral dislocation and create the gap. These techniques attempt to define new offering categories or markets. The product is transformed in a way that it satisfies new needs, desires, or persons, and/or responds to unattended ones.

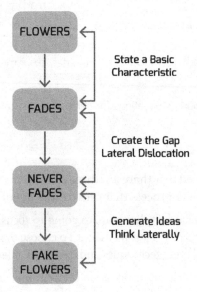

Figure 45: The Technique to Achieve Lateral Marketing

- *Substitution* - replacing the focus with something radically different, eliminating or modifying one or more elements of the product or imitating other products' attributes
- *Inversion* - thinking of the opposite, affirming the contrary, or adding a "no" to one or more elements of a product or service
- *Combination* - adding one or more elements to a product, keeping all the existing ones unchanged
- *Exaggeration* - amplifying one or more elements in a positive or negative way
- *Elimination* - removing one or more elements of a product
- *Reordering* - modifying the order or sequence of one or more elements

## 3.2.1.5 Product Innovation and the Market

Innovations can take place at two levels: inside and outside a given market. Each approach leads to a specific result. The first one hyperfragments the market by introducing product modifications; the second one, the real creator of value, though difficult to accomplish, creates a whole new market.

### Within a Given Market

Innovations developed within a given market are created without influencing any of its fundamental elements; the innovation is vertical, and the product's nature doesn't change. This type of innovation is the most common and can be of various types.

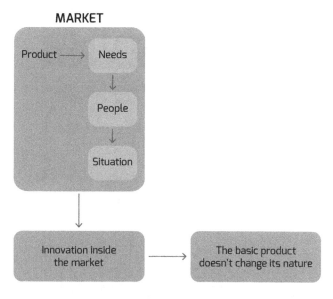

Figure 46: Innovation Inside a Given Market

- Modulation-Based Innovations
  Modulation-based innovations are variations in any basic characteristics of a product or service. These variations can be functional or physical and concern increasing or decreasing a basic characteristic.

Figure 47: Innovation Based on Modulation - Grisbí Cookies

- Sizing-Based Innovation
  Sizing-based innovation introduces a product by varying the amount/volume offered, without changing anything else - the product doesn't change.

Figure 48: Innovation Based on Sizing - Coca-Cola

- Packaging-Based Innovation
  Packaging-based innovation is the modification of the packaging design. This type of innovation doesn't modify the product but rather the perception of it, its consumption, and/or situation. The product category is the same, but the container a change allowing for volume, occasion, and situational variations.

Figure 49: Innovation Based on Packaging - Bottled Water Industry

- Design-Based Innovation
  Design-based innovation is only concerned with the visual aspect of the product. It does not concern the product size, packaging, or category - they stay exactly the same. What is altered is the design - how it looks.

Figure 50: Innovation Based on Design - Swatch Watches

- Complement-Based Innovation
  Complement-based innovation is developing a product innovation by adding some ingredients to the basic product to create a new variety.

Figure 51: Innovation Based on Complements - Coca-Cola

- Effort Reduction–Based Innovation
  Effort reduction–based innovations are based, as the name suggests, on reducing the efforts the customer makes in the process of getting to and purchasing a product or service - the time of obtaining the information, the cost of purchase risk , may increase the final purchase price

Figure 52: Innovation Based on Effort Reduction - Amazon.com

The result of this kind of innovation is a hyperfragmented and saturated market. It doesn't lead to the creation of new categories or new markets; it takes place within the category in which it competes.

The commonality between these innovations is that they deliver continuous variations on what the product is without changing its nature and essence. There is no innovation to the product, but there are improvements and/or evolutions.

| INNOVATIONS BASED ON: | | |
|---|---|---|
| Type of Innovation | Consists of | Effect in the Market |
| Based on modulation | Increasing or decreasing any characteristics of the product or service | a) amplification of targets<br>b) ability to better serve concrete segments |
| Based on sizing | Variations of volume, quantity, or frequency | a) amplification of targets<br>b) amplification of consumption occasions |
| Based on packaging | Modifications of container or packaging | a) amplification of targets<br>b) amplification of consumption occasions |
| Based on design | Modifications of design in order to communicate different lifestyles | a) amplification of targets<br>b) differentiation by lifestyle |
| Based on complements | Adding ingredients or complementing/ adding additional services | a) ability to better serve concrete segments or niches<br>b) increase in the range of products |
| Based on effort reduction | Reduction of the efforts customers make in the purchase process | a) conversion of potential buyers into current buyers<br>b) ability to reach the maximum penetration of the product or service |

Figure 53: Approaches to New Product Development

## Outside a Given Market

Innovations generated from outside a given market are a less common type of innovation. They are innovations that are the result of the alteration of a product's or service's essential components, creating and developing a market for it.

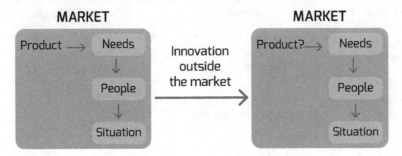

Figure 54: Innovation Outside a Given Market

I believe the best way to illustrate this is through concrete examples.

## The Dyson Vacuum Cleaner Case

Launched in 1993, DC01 was the first vacuum to not lose suction. It was first for a lot of other things too. While James was busy developing his cyclone technology, he listed all the other annoyances with conventional vacuum cleaners - then fixed them one by one. A stair hose that stretches to the top of stairs, onboard tools, a new idea. A local sawmill caught James' eye. Under the cover of darkness he sketched the timber yard's giant cyclone.

It spun sawdust out of the air, collecting it in a chamber. Could the same principle signal the end of clogging vacuum cleaner bags?

Source: www.dyson.co.uk

Figure 55: The Dyson Vacuum Line

## CHAPTER 3 — MARKETHINK

### The Kinder Surprise Case

The snack market was fragmented. In the subcategory of chocolate bars, brand saturation was quite high. Ferrero launched a novel concept: a chocolate egg with a toy inside - one of a long series of toys that kids can collect. Kinder Surprise redefined the market of candies and chocolates by creating a new subcategory where it is the leader, and no important competitor has yet appeared. Here is the story of Kinder Surprise: Michele Ferrero had the idea of selling Easter eggs not only for Easter, but the whole year. He asked his salespeople, but they discarded the idea. He asked his marketers, but they discarded the idea as well. Marketers made a search that proved consumers of Easter eggs just wanted them for Easter. Nevertheless, Ferrero went ahead and invented the famous egg kinder; two billion units sold.

Source: Interview by Lorenzo Marini, Art Director.

Figure 56: Kinder Surprise - Free Prize Inside!

### The Viagra Case

Even though Viagra has only been available since 1998, it has already gained a worldwide reputation, with sales of around £1 billion per year. Pfizer, the world's largest pharmaceutical company, has a certain amount of good luck to thank for this phenomenal success. It was by chance that they discovered its ability to treat erectile dysfunction, having developed it to treat angina.

Source: www.pfizer.com

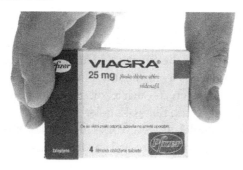

Figure 57: Viagra - The Blue Pill (Pfizer)

## The Geox "Breathable Shoe" Case

With these shoes, Geox has made a disruptive innovation. Geox succeeded in "shoe technology." During a business trip to Reno, Nevada, to promote the family's wine business at a trade fair, Mario Moretti Polegato, the founder of Geox, decided to take a walk. Bothered by his overheated feet, which were clad in rubber-soled shoes, he instinctively punctured holes into the soles to let air through. He had just discovered a simple and effective way to let excess heat out of his shoes. Mr. Polegato then developed his idea in the workshop of a small footwear company owned by the family. Once this rubber-sole technology was in place, he patented the system right away to create the world's first "breathable shoe."

Source: www.geox.com

Figure 58: Geox - The Shoe that Breaths

## The Barbie Case

It began like any other great invention does - as an idea in a visionary's head. Ruth Handler, cofounder of Mattel Toys, was watching her daughter Barbara play with paper dolls and imagine them in grown-up roles when the idea hit her - why not make a teenage doll that little girls could play with and dream about the future with? Ruth recognized the value of helping children realize their dreams and goals through play. After researching the current doll market, Ruth confirmed that while there were plenty of baby dolls available, there were no three-dimensional teenage dolls. She then resolved to create such a doll through her own company, which she cofounded with her husband, Elliott Handler. Ruth and Elliott unveiled Barbie doll, the teenage fashion model, at New York's annual Toy Fair in 1959. Initially, toy buyers were skeptical. Never before had anyone seen a doll so small, yet so sophisticated. As a teenager, Barbie was completely unlike any of the baby or toddler dolls popular at the time. Critics posed the question, would anyone buy her? Undaunted by skepticism, Mattel stood firmly behind the first Barbie doll, launching an innovative television ad campaign. Barbie quickly caught the attention of little girls across the country. She soon became a worldwide sensation, and remains as popular as ever today.

Source: barbiecollector.com

Figure 59: Barbie - The Fashion Doll

## The Walkman Case

The first affordable portable radios were introduced in the late 1950s and early 1960s. They were made possible because of the transistor, invented several years before at Bell Labs. The transistor gave them cleaner sound than vacuum tube models, and transistors rarely wore out or overheated. They also made radios much less fragile and also allowed them to be a lot smaller. There were some cassette recorders available at the time, although they were not designed for the general public. Sony called theirs Pressman and marketed it exclusively to reporters. These recorders lacked stereo sound and were very expensive. They also used (typically) microcassettes, which had no support from record companies (and were expensive to boot). With the limited choices presented to consumers, the most popular cassette tape players were either home stereos or car players.

Figure 60: Walkman - Portable Music (Sony)

## Sony Enters the Market

Sony's first stab at the personal tape player market came in 1978, with the TC-D5. It had excellent-quality sound (surpassing most desktop players) and was easy to operate. Unfortunately for most potential customers, the price was around $1,000, and it was hardly portable.

One regular user was Ibuka, then Sony's honorary chairman. He used the player on airplane trips, but he found the player too heavy for everyday use. He instructed the tape recorder division to create a smaller version for his personal use. The division, led by Kozo Ohsone, modified a Pressman to do the job. They removed the record function and added stereophonic sound. Ibuka was immediately impressed and suggested that they bring a similar item to market. By 1979, Sony's tape recorder division was flagging. There was little demand for their high-end products, while products from competing lines succeeded (boom boxes, etc.). In February, 1979, Morita, the company's chairman, encouraged the engineers to develop a player similar to the one they had developed for Ibuka. But this one had to cost less than ¥40,000 yet provide the same sound quality. He wanted the product by June 21, 1979.

Though he was skeptical that the division could create a player so quickly, Kozo Ohsone was eager to avoid having the division consolidated into another division (Sony was going through reorganization at the time) and quickly designed a portable tape player based on Ibuka's modified Pressman player. They used lower-end components to bring the price down and encased it in a small, stylish enclosure.

Source: www.sony.com

As we have seen, the lateral marketing process reorganizes existing information, and proceeds from the particulars to the more general elements through the use of more creative and exploratory approaches. But it has to be considered together with the vertical marketing approach; the traditional approach to marketing is the starting point.

# CHAPTER 3 — MARKETHINK

| | Comparison | |
|---|---|---|
| | *Vertical Marketing* | *Lateral Marketing* |
| It is based on... | a) The set of needs, persons, and situations or uses of our product<br>b) Our mission, innovating from what we want to be as a company | a) The discarded needs, persons, situations, or uses of our product<br>b) Being open to redefine our mission if necessary, but innovating from our current offer |
| It works... | Vertically, following the marketing process | Laterally, out of the marketing process |
| In an early stage it allows... | Development of markets and conversation of potential customers into current customers | Creation of markets, categories, or subcategories, and capability of reaching targets/situations non reachable with the existing products |
| In a later stage it allows... | a) Low incrementality, but it is an easy-to-sell novelty | High incrementality, but it is a more risky option |
| It s source of volume is... | Market share of product competitors, and the conversion of potential customers and situations into current ones | Totally incremental, without affecting other markets, or by taking from many other categories market share of generic competition |
| It is appropriate when... | a) Early stage of the life cycle of a market or product (growing phase)<br>b) Low-risk strategies, low resources available<br>c) For defending markets by fragmenting them | a) Mature stage of the life cycle of a market or product<br>b) High-risk strategies, high resources available<br>c) For attacking markets from outside them (with substitutes) |
| It is currently responsibility of... | Marketing departments | Not always marketing departments, but:<br>· Creative agencies<br>· Entrepreneurs<br>· Small and medium companies<br>· Engineers, R&D departments |

Figure 61: Comparison of Vertical and Lateral Marketing

## 3.2.2 "Chaotics Marketing" with John A. Caslione

*"Thriving in a turbulent economy takes more than just luck or gut intuition; it takes a new mindset, serious planning, and the right strategies". - J. A. Caslione and P. Kotler*

Companies have always had to manage and live with risk (measurable) and uncertainty (immeasurable). But since, as stated by P. Kotler and J. A. Caslione in their 2009 book, *Chaotics: The Business of Managing and Marketing in the Age of Turbulence*, we are living in turbulent times. "with its consequent chaos, risk and uncertainty". They say that "companies must build an early warning system, a scenario construction system, and a quick response system to manage and market during recessions and other turbulent conditions."[67] They define this as a "Chaotics Management System".

The "new normality," as they define it, is turbulent. It is therefore important to consider that turbulence has two major yet contrasting effects: "one is vulnerability, against which companies need defensive armor and the other is opportunity, which needs to be exploited."[68]

To get a better understanding of the concept, J. A. Caslione gives a great example:

"Recently, I was preparing to board a business flight from Chicago to Shanghai. Just then, the gate agent announced that take off would be delayed by 30 minutes because air traffic control had detected turbulence along our intended flight path. More time was needed to reroute us onto a different flight path, so that we would avoid the *detected turbulence.*

Thirty minutes later, we were flying calmly, until our plane was buffeted by severe, undetected turbulence. The turbulence was so intense that virtually all of our meals and drinks ended up on the floor. Most of the overhead luggage compartments opened, spilling out coats, briefcases, packages, and luggage on many of the passengers, who by then were screaming

We were all shaken and rattled right down to our teeth, but after what seemed like several minutes - but was probably only a mere 20 to 30 seconds - the pilots calmly told us that they had found a more favorable altitude. In fact, this new altitude was not only calmer; it had a 200-mile per hour tailwind that enabled us to land one full hour earlier than originally scheduled."

Like the Boeing 777, our businesses are also subjected to turbulence, some of it detectable and some of it undetectable. But unlike the pilots, who are trained to fly in extreme turbulence, business leaders must undertake their own form of training to prepare them to manage in a turbulent environment. Specifically, they must find

---

67  Retrieved from the book's preface found on the Chaotics website at *http://www.chaoticsstrategies.com/chaotics-the-book/preface-english/*

68  Retrieved from the book's preface found on the Chaotics website at: *http://www.chaoticsstrategies.com/chaotics-the-book/preface-english/*

and develop new business models and adopt new strategic behaviors. Otherwise, they will find themselves operating in chaos.[69]

On the other hand, when turbulence hits and a business: 1) has understood and embraced the *new normality*, and 2) is more receptive to accept and embrace new strategic behaviors - *Chaotics Strategic Behaviors*, that business will be more readily able to capitalize on opportunities created by the turbulence. Being prepared for turbulence enabled the Boeing 777 to stay on course and meet its goal. So too will a well-prepared business be able to meet its goal, in spite of any sudden turbulence.

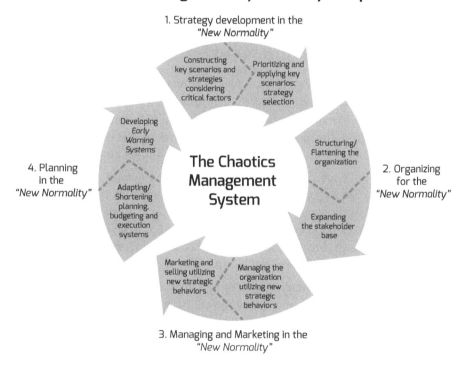

Figure 62: Key Components of the Chaotics Management System

The Chaotics Management System is a new set of strategic guidelines, or "strategic behaviors," which include a series of systems to survive in times of turbulence. The system has eight key components:

1. Development of an early warning system
2. Construction of key scenarios and strategies

---

[69] In J. A. Caslione's article, "Chaotics: The Business of Managing and Marketing in The Age of Turbulence" found on the Ivey Business Journal website at http://www.iveybusinessjournal.com/topics/global-business/chaotics-leading-managing-and-marketing-in-the-age-of-turbulence

3. Prioritization of key scenarios and strategy selection
4. Implementation of *Chaotics* management strategic behaviors
5. Implementation of *Chaotics* marketing strategic behaviors
6. Expansion of the stakeholder base
7. Flattening of the organization
8. Shortening strategic planning intervals and multiple execution scenarios[70]

"Chaotics ultimately serves as a disciplined approach for detecting sources of turbulence, predicting consequent vulnerabilities and opportunities, and developing critical and appropriate responses to ensure that the business lives on successfully and thrives for many years into the future."[71]

## 3.2.3 "Marketing 3.0" with Hermawan Kartajaya and Iwan Setiawan

Marketing 3.0 is an approach that sees the consumer as a real person and not just as a client. It acknowledges that the consumer is a human being capable of feeling and reacting to experiences at a profound level. Marketers will need to focus on the immaterial, the emotional, the experiential aspects of all their business activities, marketing efforts and strategies, products, and services.

By unconventional methods, here today, we see that you tend more to offer customers more than just a product or a service, giving them voice and listening in order to create the entire experience of the brand or product. We can already perceive that we are about to experience a marketing revolution. We clearly see that in order to get into the minds of consumers, we need to "wow" them, exceed more profound expectations, get under their skin, and become part of their reality.

Through time, society has gone through many changes and seen much progress - technologies being the major change and the main cause of it - but these evolutions are often out of our control. So marketing has to evolve and change accordingly. It has had to follow the general evolutions of society in order to stay relevant, and is currently undergoing the process of its third evolution. We are shifting into the era of Marketing 3.0, the more spiritual level; here a connection is made at a deeper, more personal and intimate level.

Let me describe the previous and present eras, so you can better grasp the concept of Marketing 3.0, spiritual marketing.

---

[70] In J. A. Caslione's article, "Chaotics: The Business of Managing and Marketing in the Age of Turbulence" found on the Ivey Business Journal website at *http://www.iveybusinessjournal.com/topics/global-business/chaotics-leading-managing-and-marketing-in-the-age-of-turbulence*

[71] In J. A. Caslione's article "Chaotics: The Business of Managing and Marketing in the Age of Turbulence" found on the Ivey Business Journal website at *http://www.iveybusinessjournal.com/topics/global-business/chaotics-leading-managing-and-marketing-in-the-age-of-turbulence*

# CHAPTER 3 — MARKETHINK

*Marketing 1.0* is also referred to as the product-centric era, rational marketing. The main objective of marketing in this period was to sell the product to the mass market as a whole as a value proposition with the use of distribution channels and the mass media. This marketing approach was based solely on the product, and the strategy was solely concerned with selling.

*Marketing 2.0*, known as the customer-centric era, is emotional marketing. In this era, today, the main objective of marketing is no longer to simply sell the product to the masses, but to satisfy a specific segment of customers and to establish relationships with the customers to gain their loyalty. Marketers know that the market is to be considered as segments rather than a whole, and that each individual has different aspirations, references, attitudes, and so on. Therefore marketing strategies have been based on differentiation and segmentation, brand identity and customer satisfaction, and experiences.

*Marketing 3.0* is to be known as the "spiritual" marketing era. In the 3.0 era, marketers need to get deeper into the consciousness and subconsciousness of the human being. They have to meet both the rational and emotional needs of customers; they need to focus on people instead of segments, offer products that not only satisfy the functional needs of the customer, but the emotional and personal rational needs as well. They need to do everything they can so the customer feels satisfied at a spiritual, deep level, with being the brand's customer and with using the product or service. They will need to feel connected to the brand and They will feel connected to the brand and what it represents for each of them. Marketers will need to consider the true value of the product in relation to the customer's deepest and most secret emotions.

We have arrived at a point at which participation and collaboration will be essential for a good marketing strategy and approach. Marketing 3.0 is all about collaboration, about letting the customers participate in the creation of what they will later use. With the Internet, the individual is automatically a customer or a potential one. Anyone is now able to create new ideas and share these ideas with the world through well-known social networks. It is important to listen to what they have to say because they are the ones who determine whether you will last or not. The marketer will soon be the customer. This is the era in which a strong codependent relationship needs to be established between the individual and the company to deliver products that not only satisfy the emotional and rational needs and wants of its customers, but that address customers' lifestyle aspirations, respecting their beliefs, human complexity, and spirituality. Marketing 3.0 is about how the brand connects and responds to all of these elements. Most of it has to do with brand credibility.

Never forget that your attitude is what matters most; make sure that everyone in your company stands by your defining values, practices them in everything they do, and promotes them. Do and behave as you promised. Avoid deception!

These are the six fundamental drivers of brand credibility:
- Trust - confidence, consistency, integrity, and authority
- Authenticity - real and sincere, informal, as advertised
- Transparency - let the sun shine in, easy to learn, easy to discover, no secrets
- Affirmation - reinforcement, community, playback, accountability, search results
- Listening - humility, empathy, welcome mat, absorbing feedback
- Responsiveness - follow-up, invitational marketing, solidifying the solution, dignifying feedback.[72]

## Marketing 3.0 Values-Based Matrix Model

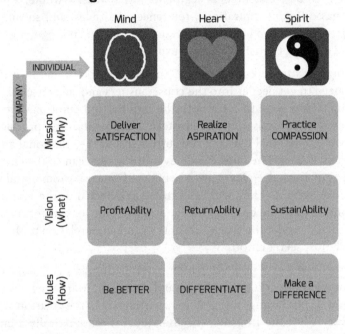

Figure 63: The 3.0 Marketing Matrix (P. Kotler and J. Caslione)

This framework can help you take a more emotionally intelligent approach to branding, satisfying the deepest and most spiritual aspirations of your targets.

The "Ten Credos of 3.0 Marketing"
- Love your customer; respect your competitors.
- Be sensitive to change and be ready to transform: when times change, change with them.
- Guard your name - be clear about who you are! Make your values clear and don't surrender them.

---

[72] By P. Blacksahw, 2008, pp. 15-38: *Satisfied Customers Tell 3 Friends, Angry Customers Tell 3,000: Running a Business in Today's Consumer-Driven World*. Doubleday.

- Customers are diverse; go first to those who can benefit most from you.
- Always offer a good package at a fair price; set fair prices to reflect your quality.
- Always make yourself available; spread the good news; help your would-be customers find you.
- Get customers, keep them, and grow them; look at your customers as customers for life.
- Whatever your business, it's a *service* business; every business is a service business, because a product delivers a service.
- Always refine your business processes in terms of quality, cost, and delivery; every day, improve your business process every way.
- Gather relevant information, but use wisdom in making decisions; wise managers consider more than the financial impact of a decision. (Kotler 2010, pp. 169–180)

## 3.2.4 Winning at Innovation: The A-to-F Model with Fernando Trias de Bes

In their latest book, *Winning at Innovation*, P. Kotler and F. Trias de Bes propose a model for managing innovation and innovation teams within a company based on the interaction of the six key roles involved in innovation. Their new model attempts to change companies and organizations' mind-set and approach toward innovation and creativity, to influence the way they think of innovation and undertake it, in a practical and direct way. It is a great framework that enables any company to manage and implement change and innovation in any functional or operational area within the whole organization.

Rather than seeing innovation as a fixed and sequential process, they suggest it should be seen as a process that allows the key roles to interact with each other freely. "

The A-F Model is a step-by-step process for developing a successful culture of innovation, bringing together the different individuals and groups across the organization for ideas to be created, developed and implemented. Offering flexibility, the model allows a back and forth flow of ideas and creativity to adapt to changing circumstances. Using this model, companies can learn how to make their innovation processes more effective, more sustainable, and more successful."[73]

The authors wrote, "the A-to-F model we introduce here is not an innovation process, but the list of the key roles we have found to exist in the companies that have shown the best innovation practices in recent years. Our proposal is that if a company wants to innovate, it must define and assign these roles to specific individuals and then, having established goals, resources and deadline, let them interact freely to create their own process" (Kotler and Trias de Bes, 2011, p. 16).

---

[73] From the book's description on the flap of *Winning at Innovation: The A-to-F Model*, 2001 Palgrave Macmillan edition

The truth of the matter is that companies need to innovate not only to win but to survive, and therefore innovation should be the number one priority of every level and area of the organization. The size or importance of the innovation is not what matters most. First of all, many small yet effective innovations lead to major improvements. Secondly, what matters most is collaboration and involvement from the top all the way to the bottom of the company. Innovation has to be promoted, encouraged, rewarded, supported, engaging, and open. It also has to be seen as a responsibility that falls on every person in the company.

## The Six Key Roles[74]

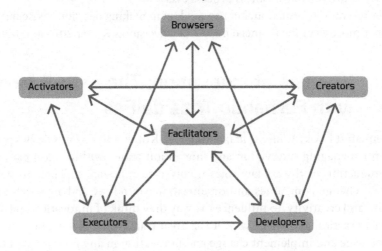

Figure 64: A-to-F Model and Interactions[75]

"(A) ACTIVATORS: These are people who will initiate the innovation process, without worrying about stages or phases." They provide the overall framework of innovation, launch the initiatives, and define the general guidelines that will condition decision making and project launching.

"(B) BROWSERS: These are the experts in searching for information. Their task is not to produce anything new, but to supply the group with information. Their mission is to investigate throughout the process and to find the information relevant both to the start of the process and to the application of new ideas." They constantly provide the required information to proceed during and at each stage of the process.

"(C) CREATORS: The people who produce ideas for the rest of the group. Their function is to ideate new concepts and possibilities and search for new solutions at

---

74 From a post by P. Kotler and F. Trias de Bes, "A-to-F Method for Innovation Success," on www.innovationexcellence.com - the world's most popular innovation website. Janurary 2, 2012. Read the full post at http://www.innovationexcellence.com/blog/2012/01/02/a-to-f-method-for-innovation-success/

75 Kotler and Trias de Bes, 2011, p. 18

any point in the process." They are constantly looking to change what is established, for opportunities and inspiration.

"(D) DEVELOPERS: People specialized in turning ideas into products and services; they are the ones who 'tangibilize' ideas, who give form to concepts and develop a rough marketing plan. Creators come up with ideas; developers invent things. Their function is to take ideas and turn them into solutions. In short - to invent." They think and work to overcome market, technological, productive, and financial constraints.

"(E) EXECUTORS: The people who take care of everything to do with implementation and execution. Their function is to implement, that is, bring the innovation under development to the organization and to the market." They deal with the production and analysis of the market's response.

"(F) FACILITATORS: Those who approve the new spending items and investment needed as the innovation process moves forward. They also manage the process to prevent it getting stuck. Their mission is the instrumentation of the innovation process." They help and support the project throughout the process in different forms and phases. (Kotler and Trias de Bes, 2011, p. 16–17)

These roles, as you can see in the figure below, correspond to the six *i*s of innovation.

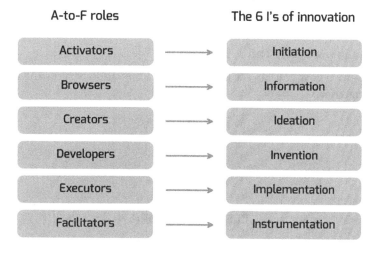

Figure 65: The Six 6 *I*s of Innovation and the A-to-F Model[76]

"The fact that the stages are a result of group dynamics among six types of roles leads to a natural and spontaneous flexibility, freeing those responsible for the innovation process from having to stick to a prescribed script and from feeling that when they move forward and backward in the process they are acting inefficiently or simply abandoning a stage-based method whose inflexibility makes it hard to

---

[76] Kotler and Trias de Bes, 2011, p. 18

follow."[77] This model conveys the essential idea that innovation is a collaborative process in which the required roles involved need to be assigned, and the individuals need to be made accountable for their responsibilities.

The creative culture of a company is something that cannot be described; it's invisible, but it can be felt and is completely recognizable. When a company is truly creative, you can feel it in the air. The interest, dedication, and proactiveness toward creativity and innovation are vivid, and ideas come from everywhere - every level and every person, regardless of his or her position or responsibilities, or whether he or she is involved or not to the area of innovation. In a creative culture, both innovation and creativity are the responsibility of every member of the organization, even the staff.

## Four Key Areas of Innovation and the A-to-F Model

For a company to become innovative, it must absolutely manage four key areas. These can be seen as the four legs of a table: if one leg is damaged, the table wobbles and is unstable. For innovation to take place successfully, these four areas need to be addresses separately, even though they complement each other:

1. Strategic planning
2. Innovation processes, e.g., A-to-F Model
3. Results
4. Metrics and rewards system

In the figure below you can see how the Total Innovation System and the A-to-F Model fit together.

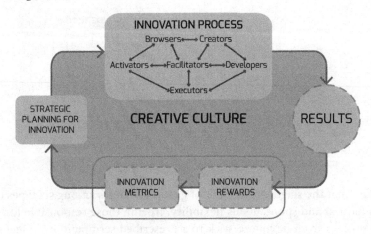

Figure 66: Total Innovation System and A-to-F Model[78]

---

77   P. Kotler and F. Trias de Bes, "A-to-F Method for Innovation Success" post: *www.innovationexcellence.com*

78   Kotler and Trias de Bes, 2011, p. 19

But this is not all; innovation also requires people and organizations being receptive to it and willing to change. People put forward seven barriers, or problems on which to work, that hinder the innovative spirit within the company and within its employees:

1. Poor knowledge of the true meaning of innovation and its reach
2. Lack of responsibilities assignment and poor accountability
3. Confusion and unclear distinction between creativity and innovation
4. Lack of a framework, absence of a unified approach to innovation
5. Lack of control
6. Poor coordination
7. Lack of customer focus (Kotler and Trias de Bes, 2011, p. 3–10)

- In the book they present many examples of the different ways in which leading companies conduct innovation and how this can be applied in any organization. These are some of the innovative companies they refer to:
- Nokia: the implementation/application of synectics to design cell phones for Indian and Chinese markets "to make the strange familiar" to lower-class users (Kotler and Trias de Bes, 2011, p. 70).
- Apple: taking the open approach and practice of innovation in the development of the iPhone and its applications. "The company decided to share its programming code with any programmer who takes an interest" in developing these applications (Kotler and Trias de Bes, 2011, p. 33).
- Nestlé: through the analysis of adjacent categories of products that are not sold by them but can provide them with the basis for the development of a potential business or product line (Kotler and Trias de Bes, 2011, p. 187).
- In summary, "the stages or phases of an innovation process must be the result of the interaction of those involved in the innovation processes. Certainly, each innovation, depending on the goals and nature of the project, will require its own ad hoc process and sequence." Thus the main idea behind this book is that "the phases or stages of an innovation process cannot be predetermined, but must emerge as a result of the interaction of a set of functions or roles performed by certain individuals."[79]

---

[79] P. Kotler and F. Trias de Bes "A-to-F Method for Innovation Success" post. *www.innovationexcellence.com*

## 3.3 Seth Godin

Figure 67: Seth Godin, best-selling author (sethgodin.com)

Seth Godin is one of the greatest marketing innovators, with an extremely pragmatic and irreverent approach. His many innovations range from his marketing concepts such as "purple cow" or "linchpin," to his book distribution tactics, to the various projects he is involved with, such as "Change This"[80] or "The Domino Project."[81] He's also an entrepreneur with Squidoo.com[82], and even covered the role of vice president of direct marketing at Yahoo! These are some of his innovative concepts and approaches:

1. Survival is not enough: zooming, evolution, and the future of your company.
2. Free Prize Inside! The Next Big Marketing Idea
3. All Marketers Are Liars: The Power of Telling Authentic Stories in a Low-Trust World
4. Small Is the New Big: And 193 Other Riffs, Rants, and Remarkable Business Ideas
5. The Dip: A Little Book That Teaches You When to Quit (and When to Stick)
6. Tribes: We Need You to Lead Us
7. We Are All Weird. The Domino Project
8. Meatball Sundae: Is Your Marketing Out of Sync?
9. Linchpin: Are You Indispensable?
10. Poke the Box
11. The Icarus Deception: How High Will You Fly?
12. Whatcha Gonna Do with That Duck?

---

80 Change This is a web-based company that is attempting to create and develop a new kind of media that uses available tools, such as PDFs, blogs, and the web, to challenge the way ideas are shared. For more information please visit their website at *http://changethis.com/*.

81 The Domino Project is a new way to think about publishing. With this project, S. Godin, in collaboration with Amazon, is "trying to change the way books are built, sold, and spread." For more information please go to *http://www.thedominoproject.com/*.

82 Squidoo.com allows anyone to build a web page about anything one is passionate about. The website also raises money for charity and actually pays royalties to its members (there are over a million). To see what this company can offer please go to *http://www.squidoo.com/*.

## Interview with S. Godin

### Seth Godin, August, 2012, New York

Figure 68: Massimo Soriani Bellavista and Seth Godin

*M.S.B.: Dear Seth, you are one of the most creative and innovative marketers, as an author, as a consultant, and as an entrepreneur. In your work, creativity is one of the most important abilities a marketing manager/entrepreneur has to have. From your point of view, how can a marketing manager or an entrepreneur improve creativity?*

*S.G.: Well, I think creativity gives people a chance to hide because they say "I am not creative," so they don't know how to do it; and I mean, define creativity as "the willingness to fail again and again until we get something right." And when we can find that, maybe we have a chance to understand it and just get over our fear of failure, and we can probably become more creative.*

*M.S.B.: I take the part of your book that talks about this and I totally agree with you when you told us today that the fear of a CEO is to lose their job. You have created lots of ideas: "permission marketing," "purple cow," etc., and you still keep creating more…In you experience, which is the concept that your fans or clients use the most?*

*S.G.: Well, I have no clients, so that's the first thing. The hard part is to distinguish between the one that is the most common, the one that is broadly understood, versus the one that has the most impact, so I think that the combination of "permission marketing" and "purple cow" is remarkable; clearly Amazon is built on it, Groupon is built on it, Facebook is built on it. And every e-mail and newsletter you get, and the growth of everything you find starts kicking off. It's all about how we make ideas that are worth spreading and we use permission to follow up. But in terms of the ones that have sort of touched the people, I've been told that they have transformed the way they think; I will say it is the dip - this idea of fear and quitting, and how we tell [ourselves] the truth about what we really want.*

# MARKETHINK
## CHAPTER 3

*M.S.B.: During the first day you said that there are lots of opportunities. Can you explain your point of view on how a manager/entrepreneur can recognize an opportunity? Right now you say we are in a world with a lot of opportunities but that people don't recognize them.*

*S.G.: I think managers do recognize them, but they don't want to; they don't want to take advantage of the opportunity.*

*M.S.B.: Why?*

*S.G.: Ah, there is a famous story of two Harvard economic professors walking down Harvard Yard, and as they were walking there was a twenty dollar bill on the ground, and they walk right by it, and the first guy says to the second, "Why don't you bend over and pick it up?" And the second guy says, "if it was a real twenty dollar bill someone would have already picked it up."*

*M.S.B.: So in your experience you have seen this situation a lot of times?*

*S.G: Every time. Opportunities don't come as a guarantee! Everyone says "I'll do it if you guarantee it is going to work." Look at Google stock, why didn't you buy Google for $ 80? Most people didn't invest and then it went to $ 500, yet everyone had the same information.*

*M.S.B.: We have worked a lot in these three days on how to communicate our business ideas. How important do you think communication ability is for a marketing manager or an entrepreneur?*

*S.G.: All we do is communication.*

*M.S.B.: You are a successful author of twelve best-selling books, but you said you had thirty publishers who refused your first books. If it is so important to mention the fear of the failure, what is your suggestion on how to manage people's fear?*

*S.G.: So when they rejected my book idea, they were not rejecting me; they were rejecting my book idea. Is there bowling in Italy?*

*M.S.B.: Yes, obviously.*

*S.G.: So if you roll the ball in bowling and you don't get a strike, that means that you are a bad person? No! It means you didn't roll the ball properly, so you roll the ball again. But to leave at the end of the day from bowling and thinking that you are a bad person because you didn't strike - this is silly. You just say "I have to practice my roll." So, for me, I don't feel personally rejected, but I realized something I did, something I executed, something I built, was rejected, so I can either think "I don't want this person to be my customer" or "I have to build something different for them."*

In the following pages, we will cover only a few of S.Godin's ideas, but we definitely recommend you dig deeper into his work and invite you to visit both his website at http://www.sethgodin.com and his blog at http://sethgodin.typepad.com.

## CHAPTER 3     MARKETHINK

## 3.3.1 Permission Marketing

S. Godin developed, in 1999, a new marketing concept: "permission marketing," in his book of the same name. It's a concept where the consumers empower the marketers with the permission to send them marketing messages of certain interest: "Permission marketing envisions every customer as shaping the targeting behavior of marketers."

Permission marketing is the opposite of "interruption marketing," but to get to the permission level, you fist need to interrupt your public. Be careful how you do it, though, and do it only once. Once you have their permission, never ever interrupt them again. To be able to avoid doing so, make sure you keep the exchange alive while respecting the wishes of the customer to maintain privacy

Permission marketing allows customers to volunteer to be marketed at with relevant messages, encourages long-term participation in and interactivity of marketing campaigns, and rewards the consumer for his or her dedicated time and attention.

Interruption marketing overwhelms the consumer with enormous amounts of irrelevant information, and therefore wastes the most coveted commodity of today's consumer: time.

The "Getting Married" Analogy and the "Dating" Metaphor

S. Godin uses an analogy to explain the difference between traditional interruption marketing and permission marketing by stating that there are two ways of getting married:

A single man walks into a bar and proposes to one woman. If she says no, he goes to the next woman and so on until one decides to pay attention and allow him in. His message is sent to a mass audience, and is mostly rejected: this is traditional "interruption" marketing. (2007, p. 22–26)

Permission marketing, on the other hand, is like dating. "It turns strangers into friends and friends into lifetime customers." Many of the rules of dating apply, and so do many of the benefits (Godin 2007, p 23). Godin lists "five steps to dating your customer":

1. Offer the prospect an incentive to volunteer.
2. Use the attention offered by the prospect, offer a curriculum over time, educate your consumer about your product or service.
3. Reinforce the incentive to guarantee that the prospect maintains the permission level he gave you.
4. Offer additional incentives to get even more permission from him.
5. Over time, leverage this permission to change the consumer behavior towards profits. (Godin 2007, p. 26)

Permission marketing is an approach to selling products or services only to those prospects who have explicitly agreed to receive your marketing messages, increasing their effectiveness, since prospects are receptive to it; they see the value of it. This approach provides the consumer the ability to volunteer to be marketed to and rewarded for paying attention to your ever more relevant messages.

The need for this type of approach came to be because marketers could no longer rely on the traditional forms of "interruption" marketing to gain customers' attention. It's irritating and no longer works. There is so much noise out there that screaming at the consumers to gain their attention no longer works. We live in a world where attention has a high level of value and time is really a scarce resource. It is important for both the consumer and the marketer to establish a relationship that benefits both - the consumer doesn't get his or her precious time stolen away pointlessly, and the marketer is sure that his or her expenditures create valuable returns. To explain why we truly need to consider a permission marketing approach, S. Godin determined the problematic elements of interruption marketing:

- Human beings have a finite amount of attention. You can't watch everything, remember everything, or do everything. As the amount of noise in your life increases, the percentage of messages that get through inevitably decreases.
- Human beings have a finite amount of money. You also can't buy everything. You have to choose. But because your attention is limited, you'll be able to choose from those things you notice.
- The more products offered the less money there is to go around. It's a zero-sum game. Every time you buy a Coke, you don't buy Pepsi. As the number of companies offering products increases, and as the number of products each company offers multiplies, it's inevitable that there will be more losers than winners.
- In order to capture more attention and more money, interruption marketers must increase spending. Spending less money than your competitors on advertising in a cluttered environment inevitably leads to decreased sales.
- But this increase in marketing exposure costs big money.
- Interruption marketers have no choice but to spend a bigger and bigger portion of their company's budgets on breaking through the clutter.
- But, as you've seen, spending more and more money in order to get bigger returns leads to ever more clutter.
- Catch-22: The more they spend, the less it works. The less it works, the more they spend. (2007, p. 16)

S. Godin defined permission marketing with three concepts. It has to be "anticipated" by the people; they need to look forward to hearing from you. It must be "personal," directly related to the individual's characteristics, preferences, and choices. And last but not least, it has to be "relevant"; it will only be successful if what you are saying has true meaning to the individual and he or she is actually interested in your promotional message (Godin 2007, p. 21).

## Permission Levels

In his book, S. Godin established and described different permission levels. The goal of this strategy is "to move customers up the 'permission ladder' from strangers, to friends, to customers. And then, from customers to loyal customers. At every step of the ladder, trust grows, responsibility grows, and profits grow" (2007, p. 75).

- *Intravenous level* - the marketer makes the purchasing decision on behalf of the customer; he or she cannot say no. Examples of this are book clubs and magazine subscriptions.
- *Purchase upon approval* - a less invasive level compared to intravenous. At this level a second authorization is required by the customer before sending and billing them for the product. They are free to refuse the offer.
- *Points level* - the customer earns points for purchasing or giving his attention to the marketer. Customers buy more in response to the incentives and personal attentions. The marketer rewards his or her customers.
- *Points liability model* - the points have a real value; the reward is reachable and considered valuable to the customer.
- *Points chance model* - there is no guarantee of wining, but the more the customer purchases, the more chances he gets of winning the reward.
- *Personal relationships level* - thanks to the established relationship, the marketer temporarily gets a customer's attention, but it depends entirely on the individual and his state of mind, mood, and present desires; the marketer has little or no control over the individual.
- *Brand trust level* - trustworthiness takes years to build, is hard to measure and manipulate but leads to brand extensions. If they are using your product - giving you permission - why shouldn't they use its line extension?
- *Situation level* - this is the permission given when the customer engages, establishes, and/or asks for the conversation/exchange to take place, when the customer calls the customer service department, for example.

## Rules of Permission Marketing

- Make sure the names on your list really belong there - the names should only be of people who have agreed to receive your marketing message.
- Give your customers the ability to choose how they receive your promotional message - what format, where, etc.
- Give the customers the ability to "opt out" of future mailings - understand and respect that opting in is their choice. An attempt to keep them interested is a loss of time, and it's better to concentrate on potential and actual permission givers.
- Let your customers know what you intend to do with the information they share with you - don't deceive them; reassure them and respect their privacy.

Permission is nontransferable; they have given permission to you and only you. It is a process rather than a moment, and it can be cancelled and retrieved at any time. Permission marketing is all about obtaining the customers' consent to receive information from the company, instead of using the traditional interruption marketing approach. It is about establishing and maintaining a positive relationship and about increasing the depth of this relationship with the customers, so they welcome you in their life and make their most valuable resource available to you by taking the time to listen to what you have to say. As S. Godin puts it, it's "turning strangers into friends, and friends into customers." It enables marketers to get messages across, bypassing the large amounts of marketing messages.

## 3.3.2 "Ideavirus"

The concept of the "ideavirus" introduced by S. Godin in 2000 in his book, *Unleashing the Ideavirus*, offers a new perspective, an addition to the already well-known word-of-mouth and viral marketing, as well as a complement to bring permission marketing to another level. With permission marketing, as we have seen, he explains the need to turn strangers into friends and friends into customers once you have their attention, but it lacked the "how" - how to attract their attention and interest. We live in an age where consumers are becoming less permeable to marketing messages, yet they are always more interconnected.

The aim is no longer to impose your ideas on consumers no matter what, but to create ideas strong enough that consumers want to pass them on. "We live in a world where consumers actively resist marketing. So it's imperative to stop marketing at people. The idea is to create an environment where consumers will market to each other" (Godin 2000, p. 14). To resolve this problem, he proposes the "ideavirus," which is *a creation that not only makes prospects give you permission to invade their spaces, but causes them to ask you to do so.*

"The notion is to come up with a new idea and then spread it through the Internet, using e-mail and viral marketing techniques. The object is to get people to embrace the idea and support it."[83] This idea spreads through the masses, penetrates the marketing noise and infects the appropriate host. "Stop marketing at people! Turn your ideas into epidemics by helping your customers do the marketing for you."[84] Creating an ideavirus means turning your idea into a "virus worthy" idea that is worth talking about because it is "attractive."

---

83   Definition from Netlingo.com at *http://www.netlingo.com/word/ideavirus.php*
84   It's part of the title: *Unleashing the Ideavirus: Stop Marketing at People! Turn Your Ideas into Epidemics by Helping Your Customers Do the Marketing for You.*

| CHAPTER 3 | MARKETHINK |

## The Formula

Figure 69: Viral Marketing (Depositphotos.com)

It is definitely not an exact science, nor a definite step-by-step guide, but rather a set of key elements that puts you in the right path for success, a great way to increase your chances of spreading your idea and infecting your target. What is definitely imperative, though, is a valuable idea, loads of imagination, a clear vision, good communication skills, and commitment. The ideavirus formula is a combination of eight variables that you have to tweak and adapt to your needs to unleash, infect, and spread your idea. Each variable has a specific fundamental role.

1. *Hives* - "people are not one amorphous mass. We're self-organized into groups, or hives that have several things in common: a way to communicate among ourselves, spoken or unspoken rules and standards; a common history; fashion leaders" (Godin 2000, p. 42). "A hive that respects the core value of your virus is a critical first step in laying the foundation for promoting the idea" (Godin 2000, p. 90).
2. *Sneezers* - "some people are more likely to tell their friends about a great new idea. These people are at the heart of the 'ideavirus'. Identifying and courting sneezers is a key success factor for idea merchants" (Godin 2000, p. 37).
3. *Velocity* - "is the measure of how fast the idea spreads from one party to another. If an idea is going to hit ten people before it gets to me, the multiplier effect is large indeed - fast steps lead to more people being infected before it dies out" (Godin 2000, p. 26).
4. *Vector* - "as an 'ideavirus' moves through a population, it usually follows a vector. It could be a movement toward a certain geographic or demographic audience, for example. Sometimes an 'ideavirus' starts in a subgroup and then breaks through that niche into the public consciousness. Other times, it works its way

through a group and then just stops" (Godin 2000, p. 51). This is important because there is "plenty you can do to influence its vector, and the vector you choose will have a lot to do with who 'gets' the virus. The vector controls the hives through which the idea flows" (Godin 2000, p. 94).

5. *Medium* - "In order to move, an idea has to be encapsulated in a medium. It could be a picture, a phrase, a written article, a movie, even a mathematical formula (e=mc2). The Medium used for transmitting the 'ideavirus' determines how smooth it is as well as the velocity of its growth" (Godin 2000, p. 13). "The key to the entire virus spreading process."

6. *Smoothness* - "how easy is it for an end user to spread this particular 'ideavirus'? Can I click one button or mention some magic phrase, or do I have to go through hoops and risk embarrassment to tell someone about it? The smoothest viruses, like Hotmail, spread themselves. Just the act of using the product spreads the virus. There's an obvious relationship between smoothness and catchiness. A product that's easy to recommend is often a product that's easy to get hooked on" (Godin 2000, p. 27).

7. *Persistence* - of the virus - "how long does a sneezer sneeze?" (Godin 2000, p. 80). This "matters because the longer people are sneezing about your idea, the more people they infect" (Godin 2000, p. 61).

8. *Amplifier* - "a system that allows the positive word of mouth to be amplified (and the negative to be damped!)" (Godin 2000, p. 102). To get bigger, for your "ideavirus" and to reinforce "the recommendations to a far larger audience: TV, press, web" (Godin 2000, p. 55).

To successfully "unleash" your ideavirus and get it spreading, there are some key points to figure out:

- Understand and admit that ideavirus don't last forever, that they have a life of their own, and that you cannot have control over how they spread.
- Do not unleash an idea if it is not remarkable; make good stuff. Make sure your idea stands out, that it has the "wow!" factor.
- Acknowledge that there are no guarantees. It is not because you have a great idea that it will become an epidemic. There are many factors that influence the level of infection: wrong time, wrong target, incomprehension from the market, etc.
- Be certain that your idea is easy to spread, that the message is clear - what is it? Determine what you want your sneezers to say and how; give them the necessary tools and information to spread your idea.
- Establish a relationship with your sneezers; listen and understand them. What motivates them and how do they behave?
- Be persistent, make yourself visible, and always amaze your public. Constantly reinforce your virus and keep the "infection" spreading. Don't do things halfway. Always nurture your followers, their attention, and their interest. Value their permission. Keep them enthusiastic.
- "Fill the vacuum." Fill the empty space; satisfy unfulfilled needs, because "it's very

# CHAPTER 3 — MARKETHINK

hard to keep two conflicting 'ideaviruses' in your head at the same time. So if an idea already inhabits space in your consumer's brain, your idea can't peacefully coexist" (Godin 2000, p. 52).

The ideavirus concept is based on the implication - of increasing interest - that ideas are the new currency in the business world. S. Godin establishes that there are five fundamental principles that need to be understood by all "idea merchants."[85]

1. Idea merchants understand that creating the virus is the single most important part of their job. So they'll spend all of their time and money creating a product and an environment that feed the virus.
2. Idea merchants understand that as long as they can recognize and manipulate the key elements of idea propagation - the sneezers, the persistence, the smoothness, the vector, and the velocity - they can dramatically improve a virus's chances of success.
3. Idea merchants remind themselves on a regular basis that digital word of mouth amounts to a permanent, written record online, a legacy that will follow the product, for good or for ill, forever.
4. Idea merchants realize that the primary goal of a product or service is not just to satisfy the needs of one user. The goal is to deliver so much wow, to be so cool, to be so neat, and to be so productive that the one user tells five friends. Products market themselves by creating and reinforcing ideaviruses.
5. Idea merchants know that because an ideavirus follows a life cycle, they will have to decide when to shift from paying to spread it to charging users and profiting from it.

To test his concept, S. Godin made his book itself an "ideavirus." The book was an e-book released for free on the web as a PDF, the volume of which was small enough for people to e-mail it to each other, because he also gave them explicit authorization, and maybe a little push, to share it with others.[86] His strategy worked; the first ideavirus unleashed had its results: it is the most popular e-book ever written![87]

An ideavirus is an idea that spreads like a virus and infects the most appropriate hosts, ensuring increased and continuous contagion. You have to "create an 'ideavirus' so focused that it overwhelms that small slice of the market that really and truly will respond to what you sell" (Godin 2005, p. 31).

---

[85] From an article by S. Godin in 2000. "Here's a Big Idea: Ideas Are Driving the Economy. Here's a Bigger Idea: Ideas That Spread Fastest Win," for *Fast Company Magazine* at http://www.fastcompany.com/magazine/37/ideavirus2.html?page=0%2C1

[86] The book is still available for free at *http://www.sethgodin.com/ideavirus/downloads/IdeavirusReadandShare.pdf*

[87] Nick Douglas, in a 2007 article, "How the Top Self-Branders Sell Themselves" on Gawker, found at *http://gawker.com/self_evangelism/*

## 3.4 Purple Cow

Figure 70: A Purple Cow is Remarkable (Depositphotos.com)

In his book *Purple Cow*, S. Godin gives us the key idea behind this rather strange concept: "When was the last time you noticed a cow? Saw a cow on the side of the road, pulled over and gawked...Not likely. Cows, after you've seen them for a while, are boring. They may be well-bred cows, Six Sigma cows, cows lit by a beautiful light, but they are still boring. A Purple Cow, though: Now, that would really stand out. The essence of the Purple Cow - the reason it would shine among a crowd of perfectly competent, even undeniably excellent cows - is that it would be remarkable. Something remarkable is worth talking about, worth paying attention to. Boring stuff quickly becomes invisible."[88]

"Does everyone like Hooters? No way. That's part of what makes it remarkable. If everyone liked it, it would be boring" (Godin 2005, p. 102).

S. Godin states that the traditional marketing mix is missing some key elements. For him, marketers should consider publicity, packaging, and permission as individual key elements of the mix, to be added to the previous and well known four *p*'s, making them a total of seven *p*'s. But he still feels that something is missing, so, with his new approach, he has determined the eighth and newest *p*: the "purple cow." This *p* is all about being remarkable, about delivering, creating, and conceptualizing something exceptional and worth talking about - *du jamais vu*. He defines remarkability as "something worth talking about. Worth noticing. Exceptional. New. Interesting. It's a Purple Cow. Boring stuff is invisible. It's a brown cow" (Godin 2005, p. 3).

"Remarkable marketing is the art of building things worth noticing right into your product or service" (Godin 2005, p. 3).

---
[88] Bull Market 1st ed. May, 2004. "Companies That Can Help You Make Something Happen," compiled by S. Godin. *http://www.motivational-speaker-resource.com/docs/pdfs/BullMarket.pdf*

A good example of a "purple cow" is the Curad case study:

When Curad wanted to challenge the Band-Aid brand for the market for adhesive bandages, most people thought Curad was crazy. Band-Aid was a household institution, a name so well known it was practically generic. And the product was terrific. What could Curad hope to accomplish? Curad developed a purple cow - bandages with characters printed on them.

Kids, the prime consumers of small bandages, loved them. So did parents who wanted to make the boo-boos get better even faster! And of course, when the first kid with Curads wore them to school, every other kid wanted them, too.

It didn't take very long at all for Curad to grab a chunk of market share away from the market leader. (Godin 2005, p. 74)

## The Steps to the Purple Cow

Figure 71: Funny Purple Cow (Depositphotos.com)

The first step is to "be the cow!" Bring the cow to work, create a purple culture, look for purple opportunities and don't be afraid of being remarkable.

The second is to break with the traditional ways and realize that you have to get out of the "TV-industrial complex." Get out of the vicious circle - buying ads, getting more distribution, selling more products, making profits, buying ads, increasing distribution, and so on. It's not about creating safe, ordinary products supported by great marketing anymore; this creates an average product for the average consumer. The new rule is all about creating a product so remarkable that people look for it and desire it deeply.

"Making and marketing something remarkable means asking new questions - and trying new practices." Here are ten suggestions to "raise" the purple cow:[89]

---

[89] Retrieved from Business Summaries at http://www.bizsum.com/trial/022005/pdf/PurpleCow_BIZ.pdf

# MARKETHINK CHAPTER 3

1. Differentiate your customers. Find the group that's most profitable. Find the group that's most likely to influence other customers. Figure out how to develop for, advertise to, or reward either group. Ignore the rest. Cater to the customers you would choose if you would choose your customers.
2. If you could pick one undeserved niche to target (and to dominate), what would it be? Why not launch a product to compete with your own that does nothing but appeal to that market?
3. Create two teams: the investors and the milkers. Put them in separate buildings. Hold a formal ceremony when you move a product from one group to the other. Celebrate them both, and rotate people around.
4. Do you have the e-mail addresses of the 20 percent of your customer base that loves what you do? If not, start getting them. If you do, what could you make for them that would be super special?
5. Remarkable isn't always about changing the biggest machine in your factory. It can be the way you answer the phone, launch a new brand, or price a revision to your software. Getting in the habit of doing the "unsafe" thing every time you have the opportunity is the best way to see what's working and what's not.
6. Explore the limits. What if you're the cheapest, the fastest, the slowest, the hottest, the coldest, the easiest, the most efficient, the loudest, the most hated, the copycat, the outsider, the hardest, the oldest, the newest, or just the most! If there's a limit, you should (must) test it.
7. Think small. One vestige of the TV-industrial complex is a need to think mass. If it doesn't appeal to everyone, the thinking goes, it's not worth it. No longer. Think of the smallest conceivable market and describe a product that overwhelms it with its remarkability. Go from there.
8. Find things that are "just not done" in your industry, then go ahead and do them. For example, JetBlue Airways almost instituted a dress code, for its passengers! The company is still playing with the gift cards. A book publisher could put a book on sale for a certain period of time. Stew Leonard's took the strawberries out of the little green plastic cages and let the customers pick their own. Sales doubled.
9. Ask "Why not" questions? Almost everything you don't do has no good reason for it. Almost everything you don't do is the result of fear or inertia or a historical lack of someone asking - "Why not?"
10. What would happen if you simply told the truth inside your company and to your customers?

It's neither a plan nor the secret formula to the purple cow; it is a process composed of a few steps. "Go for the edges. Challenge yourself and your team to describe what those edges are (not that you'd actually go there), and then test which edge is most likely to deliver the marketing and financial results you seek" (Godin 2005, p. 85). It is reviewing every one of your $p$'s and seeing where your edges are, comparing them with those of competitors, and selecting your purple cow $p$ accordingly.

Understand that it requires compromise. "In almost every market, the boring slot is filled. The product designed to appeal to the largest possible audience already exists, and displacing it is awfully difficult, because the very innocuousness of the market-leading product is its greatest asset. How can you market yourself as 'more bland than the leading brand?' the real growth comes with products that annoy, offend, don't appeal, are too expensive, too cheap, too heavy, too complicated, too simple - too something. (Of course they are too *too* for some people, but just perfect for others)" (Godin 2005, p. 92).

## The Cow's Barriers

The purple cow can become the best competitive advantage, but unfortunately marketers don't develop purple cows often, or easily. Not because they cannot come up with them, but because of their personal fear of taking the leap, of assuming risks and consequences, and of going against established approaches and procedures. These are the main barriers to developing the purple cow, according to S. Godin:

*Fear of criticism* - those who stand out are almost always criticized; criticism leads to failure, and we are taught, from a very young age, to play it safe and to avoid failure. You have to accept that ideas will always be criticized and that ideas fail, but understand that what fails is the idea, not you. Now stop playing it safe and start challenging yourself and the rules. Fear has many variables and affects people differently; there is fear of failure, fear of rejection, or even an inexplicable fear within. It can be fear of losing your job, or at a deeper level, fear of personal judgment and attacks by others.

*Following the leader* - following the rules and not taking the risk of being remarkable, playing on the safe side. Waiting for the market leader to come up with the purple cow, with the breakthrough ideas, and attempting to copy him. How exactly can you compete by being the same? Stop following and start being different. Again, stop playing it safe and start challenging yourself and the rules.

*Catch-22 of the Purple Cow by J. Spolestra in "Marketing Outrageously"* (Godin 2005, p. 46). Being remarkable is encouraged in good times and discouraged in tough times. It shouldn't be like this! You need to challenge situations, to make propositions always - in good and in bad times. Looking for the cow should be a constant process and only like that will you be able to really see what you can do. When times are bad, why would you challenge situations? Think about it. Isn't that exactly the right moment to come up with the genius idea that can help make bad times good ones?

S. Godin is not giving us the purple cow formula or the solution to all our problems; he is telling us that we have to find a way to be remarkable and that each one of your products must be unique in their own way, create the "wow!" factor, and exceed expectations. He is also saying that it is risky, but that playing it safe is riskier!

You cannot oblige people to listen to you; what you can do is make sure you find who is most likely to pay attention to what you have to say and give them the unexpected by creating the purple cow especially for them. Remember, they will listen to your story only if it's remarkable. If it's not, then you are invisible.

## 3.5 Guerrilla Marketing by Jay Conrad Levinson

*"Guerrilla creativity combines art, the science of human behavior and business sense to create good marketing - strategies that will generate enough confidence and trust that people will have good reason to buy your product or service. It drives marketing strategies to their goal." - J. C. Levinson*

*"The soul and essence of guerrilla marketing which remain as always - achieving conventional goals, such as profits and joy, with unconventional methods, such as investing energy instead of money." - J. C. Levinson*

Guerrilla marketing is an unconventional tactic pushed to another, higher level established by J. C. Levinson in 1994 in his book of the same name: *Guerrilla Marketing*. This concept relies on the use of clever marketing tactics that get the public curious, interested, and engaged. It is based on the use of exceptional and unusual techniques when performing marketing activities. It provides the possibility of obtaining maximum output from minimum input invested (resources), creates buzz, and starts the word-of-mouth effect. Guerilla marketing is a nontraditional, low-cost, and highly effective marketing approach. It relies on the use of good creativity and innovation techniques to introduce the brand and its products, service, or concept to the people and gain public awareness. This allows you to get exposure, create buzz, and become a subject of discussion.

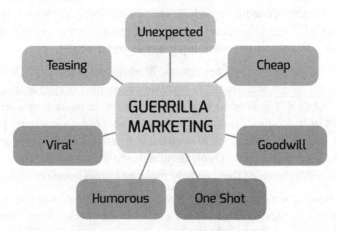

Figure 72: Elements of Guerrilla Marketing

It is important to be clear on the fact that not every innovative and shocking campaign is a guerrilla marketing campaign. Consider the long, controversial marketing campaign designed by O. Toscani for Benetton. It was created to be controversial, but it was not part of a guerrilla marketing plan. It was a different way of consolidating their brand identity and standing out compared to competitors. A guerrilla marketing campaign has to have some key ingredients according to A. Reidl.

*Unexpectedness* - they have to be totally unexpected. The element of surprise tends to raise people's attention. It happens when participants have no clue they will witness something - placing odd objects in unusual places or at unusual times, for example.

*Drasticity* - the word "drastic" means "likely to have a strong or far-reaching effect; radical and extreme." It is an element that enables marketers to reach a large number of recipients with a constrained budget, and it maximizes the relevancy of the product in the eyes of the target audience; those showing a reaction are part of your target who are getting your message. It creates a high degree of interest and attention.

*Humor* - this is an element that can reduce the existing barriers between the sender (the company) and the recipient (the actual or potential customers). It helps differentiate the activities from competitors'. Humor creates the "it" factor and willingness to share it.

*One-shot game* - any guerrilla marketing campaign has a determined life span, which is usually short. It must be performed in a strictly limited period of time to have the most effect, and should absolutely not be duplicated or replicated in any way. The true impact comes from its uniqueness.

*Goodwill* - you have to show a high degree of goodwill, showing that you care, but above all it has to be felt. This is very hard to accomplish, but if you manage to transmit that feeling, then you have done a great job. Goodwill leads to establishing a positive reputation, which becomes an invaluable asset for the company - its attractive force.

*Tease* - it has to tease the consumer, meaning that it has to be playful, provocative, and somewhat annoying; it has to entice curiosity. It is about dangling something in front of them; make them want to know more and desire it, but don't completely fulfill the desire. When you tease the prospective consumer, you have to make sure you amuse him or her. Teasing customers is a great way to distract them and get their willing attention. You distract them from their routine and preoccupations (even if only for a little while), and mainly their attention is diverted from the actual marketing activity they are being subject to, more you can make them receptive to your message and willing to participate. When you tease the consumer, make sure you don't do it in a harmful and overintrusive manner. It's all about amusing and surprising them, about making something different happen that they will notice. You want them to want more and become an active consumer, and therefore a customer.

*Viral* - we will cover this point in more detail in the following pages, but for now we want to highlight the importance of this element. Your guerrilla marketing activities need to be easy to share, experience, and be a part of. You have to make sure you create, distribute, and make available as much material as possible (before and after), such as posts, images, and videos, to get the widest reach.

*Cheap* - guerrilla marketing is a support to a strategic marketing plan, and the actual ROI is not clear-cut (it does have positive effects and results, but they are hard to monetize). It is therefore important not to invest too much of your budget on it. Guerrilla marketing is about making noise, and the more noise you make regularly in surprising ways, the better. We previously said that it is a one-shot effort, meaning that even if it is absolutely the best guerrilla stunt, you cannot reproduce it, because it would be a waste of your investment since it is something that "dies" there, therefore limiting further investment in this type of activity. But be careful; by cheap we don't mean that you reduce the quality of it and deliver something that is poorly executed or distasteful and unappealing. We mean that the overall guerrilla marketing campaign should consist of inexpensive activities achievable with few resources and little effort, time, and money, while always aiming for good quality marketing, in line with the corporate identity. The main advantage of this marketing method is definitely the unexpected effect that catches the person of guard, causing an emotional response and leaving a mark. Guerrilla marketing is all about catching the interest of the public better and for a longer stretch of time than your competitors.

Guerilla marketing means putting in action creative moves to get an emotional reaction from the target market(s) with the use of humor, controversy, shock, and entertainment. It's all about being memorable and relevant to inspire a strong desire to share and be part of it.

## The Nineteen Secrets of Guerrilla Marketing

J. C Levinson established the nineteen secrets, or concepts, if you will, of a guerrilla marketing campaign, and he believes that "if you memorize these secrets, you will exceed your most optimistic expectations in business."[90] The secrets are as follows:[91]

| 1. Commitment | 6. Assortment of Weapons | 11. Involvement | 16. Augment |
|---|---|---|---|
| 2. Investment | 7. Convenient | 12. Dependent | 17. Congruent |
| 3. Consistent | 8. Subsequent | 13. Armament | 18. Experiment |
| 4. Confident | 9. Amazement | 14. Consent | 19. Implement |
| 5. Patient | 10. Measurement | 15. Content | |

Figure 73: J. C. Levinson during the 2009 Annual Sales and Marketing Conference in Santiago

---

[90] Shared by J. C. Levinson during the 2009 Annual Sales and Marketing Conference in Santiago, Chile, and transcribed by S. Gibson, found at *http://www.closingbigger.net/2009/07/19-guerrilla-social-media-marketing-secrets/*. S. Gibson is a keynote speaker on social media and sales performance, as well as a writer, a coach and trainer, and a blogger (specialized in guerrilla marketing).

[91] For more information please go to http://www.closingbigger.net/2009/07/19-guerrilla-social-media-marketing-secrets/.

## 3.6 Experiential Marketing

Experiential marketing is a distinctive approach to the marketing of goods and services, an approach that integrates the concepts of emotion, logic, and the senses. It is the application and combination of these three concepts that trigger a sensorial reaction and establish an emotional connection in the minds of consumers. This connection is made on both the rational and emotional level, but it's important that these connections are relevant and coherent, memorable, and emotional as well as interactive.

"The term 'Experiential Marketing' refers to actual customer experiences with the brand/product/service that drive sales and increase brand image and awareness. It's the difference between telling people about the features of a product or service and letting them experience the benefits for themselves." "Experiential marketing allows customers to engage and interact with brands, products, and services in sensory ways that are the icing on the cake of providing information."[92]

Experiential marketing is not like some theatrical stunt, but rather like a well-thought plan that support marketing efforts in order to establish a during relationship through genuine experiences.

It is an approach that engages the consumers' senses with visual elements, sounds, smells, textures, and more as long as it activates one of the human senses. It aims to create a unique "world," to establish a strong bond in the mind of consumers by connecting them with the product and brand on multiple levels by the means of an in-depth experience. Give them a lot more than just tangible information to activate their buying behavior.

Experiential marketing doesn't limit itself to just communicating the features and benefits of a product from the company's point of view; it allows consumers to experience them, "live" the product, and see for themselves, to determine what their point of view is. Remember it is what the customers think that counts; remember that "perception is reality."

In 1999, B. H. Schmitt determined that there are five dimensions to an experience, referred to as "sense, feel, think, act, and relate."[93]

---
92 Definition given by Erik Hauser, "a recognized thought leader in the field of experience/experiential marketing" on the Experiential Forum website found at *http://www.experientialforum.com/*
93 B. H. Schmitt, 1999. *Experiential Marketing: How to Get Customers to Sense, Feel, Think, Act, Relate to Your*

*Sense* - he experience includes aesthetics and sensory qualities and elements: visual, olfactory, auditory, and tactile aspects.

*Feel* - the experience includes and triggers moods and emotions; it plays on the affective side of the individual.

*Think* - it relates to cognitive aspects; the experience includes convergent-analytical and divergent-imaginative thinking elements: surprise, curiosity, etc.

*Act* - it provides physical and behavioral reactions and experiences.

*Relate* - it refers to the social aspect of the experience and the customer's sense of belonging.

According to B. Schmitt, "the term 'customer experience management' represents the discipline, methodology, and/or process used to comprehensively manage a customer's cross-channel exposure, interaction, and transaction with a company, product, brand, or service."[94]

P. Kotler's take on experiential marketing is that "marketers need to think more about designing and delivering a positive experience for the customer than about simply selling a product or service" (2008, p. 26). This means that they need to consider what the customer experiences when they are in the process of choosing a product or service. Focus on what it is that can deliver a stimulating experience to influence their behavior.

Experiential marketing focuses on the whole customer experience and the customer's response to it, rather than just the marketed product. It is interacting directly with the person and giving life to the brand and its products. "The aim of experiential marketing is to add drama and entertainment to what otherwise might pass as stale fare." "All merchants offer services; your challenge is to escort your customer through a memorable experience." (Kotler 2003, p. 62)

For a good experiential marketing campaign you need to do the following:
- Give people something to talk about - a unique feature or attribute, benefits and value proposition, design, etc.
- Focus on creating a two-way dialogue.
- Let people experience the product and facilitate their talking about their experience publicly.
- Establish a platform to drive people to talk about their experience.
- Collect feedback for your sources in the viral domain and make it available for others to access when they are making their purchasing decision.
- Be ready and willing to hear negative things and to accept criticism.
- Be prepared to acknowledge questions and complaints, and be open to suggestions.

---

*Company and Brands*, The Free Press

94 B. H. Schmitt, 2003. *Customer Experience Management: A Revolutionary Approach to Connecting with Your Customers*, John Wiley & Sons

- Consider customers contributions, ask them to participate further, and push to find what opportunities lay behind your product.
- Make sure you listen to what people say to deliver "innovations" and give them something else to talk about.

To give you a better idea of this approach, here are some examples:

## HP Experiences Exstreamly[95]

When enterprise software providers try to show current and potential customers their capabilities, standard sales presentations often aren't enough. HP Exstream and Pro Motion Inc. recently took that standard sales presentation to a whole new level with their own mobile trade show, the HP Exstream Results Tour.

After Pro Motion outfitted a forty-five-foot deluxe motor coach with the latest computer hardware and HP Exstream software, the tour hit the road April 12 through May 26. With key HP staff on board, the tour traveled ten thousand miles to more than forty current and potential financial-services clients in twenty-three cities. Setting up in each customer's parking lot, this mobile trade show gave HP Exstream the opportunity to show current software offerings and upcoming new upgrades in a low-pressure, entertaining, and comfortable "living room" environment.

"For Business-to-Business clients, taking their products directly to their customers without the clutter of competition provides the opportunity to really showcase their brands. It also attracts senior level decision-makers who may not go to trade shows," says Steve Randazzo, president of Pro Motion. "We've found this strategy dramatically enhances the return on investment for our clients."

- The results far exceeded HP Exstream's expectations.
- More than six hundred financial services and insurance customers and prospects visited the coach.
- The tour resulted in three closed sales, adding up to more than $2 million, in addition to many more millions in sales that moved along the funnel.
- The tour earned forty-eight meetings, including twenty new business prospects.
- From those, nine major HP/Exstream revenue opportunities developed, with several others moving significantly toward completion.
- The tour returned ten times the investment.

## Sanctum in 3D[96]

Universal was looking for a mobile venue that would allow them to take this amazing 3D underwater journey to top cities across the United States, and they chose "Cinetransformer" to promote their latest 3D adventure: *Sanctum*.

---

95  Example taken from Pro Motion's (the experiential provider's) website at *http://www.promotion1.com/wow/hp---exstream-results-tour/*

96  This example was taken from Cinetransformer website at *http://cinetransformer.com/sanctum.html*

Their goal was to submerge the audience into a cave-like atmosphere that would enhance the feeling of being trapped underwater and allow every guest to feel like part of this adventure.

To recreate this effect, the Cinetransformer was fully decorated outside and inside. High-resolution graphics applied to the floor and walls of the theater allowed guests to be drawn into the inner world of *Sanctum* as they experienced exclusive 3D scenes from the film, introduced by three-time Oscar winner James Cameron (*Avatar*), while enjoying free popcorn and receiving free *Sanctum* pens.

Press from all over the world enjoyed this unique experience firsthand, as executive producer James Cameron, director Alister Grierson, and writer and producer Andrew Wight took part in the press conference for a Q&A session after the show inside the Cinetransformer.

The response from the audience was incredible; every guest coming out of the theater was eager to go see the film, and thousands of people were transformed into *Sanctum* fans! The tour generated tons of PR, including interviews on local TV stations, newspapers, and magazines as well as millions of impressions on Facebook and across the web.

## 3.7 Green Marketing

**Green Marketing, a.k.a. Ecological, Environmental, Sustainable**

Figure 74: Green Label (Depositphotos.com)

The American Marketing Association (AMA) defines green marketing in three ways:

1. Retailing definition - marketing products that are presumed to be environmentally safe

# CHAPTER 3 — MARKETHINK

2. Social definition - the development and marketing of products designed to minimize negative effects on the physical environment or to improve its quality
3. Environmental definition - the efforts by organizations to produce, promote, package, and reclaim *products* in a manner that is sensitive or responsive to ecological concerns

Green marketing is the trendy approach of selling goods based on their environmentally friendly and sustainable attributes and benefits - such as ecologically safer products, recyclable and biodegradable packaging, energy-efficient operations, and pollution control among them. It is the promotion of environmentally safe and beneficial products for the welfare of consumers and the planet. Therefore, green marketing incorporates a wide range of activities, from product modification, to the production process or packaging or distribution, as well as advertising and promotional tactics.

There are four fundamental assumptions to green marketing:

- Potential customers see the product's "green" aspect as a real benefit and base their buying decision accordingly.
- Consumers are willing to pay more for the "green" aspect of a product and will be increasingly willing as awareness of environmental issues grows
- "Green" topic connects consumers, creating communities that want a lifestyle that is ecologically responsible and respectful of the environment.
- Our resources are limited, and human wants are unlimited; the efficient use of resources will be a definite competitive advantage.

## Elements of the Mix

When determining a green marketing approach, the basic elements of the product mix change a little.

- The product's objective is to reduce resource consumption and environmental pollution, and to finding ways to preserve scarce resources.
- The price is based on the effective "greenness" of your product and the way the consumers perceive this as more valuable.
- The promotion of green marketing can be done in three ways: promote the green lifestyle, communicate the corporate stand on environmental responsibility and respect, and show the correlation between the product and its impact on the biophysical environment.
- The place is all about how, when, and where to make the green product available in a way that is consistent with the green approach. Logistics and placement are key.

Green marketing is a marketing strategy that bases its focus on the environment and the specific customers' inclination toward ecology, the planet, and their personal health and well-being. It is a way of developing a sustainable, intelligent, and lasting business, as long as you truly focus on delivering exactly what you commit to in terms of ecological responsibility and the marketing of products that really do cause less damage to the planet and benefit a person's well-being. This approach to marketing gives you access to new markets, increases your profit's sustainability, and gives you a strong competitive advantage. Be careful, though; being a green marketer has its challenges. Green products require costly renewable and recyclable materials and huge investments in technology and R&D.

Here are some examples:

The Toyota Prius is a full hybrid electrical car, which combines a conventional internal combustion-engine propulsion system with an electrical one, making it the cleanest vehicle on the market based on smog-forming and toxic emissions.

## Energy-Efficient Lightbulbs

Energy-efficient describes lightbulbs that consume less energy than the old incandescent ones to produce the same amount of light. But they also save on material consumption and maintenance costs, since they last about eight times longer than the traditional ones. The most efficient are the compact fluorescent light (CFL) bulbs.

## Fundamentals

To be a green marketer a company needs to respect four fundamental concepts:

- Be genuine! Do what you are claiming to be doing: don't deceive! Make sure that the whole business functions consistently with all your claims.
- Educate your customers! Don't just educate them by informing them that you have adopted the "green" approach to your marketing because you care for the environment, but educate them on why it is important to be environmentally friendly as a company and as a consumer, for humanity. Avoid the "so what" factor.
- Give your customers the ability to be a part of the movement, to be environmentally friendly, and to help preserve the planet. Be part of the change.
- Be green everywhere, from the materials you use, to the distribution methods you employ, to the message you send. But above all, be and behave green.

# CHAPTER 3 — MARKETHINK

## 3.8 "Buyology" by Martin Lindstrom

Figure 75: M. Lindstrom and Buy.Ology (martinlindstrom.com)

"Buyology" is the meeting between neuroscientists and marketing experts that has and will shed new light on how and why we, the consumers, the human beings, make decisions about what we buy. The term "buyology" is based on the groundbreaking neuromarketing study conducted by M. Lindstrom, the global marketing research expert. With this neuroscientific research, named "Project Buyology," M. Lindstrom has created a very powerful tool to understand consumer buying patterns and behaviors and what it is that triggers the decision-making process. For this research he made use of the most advanced and expensive brain imaging technology - *neuroimaging* - to "shed light on the truth and lies about why we buy."[97] Neuroimaging refers to all the medical techniques used for creating structural and functional images of the brain. Its aim is to examine the true and deep desires of the consumer.

### Understanding Neuromarketing

The word "neuromarketing" was coined by A. Smidts in 2002. It refers to a new field of marketing that studies consumers' brain activity and reactions, their sensory motor responses, and cognitive and affective responses to marketing stimuli. It's all about the use of technologies to understand what happens to the brain when it's stimulated by particular elements, to learn why consumers make the decisions

---

[97] Found in "Change This" Manifesto, no. 54.02: "This is your Buyology" by Martin Lindstrom, published on January 15 2009. You can find it at http://changethis.com/manifesto/show/54.02.YourBuyology. "Change This" is a community, based on S. Godin's ideavirus concept, where good ideas are summarized/explained through manifestos and archived for people to share and enjoy - we strongly recommend you visit it.

they make and do what they do, and what part of the brain is telling them to do it. Neuromarketing is where science meets marketing, with the aim of uncovering the "secrets" of buying.

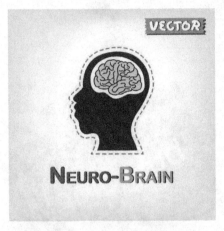

Figure 76: Neuro Brain (Depositphotos.com)

- Neuromarketing will be used by marketing analysts to gain a more accurate measure of consumers' preferences and reactions to stimuli - the verbal response to questions may not always be the true answer due to cognitive bias.
- Neuromarketing will let the marketer know exactly what the consumer reacted to. For example, was it the color of the packaging, or the sound of the packaging opening, or the idea that they will have something their coconsumers won't?
- The knowledge gained by neuromarketing will help marketers create products that are designed more accurately and effectively. Marketing campaigns will focus on their customers' brains' responses to their stimuli.

This concept has proven that many, if not all, the assumptions we have about the way we decide to buy are completely misleading. It shows how our brain reacts in different and unexpected ways to different stimuli, giving us more profound knowledge on how our brains work and create unexpected physical connections that then influence our behavior.

This knowledge will definitely change the marketplace, what marketers will do to attempt controlling our minds, and how we will react or adapt to their future efforts at getting to us.

Buyology is an approach that will help marketers decode what the consumer really thinks and feels even before he is confronted with the new product, logo, brand, lifestyle concepts, visual manifestations, and marketing messages. It will give marketers access to information about the subconscious needs and desires of individuals, enabling them to offer their consumers products and services that are truly meaningful to each customer's inner self. Therefore the products will deliver a

# CHAPTER 3 — MARKETHINK

higher level of satisfaction and reduce costs and waste of resource and cash used to push a product or packaging that is not desired.

Neuromarketing is the medical knowledge of the brain put together with technology and marketing to uncover what our brains want, and it gives companies the ability to deliver it. Buyology is the "subconscious thoughts, feelings, and desires that drive the purchasing decisions we make." These are some interesting outcomes of the study. The most interesting one is that our brain operates in a non-conscious level for the 85 percent of the time, but through this research we know there are things that can be done to influence the people's "subconscious" works:

- Visual images are more effective when combined with another sense - such as visual and sound, or visual and smell. This is called sensory branding; an example of this is the Motorola portables and their tone: *"Hello Moto."*
- Colors truly increase product and brand recognition, as well as the perception items, known as "color me crazy." But also shapes have a strong impact on the brain: think of the Coca-Cola bottle that looks like a woman's silhouette.

Overall what M. Lindstrom has done with his "Project Buyology" is make the consumer more vulnerable to future marketing efforts by putting into light that about 90 percent of our buying behavior is unconscious. Now marketers are going to do everything to control that 10 percent. Fortunately advertisers and marketers don't know how to take control of our unconscious, but they now have new tools and information to attempt to slightly influence our "buyology," our buying patterns and habits.

Figure 77: M. Lindstrom Illustrates Buyology (martinlindstrom.com)

## 3.9 "Lovemarks" by Kevin Roberts

*"The essential difference between emotion and reason is that emotion leads to action while reason leads to conclusions." - D. Calne*

Is there a brand or a product that makes you vibrate? One you couldn't live without?

That is a "lovemark," a brand that is part of who you are; that manages to position itself in you, in your heart, in your life. A lovemark is one of those brands (or products) to which we are emotionally connected - a connection that establishes a profound sense of loyalty that transcends all forms of rationality.

A lovemark is not just a new brand concept or marketing tactic, nor is it a "technological or economic phenomenon." It's a new business philosophy, a "social or attitudinal - even spiritual -transformation."[98] It's a "game-breaking opportunity to reinvent branding."[99]

The term "lovemark" was coined and developed in 2004 by Kevin Roberts, the worldwide CEO of Saatchi & Saatchi to describe an approach that "inspires loyalty beyond reason" and that commands respect and great love [100]. "Lovemarks "are super-evolved brands that offer emotional differentiation"; they reach the heart and "evolve out of a long-term commitment built on respect and love."[101]

"If you want to stay in the game, then respect is no longer sufficient. In this age of relationships, you must take your brand into the territory of the emotions. Brands must invite loyalty and invoke a sense of ownership."[102] K. Roberts states very clearly why there is a real need for brands to transform into "lovemarks":

You have to really dig in to emotional connections with consumers. The rational side of life isn't enough. We've got too much information. We do not live in the information age anymore, nor do we live in the age of knowledge. We've gone hurtling past that. Once everybody has information and knowledge, it's no longer a competitive advantage. We live now in the age of the idea. What consumers want now is an emotional connection. They want to be able to connect with what's behind the brand, what's behind the promise. They're not going to buy simply rational. You feel the world through your senses, the five senses, and that's

---

98 From the 4Front Q&A with Kevin Roberts, April 2001. "Transactions to Relationships, Brands to Lovemarks." You can download the full article on *http://www.lovemarkscampus.com/4front-transactions-to-relationships/*.

99 From *www.lovemarks.com*

100 Saatchi & Saatchi, the global advertising agency network

101 From the Saatchi & Saatchi Dutch website FAQ page on Lovemarks at http://www.saatchi-amsterdam.nl/lovemarks/

102 From the 4Front Q&A with Kevin Roberts, April, 2001. "Transactions to Relationships, Brands to Lovemarks." You can download the full article on *http://www.lovemarkscampus.com/4front-transactions-to-relationships/.*

what's next. The brands that can move to that emotional level, that can create loyalty beyond reason, are going to be the brands where premium profits lie.[103]

## 3.9.1 The Lovemarks graph

To illustrate his concept and differentiate it from past approaches, K. Roberts uses a simple "graph that plots a brand along two axes, one measuring respect, and the other measuring love. Brands with a future will be those that can migrate to the quadrant formed by the intersection of high respect and high love - the Lovemark quadrant."[104]

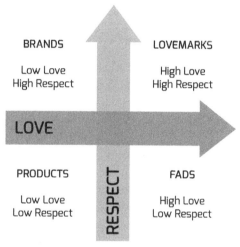

Figure 78: Lovemarks in a Graph (lovemarks.com)

For a better understanding, it is important to be clear on what is meant by both terms. Note that "Love needs Respect right from the start. Without it we're not talking Love, we're talking a fad or infatuation. Compelling and fun but certainly not capable of inspiring loyalty of any kind."[105]

"In a philosophical context, love is a virtue representing all of human kindness, compassion, and affection."[106] Love is a strong feeling of affection based on admiration or common interest, an unselfish and loyal attachment toward someone or something. It's a deep, ineffable feeling of affection and solicitude toward someone or something, an intense, wholehearted emotional feeling of devotion.

---

[103] From the Public Broadcasting Service (PBS) interview with Kevin Roberts in December, 2003. You can read the full interview at http://www.pbs.org/wgbh/pages/frontline/shows/persuaders/interviews/roberts.html.

[104] From the 4Front Q&A with Kevin Roberts, April, 2001. "Transactions to Relationships, Brands to Lovemarks." You can download the full article on http://www.lovemarkscampus.com/4front-transactions-to-relationships/.

[105] From the Lovemarks website www.lovemarks.com

[106] Definition from Wikipedia at http://en.wikipedia.org/wiki/Love

The love one has for a brand leads to loyalty, a feeling of allegiance that goes "beyond reason," which makes it a lovemark. When a brand becomes a lovemark, the relationship with the consumer changes: he or she becomes passionate, and his or her decisions are no longer based on reason, but rather they are purely emotional. Love is the key, because love is the main engine that moves our world!

Respect is a feeling of deep admiration and esteem toward someone or something, elicited by their abilities, qualities, or achievements. It's thinking highly of or valuing something, having regard for something, or admiring something or someone at a rational level. Respect leads the way to love; it is obvious that there can be no love if there is no respect.

## 3.9.2 The Lovemarks Trinity

Commanding both respect and love is what makes a brand a lovemark, and to do this, K. Roberts proposed the "Lovemarks Trinity," the three ingredients required to transform: mystery, sensuality, and intimacy.

### Mystery

Mystery is the quality of something kept secret to provoke interest and/or excitement. It is a profound, inexplicable, or secretive quality difficult to understand, grasp, or explain. It refers to something purposefully left untold or unexplained to arouse curiosity or speculation; think of the Coca-Cola secret formula.

K. Roberts defines "mystery" as what "draws together" the following:[107]

- Past, present, and future - to locate the brand in time and space Great stories - for context and meaning
- Dreams - which create action, which in turn inspires dreams
- Myths and icons - a reference library of the heart
- Inspiration - the spark that sets lovemarks on fire

A brand that can keep some mystery is able to continuously recapture our attention, breaking the walls of mass communication noise, holding high our curiosity and desire to discover what is "occult," because it might just be around the corner. "Great relationships are about learning and anticipation. When you know everything, there is nothing left to discover. No more surprises, no more wonder, no more opportunities. In a world suffering from information overload, the most powerful attention-grabbers are the things you don't know. It's the Mystery component of a Lovemark that keeps you guessing, keeps you intrigued and keeps you going back for more."[108]

---

107 From the Lovemarks website *www.lovemarks.com*

108 Lovemarks explained by Brand Express in "Beyond Brands - Lovemarks." To read the full article go to *http://www.brandxpress.net/2005/06/beyond-brands-lovemarks/.*

## Sensuality

In K. Roberts's words, sensuality is "a portal to the emotions"; it's "how human beings experience the world." It pertains to the gratification, arousal, excitement, and/or stimulation of the senses. It's a sensually pleasing or fulfilling experience that appeals to our senses: sight, smell, hearing, taste, and touch. Our senses are the highway to human emotions; most of what we know and feel comes through our senses.

"Emotional connections are at the very heart of a Lovemark. So it makes sense that the crucial elements of design, scent, texture and flavor - things that appeal directly to the senses - will influence your response over and above the more 'rational' product arguments (better, stronger, newer, cheaper...)."[109]

## Intimacy

Intimacy plays a central role in all of our lives, because intimate relationships provide strong emotional attachments that fulfill a universal need of belonging and affection.

"Intimacy generally refers to the feeling of being in a close personal association and belonging together. It is a familiar and very close affective connection with another as a result of a bond that is formed through knowledge and experience of the other. Genuine intimacy in human relationships requires dialogue, transparency, vulnerability and reciprocity."[110]

In K. Roberts's words, intimacy is "where thinking and feeling come together most closely. Real love needs intimacy - the small moments with emotional resonance."[111] Intimate relationships are based on three fundamental elements: commitment, empathy, and passion - the company's commitment to its audience, true empathy between them, and a shared passion. *K. Roberts gives the following reasons why each element is important:*[112]

- Empathy to understand and respond to other people's emotions
- Commitment to show that you are in the relationship for the long haul
- Passion to energize the relationship

It's about creating intimate experiences capable of building long-standing emotional ties with consumers. This is expressed by the brand's ability to get in close contact with its customers' inspirations and personal aspirations, therefore establishing a deep sense of closeness, affinity, and understanding. The communion is such that it resembles the intimacy two people in love have.

---

[109] Lovemarks explained by Brand Express in "Beyond Brands - Lovemarks." To read the full article go to *http://www.brandxpress.net/2005/06/beyond-brands-lovemarks/*.
[110] Definition from Wikipedia *http://en.wikipedia.org/wiki/Intimacy#Intimacy*
[111] From the Lovemarks website *www.lovemarks.com*
[112] From the Lovemarks website *www.lovemarks.com*

### 3.9.3 The Tool

K. Roberts developed a tool, "The Lovemark Profiler," that puts the brand to the test to find out in which key ingredient love is needed. To test your brand and find out if and where you need to work to become a "lovemark," please go to http://www.lovemarks.com.

### 3.9.4 "Lovemarks by the Numbers"

In his blog[113], K.Roberts presented the work done by professors Peter Boatwright and Jonathan Cagan on creating loyalty beyond reason.[114] In their book, *Built to Love: Creating Products That Captivate Customers*[115], the authors give many "insights on the benefits of creating products, services, and technologies that inspire love," what they call high-emotion companies.

What is more interesting in this context is their "High Emotion Index" and what emerged from it. K. Roberts summarizes it very well: the index "compares the stock performance of companies that provide more emotion with those that provide less. They compiled a list of forty promising, innovative consumer product companies based on rankings from BusinessWeek and Interbrand. Then they surveyed consumers to identify which brands elicited the most powerful emotional response." Furthermore, "it turns out that you would have been wise to invest in one of the high-emotion companies Boatwright and Cagan write about. Between 1997 and 2007, over 80 percent of investors in high-emotion companies did better than the Dow Jones index, the NASDAQ, and the S&P 500. A solid example of the premiums powered by emotional connections."[116]

Some examples of "creative, engaging, stimulating, and genuinely loved" brands are below:

Figure 79: Examples of Lovemark Brands

---

113  Kevin Roberts's blog *www.krconnect.blogspot.com*

114  Understanding how emotions are linked to decision making has become quite important, and many of the findings support the lovemarks concept and how it is, today, truly a matter of connecting and eliciting emotions.

115  P. Boatwright and J. Cagan, *Built to Love: Creating Products That Captivate Customers*, Berrett-Koehler Publishers, 2010

116  On "Lovemarks by the Numbers," posted on November 7, 2010, by Kevin Roberts on his blog. You can read the full post at *http://www.krconnect.blogspot.com/search?q=Lovemarks+by+the+Numbers*.

"Remember, we're living in the attention economy. You are bombarded with messages left, right and center. Wherever you go, you're surrounded by brands and media. You've got about three seconds to connect with a consumer emotionally and then to interest her. You've got to dig deep and go into homes, and you've got to have people who are curious, who are really interested and who can get on with the consumer and can really understand them, can predict, can interpret - not just a lot of quantitative stuff. And you've got to be able to figure out how do you feel what they're thinking, rather than how do you enumerate it."[117]

# 3.10 Sustainable Marketing by Walter G. Scott

*"Marketing is... the process through which economy is integrated into society to serve human needs." - P. Drucker*

In the twentieth century, mankind witnessed a process of change unprecedented in history. Extraordinary technological and scientific developments allowed man to land on the moon and to orbit the Earth, to construct buildings hundreds of meters high, to build high-velocity trains and giant airplanes, to transplant hearts and other vital organs, to lay the foundations of the "information and knowledge society," and all as a result of a succession of scientific and industrial revolutions that have marked the past hundred years.

However, the astonishing progress is not altogether free of negative effects - on the physical and natural environment and on society and the economy. The main effects of scientific progress on the environment may be described as follows:

- A change (probably irreversible) in the composition of the atmosphere and consequently of the climate
- A depletion of the ozone layer, the shield protecting the Earth from ultraviolet radiation
- Soil degradation and increased desertification
- Increased air and water pollution
- A reduction in the availability of fresh water
- Increasing depletion of physical and natural resources, from oil to copper, to timber, and so forth

The effects on society and on the economy may be defined as follows:

- A growing gap between "rich" and "poor," within both the more developed countries and those in which economic development has yet to start or is still in its infancy

---

[117] From the Public Broadcasting Service (PBS) interview with Kevin Roberts in December, 2003. You can read the full interview at *http://www.pbs.org/wgbh/pages/frontline/shows/persuaders/interviews/roberts.html*.

- Increasing political instability, ethnic conflicts, and terrorism in many regions of the world
- Increasing expansion of urban centers, mostly characterized by a deterioration in quality of life
- Persisting inadequate sanitary conditions in most "poor" countries and a parallel rise in the incidence of illnesses related to high living standards (e.g. tumors, cardiovascular disease, mental illness) in rich countries
- Workforce exploitation and the spread of child labor, especially in so-called "emerging countries"
- Persisting high levels of total or partial illiteracy, in "poor" as well as "rich" countries

Together, the effects described above determine what might be defined as *three basic gaps in the modern world*:

1. The gap between the availability of the Earth's physical and natural resources and the degree to which they are exploited (*ecological gap*)
2. The gap between individual and collective needs (*quality-of-life gap*)
3. The gap between "rich" and "poor" (*social and ethical gap*)

The first gap pertains to an issue that has attracted growing attention since the publication, in 1972, of the first Club of Rome report, *The Limits to Growth*.[118] Since then, the issue of ecology and the environment has assumed ever-increasing importance, both in public opinion and in scientific and institutional circles. The business world has also shown significant early signs of interest, albeit not enough to effect fundamental strategic change.

With regard to the second gap, over the course of the twentieth century, the entrepreneurial system focused primarily on consumer markets, which it flooded with a growing quantity of goods and services intended to serve personal needs. While this resulted in an improved quality of life, the improvement was not as great as it could have been, had a more balanced process of development been adopted. Consider the words of J. K. Galbraith, written as early as 1955, which - although referring to the United States - are certainly applicable to other Western countries as well: "The family which takes its mauve and cerise, air-conditioned, power-steered and power-braked automobile out for a tour passes through cities that are badly paved, made hideous by litter, blighted buildings, billboards, and posts for wires that should long since have been put underground. They pass on into a countryside that has been rendered largely invisible by commercial art. They picnic on exquisitely packaged food from a portable icebox by a polluted stream and go on to spend the night at a park which is a menace to public health and morals. Just before dozing off on an air mattress, beneath a nylon tent, amid the stench of decaying refuse, they

---

[118] D. H. Meadows, D. L. Meadows, J. Randers, and W. W. Behrens III, 1972. *The Limits to Growth*, University Books, New York

may reflect vaguely on the curious unevenness of their blessings."[119]

This gap holds great promise, should businesses and institutions come to appreciate the high, unmet demand for goods and services to satisfy collective needs, as a basic strategy of economic and social development.[120]

As for the third gap, we shall simply point out that poor countries as a whole, as well as the remaining pockets of poverty in more developed areas, offer great potential in terms of both supply and demand. This potential can be only realized if new, advanced institutional and entrepreneurial approaches are adopted.[121]

Although the three gaps present different characteristics and dynamics, they are clearly interrelated. For example, the widespread satisfaction of individual transportation needs, achieved through the proliferation of private cars, resulted in the saturation of road systems - on both an urban and an interurban level - and an ensuing reduction in the quality of public transport services, not to mention other negative side effects such as air and noise pollution, road accidents, environmental disfigurement, and so forth.

Having thus framed our discussion, we must now ask ourselves whether and how it may be possible to modify and rectify this age-old development process to introduce the ever more crucial changes necessary to avert its collapse - and whether it would be possible to do so while preserving at least some of the concepts, processes, and tools that have afforded a part of humanity unprecedented well-being and quality of life. In other words, we must ask ourselves the following question: Is it possible to devise a system for sustainable development, capable, in time, of bridging the "three gaps"?

## 3.10.1 The Meaning of Sustainable Development

According to the common definition introduced in 1987 by the Bruntland Commission, sustainability may be defined as "progress that meets the need of the present without compromising the ability of future generations to meet their own needs."[122]

This definition considers sustainable development a long-term process, based on the ethical principle of the equity between present and future generations. In-

---

[119] J. K. Galbraith, 1958. *The Affluent Society*, Houghton Mifflin Company, p. 253

[120] J. B. Quinn, an eminent American scholar in the field of industrial economics, stated a few decades ago, "Since many consumer markets are approaching the saturation limit, the public markets of environmental goods could become the driving force of US economic growth in the next decades." ("Next Big Industry: Environment Improvement," in *Harvard Business Review*, September–October, 1971, p. 122). These ideas are still as valid as ever, and not only in the United States.

[121] For an in-depth discussion of such approaches, see C. K. Prahalad's 2005 pioneering work, *The Fortune at the Bottom of the Pyramid*, Wharton School Publishing, Upper Saddle River

[122] *The Report of Brundtland Commission: Our Common Future*, Oxford University Press, New York, 1987.

deed, development would be pointless if it were based on the devastation of the physical, natural, and resources of the "civilization" enjoyed by a part of humanity, without the slightest concern for future generations. Furthermore, the notion of sustainable development implies an extension of the concept of "needs" to include a healthy environment, a more just society, and a more prosperous economy.

The view of sustainable development is perfectly consistent with the concept of the "three gaps," discussed above. In other words, the realization of a process of sustainable development implies, if not closing, at least gradually narrowing the three gaps.

As far as the ecological gap is concerned, "the importance of ecological sustainability follows from the fact that the economy and society depend ultimately on the integrity of the biosphere and the ecological processes occurring within it. Nature provides human societies and economies with a complex life support system, comprising among other things air, water, food and a suitable climate for survival, as well as the physical resources which are currently the foundation of economies. We interfere with these natural systems at our own risk."[123]

That is why sustainable development must focus on the ecological aspect, which is, as it turns out, a decisive factor in the bridging of the other two gaps. In other words, sustainable development has biophysical limits. Thus, the state of the physical and natural environment will determine whether a society is sustainable or not. This does not mean that environmental conservation will necessarily result in the restriction of economic and social development. On the contrary, an intelligent and progressive effort to protect the environment and maximize its potential can sustain and accelerate economic development, if translated into the promotion of new processes of production, consumption, and reutilization of goods.

If we now consider the relationship between sustainability and the quality-of-life gap, we will see that one of the shortcomings of the approach to need-satisfaction hitherto practiced by the more developed countries lies in their essentially having favored the production of goods and services for individual consumption. To return to the example of the car, the emphasis that industrialized societies have placed on the development of private, as opposed to public, transport is now backfiring, resulting in a reduced level of satisfaction of individual as well as collective transportation needs. The emergence of new paradigms, capable of meeting both target conditions - the maximum level of satisfaction of needs and the respect for the constraints dictated by sustainability - marks the start of a new chapter in the development of processes of production, distribution, and use of goods and services to meet human needs.

---

123 M. Diesendorf, "Sustainability and Sustainable Development," in D. Dunphy and J. Benveniste, Eds., *Sustainability: The Corporate Challenge of the 21st Century*, Allen & Unwin, London, 2000, p. 23.

Finally, the gradual elimination of the third gap - the social gap, embodied in the phenomenon of poverty, still affecting more than two thirds of world population - may constitute one of the most solid foundations for sustainable development, for a number of reasons. First, from an ethical standpoint, it is in fact unacceptable that only slightly more than eight hundred million of the more than six billion inhabitants of the globe enjoy above-subsistence-level incomes. The second reason is of an economic nature: the gradual incorporation of such a large segment of the world's population into the global economic system would mean engaging in a virtually inexhaustible process of production, distribution, and utilization of wealth.[124] A third reason lies in the fact that a considerable proportion of the areas needing environmental rehabilitation and conservation are situated in less developed countries. Employing the abundant workforce available in these regions, in order to narrow the ecological gap, may also turn out to be an excellent investment.

## 3.10.2 The Role of Businesses in Sustainable Development

The entrepreneurial system obviously plays a fundamental role in shaping both the positive and the negative effects of economic development. With regard to the positive effects, suffice it to mention the "thirty golden years" - as Jean Fourastié termed the years following the Second World War - during which the inhabitants of developed countries attained unprecedented levels of material well-being, dignity, and freedom.[125] This was made possible by the development of an entrepreneurial system that - spurred by growing demand and facilitated by an abundance of financial resources, technological innovation, labor, and raw materials - was able to provide the market with the goods and services required to meet the basic needs of the population.

The negative effects of economic development concern the environmental and social impact of certain business choices regarding raw materials, the location of production and administration facilities, reclamation and recycling, and behaviour toward stakeholders (e.g., clients, employees, suppliers, brokers, communities, and institutions).

---

[124] For an in-depth discussion of these essential issues, see the recently published texts below. The books present different approaches and possible courses of action, addressing the problem of world poverty, all extremely interesting: C. K. Prahalad, op. cit.; S.L. Hart, *Capitalism at the Crossroad*, Wharton School Publishing, Upper Saddle River, 2005; D. Bornstein, *How to Change the World*, Oxford University Press, New York, 2004; J. D. Sachs, *The End of Poverty*, The Penguin Press, New York, 2005; C. Prestowitz, *Three Billion New Capitalists - The Great Shift of Wealth and Power to the East*, Basic Books, New York, 2005. It may also be helpful to read or reread the classic *The Nature of Mass Poverty* by J. K. Galbraith (Harvard University Press, Cambridge, Mass. 1979).

[125] J. Fourastié, 1979, *'Les Trente Glorieuses, ou la révolution invisible de 1946 à 1975* (The Glorious Thirty, or the Invisible Revolution from 1946–1975), Fayard, Paris

But what role can business play in the framework of a process of sustainable development? What strategic choices should be made, and what tools should be employed to this end?

There is no doubt that modern businesses should bear a substantial share of the task of building a sustainable society - in light of its nature and key role in the development of values essential to human society's ability to continue meeting its own needs.

In fulfilling this task, businesses should operate in conjunction with other social institutions, from political and public institutions to those representing the different components of society. A first possible contribution on the part of businesses toward sustainable development might be the improvement of its own operations in terms of quality and efficiency.

Enlightening in this contest are the remarks of Pierangelo Andreini, professor of technical and industrial physics at the Polytechnic University of Milan, in his introduction to a recent handbook on quality: "The most reliable economic scenarios predict that in the next twenty years markets and consumption will be shaped by three essential requirements: health, safety, and sustainability. This requires sustainable management of resources as well as the adoption of more responsible patterns of production and consumption, following the principles of intergenerational equity, that is, the right of future generations to satisfy their needs to the same extent as the present generation. These requirements derive from the knowledge that current modes of economic development drive us to exceed the ecosystem's 'carrying capacity' - not only on a local scale, as in the past, but increasingly on a regional and global scale as well. The very stability of the global climate is threatened by the 'greenhouse effect,' exacerbated by human economic activity, mainly due to the consumption of energy and raw materials. The primary objective should thus be one of minimizing wastefulness and environmental pollution, adopting patterns of production and consumption based on technologies for the efficient use of energy and raw materials, favouring the existing trend of the dematerialization of economies. Ultimately, producers and service providers should aim to adopt production and operation methods that minimize pollution and waste production. This may be achieved by creating entrepreneurial systems capable of fully exploiting raw materials, through networks in which the waste materials and emissions of one industry serve as raw materials for another, and so forth, until the circle is closed."[126]

A key aspect of the role of businesses in sustainable development, often overlooked, is the fact that sustainability can be a source of profit for those businesses, and additionally those who consider it the principal challenge of the twenty-first century. Just as industrial development from the late nineteenth to the last quarter of the twentieth century met the challenge of satisfying basic needs, so too future development

---

126 P. Andreini (ed.), 2004: *Qualità, Certificazione, Competitività*, Hoepli, Milano, p. 1

will need to meet the challenge of the three gaps: ecological, quality of life, and social.

Returning once again to the example of car industry, a sector that may rightly be regarded as the symbol of the industrial era, a car manufacturer may develop the following strategies for sustainable development[127]:

- Develop production processes based on the principles of sustainability, including the design of cars ready to be dismantled for recycling[128]
- Adopt energy-efficient production processes
- Reduce the various forms of internal and external pollution at its manufacturing, administration, and service facilities
- Design nonpolluting engines and batteries
- Design vehicles that are more suitable, or less unsuitable, for urban traffic
- Design safer vehicles
- Develop forms of sustainable marketing (car sharing, car rental, new and more advanced parking methods, consultancy services on sustainability, etc.)
- Promote agreements of *comarketing for sustainability* with other agents operating in related fields (railways, highways, airlines, hotel chains, etc.)

Similar ideas can certainly be developed for many other sectors, from the more traditional to the more advanced and innovative, not to mention the new field of entrepreneurial actively likely to emerge in a society that is increasingly aware of the inexorable need to follow the path of sustainable development, i.e., the path toward eliminating the three gaps.

## 3.10.3 A Model for Sustainable Marketing

Before outlining a model for sustainable marketing, it is worth noting the conclusions of Alfred Chandler, a leading scholar of modern corporations. According to Chandler, the fact that the industrial production of consumer goods - and hence of industrial goods as well - was able to reach such outstanding levels of development is largely due to the progress made by corporations in the fields of marketing and mass distribution. In other words, mass production and mass marketing constitute two closely related and complementary aspects of the same phenomenon, that of advanced market capitalism.[129]

The contribution of marketing to the definition of business strategies in the era of sustainable development will therefore assume different characteristics, depend-

---

127 See W. G. Scott, 1991, *FIAT UNO - Innovazione e mercato nell'industria automobilistica*, Isedi, Torino

128 Following the example of the practices that have long been implemented by Xerox with success in the sector of photocopying machines

129 In particular, see A. D. Chandler, 1977, *The Visible Hand - The Managerial Revolution in American Business*, and 1990, *Scale and Scope - The Dynamics of Industrial Capitalism*, Belknap Press, Cambridge. For an interpretation of Chandler's work according to the marketing paradigm see W. G. Scott, 1997, "*Marketing & Competizione, Vita e Pensiero*, Milan, pp. 115–127.

ing on the sector in which the company is active, its size, level of technological advancement and innovation, degree of market orientation, management and organizational culture, etc. For example, a company with a long-standing client-oriented approach, or one that has adopted the principles of corporate social responsibility (CSR), is likely to have an easier time applying the principles of sustainable development.[130] In this context, marketing could provide the following:

- An evaluation of the relevance of different issues of sustainable development to the company's activities
- An analysis of the attitudes and behaviors of the company's different stakeholders vis-à-vis the issues of sustainable development (both general and more specific issues, such as the biodegradability of the materials used for packaging and wrapping)
- An evaluation of the extent to which different products manufactured by the company may be designed/produced/distributed/installed/substituted/recycled following the principles of sustainability, and how this may affect cost/prices/revenues
- An evaluation of the company's relations with research centers, institutes, organizations committed to environmental, social, and civil concerns, public institutions operating in the various fields of sustainable development, and the media
- An evaluation of programs to promote the idea of sustainable development, in which the company has participated, directly or indirectly

Having established the above basis for evaluation, a corporation could then formulate a strategic plan that would define a) its general objectives, in terms of sustainability - for example, the production of low-cost medicines for African populations, the production of submerged pumps for irrigation and water conservation programs, the production of electric engines to replace gasoline-powered ones, the development of fair forms of trade, etc.; b) financial, organizational, and management solutions; and c) a marketing plan it wishes to implement.

The sustainable marketing plan, defining the ways in which to apply the basic steps of the "marketing mix," includes choices that the company will make regarding:

- Products (assortment and design)
- Materials used in products, packaging, and wrapping (reusability and recyclability)
- Prices (incentives designed to encourage behaviours consistent with sustainable development)
- Distribution, personal selling, and direct marketing
- Logistics, assistance, and service
- Promotion, advertising, public relations, and sponsorships[131]

---

[130] For an in-depth analysis of the issue of CSR, see: P. Kotler and N. Lee, 2005, *Corporate Social Responsibility - Doing the Most Good for Your Company and Your Cause*, Wiley, Hoboken

[131] On prospects in the area of product and production processes innovation, see American architect William McDonough and German chemist Michael Baungart's creative suggestion, centered on "ecoefficacy."

- Materials used in products, packaging, and wrapping (reusability and recyclability)
- Prices (incentives designed to encourage behaviours consistent with sustainable development)
- Distribution, personal selling, and direct marketing
- Logistics, assistance, and service
- Promotion, advertising, public relations, and sponsorships

This is only a very preliminary list of strategies and programs by means of which businesses can live up to the challenge of sustainable development. Much time and effort is still needed before these new approaches take root, driven by evidence and concerted action. Then again, hasn't successful business always been about being ahead of one's time, reaping the benefits of innovation?

We should also bear in mind that marketing strategy requires a unified approach, whereby the company's different functions - finance, research and development, operations, and marketing and sales - may integrate and complement one other, sharing an unified vision of environmental concerns and the market.

As we have previously seen, there is a vast and problematic scenario, capable of challenging even the most sophisticated macrotrend analyst. It is thus essential that *companies employ the valuable experience* gained by the entrepreneurial system over the past fifty years in converting material resources into means to satisfy the needs of humanity be employed as a basis to meet the challenges of the present. To this end, the efforts of those working in the field of marketing, be it as policy makers, scholars, or marketers, will have to be channelled toward the ongoing development of an approach centered on the interests of society, with the knowledge that the principles of marketing can contribute substantially to the promotion of these interests.

---

Ecoefficacy is based on the following concepts: 1) the design of production processes involving the reintroduction of waste by-products as raw materials in successive production cycles; 2) the net separation between "biological metabolism" and "technological metabolism"; and 3) a shift away from the notion of "selling products" to that of "selling services" (W. McDonough and M. Braungart, 2023, *Cradle to Cradle*, North Point Press, New York.)

## 3.11 Disruption by Jean Marie Dru

Jean Marie Dru, the worldwide Chairman of the TBWA[132] ,, has written quite a few books, one of the most important and influential being *Disruption, Overturning Conventions and Shaking Up the Marketplace*, which focuses on creativity and management in the field of advertising. J. M. Dru's objective is to help in the creation of marketing campaigns (more specifically in advertising) that sell ideas.

In J. M. Dru's words, "the Disruption methodology is a three-step process which consists of studying successively and systematically the convention, the disruption, and the vision, then, for each given problem, finding the link that will bring together the three notions, thus revealing how the vision refers to the convention that itself inspired the disruption" (Dru 1997, p. 56).

### 3.11.1 The Disruptive Process

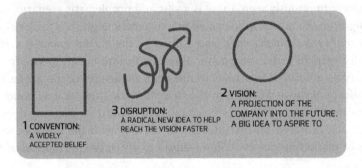

Figure 80: Disruption, the Three-Step Process

Convention - what freezes the mind, common sense, rules of the game.

At this stage you have to identify the dominant thinking conventions that exist in your industry or market. This step might seem easy, but it requires digging deep and validating the assumptions and principles that are taken for granted and that reinforce the status quo that normalizes the markets. Apple went against the convention that computers where only for specialists.

Disruption - challenge and overturn conventions with disruptive ideas.

Once the assumptions and conventions have been identified, you have to challenge them by questioning and analyzing each and every element that characterizes them. The challenge or disruption must be a violent process that creates a rupture with the past; this means that there will be a broad array of elements to be questioned, opening the door to many possibilities and opportunities. Richard Branson's

---

132  TBWA is an international advertising agency and a unit of the Omnicom Group.

# CHAPTER 3 — MARKETHINK

Virgin moves along these lines with their communication campaigns.

Vision - adjust the disruptive ideas to the direction given by the vision.

This step of the process is better explained in the words of the author:

We start with a convention, then try to find a way to disrupt it. But we have to remain true to the brand and to the way we would like people think about the brand. We therefore have to be very clear about the long term vision. Formulating that vision is the third step. The vision is a leap of the imagination from the present to the future. It's picturing where the brand will be over time. It's imagining the brand on a larger, more ambitious scale

IBM decided that it no longer wanted to be seen only as the mainframe computer manufacturer; instead, it wanted to become the provider of "solutions for a small planet." NASDAQ does not want to be seen as the second-biggest stock market in the United States, but rather as "the stock market for the next hundred years." (Dru 1997, p. 58)

The genesis of the concept is to challenge the established status quo and break away from the uniformity of thinking; the disruption method is just that, a way to "define what share of the future a brand can envision and to find disruptive ways of accelerating that brand on the road to its chosen future" (Dru 1997, p. 56).

## 3.11.2 The "Disruption World Bank"

The "Disruption world bank" was developed by J. M. Dru's team because they wanted to "provide planners with a tool that comes in handy at exactly the right point in their work process. It is a collection of five-minute video case histories showing and explaining strategic breakthroughs from around the world, where each case traces the convention and/or vision that led to a disruption and describes the disruption itself and the results of the campaign. Their database is a reflection of their "Disruption approach to strategy" where the cases studies are classified according to the type of convention, disruption, or vision they represent, facilitating the association of seemingly unrelated ideas, as well as "reinforcing the Disruption mind-set" (Dru 1997, p. 142).

We are giving importance to this method and to the "disruption world bank" especially because it is a good example of an "Ideabase" that was a head of its time, and that was already concerned with the generation of innovative ideas and stimulating new associations. The Ideabase that we developed to map marketing and sales innovations from around the world has a broader mission that goes beyond advertising and cross-references hundreds of more complex variables (versus disruption's three) - market segment, industry, creative concept, and marketing level. What we want to point out, in this context, is the conceptual alignment that exists between this very interesting model and ours.

# 3.12 A little about Digital Marketing

By Fabrizio Bellavista and Massimo Soriani Bellavista

*"Social media are revolutionizing the theory and the practice of marketing."* - Philip Kotler

*"Markets are conversations.*

### The Cluetrain Manifesto[133]

Until now, in many chapters of this book, the concepts of "relation" and "sharing" have gained increasingly important but variable roles at the same time. The process is ongoing and can be summarized as follows: starting from the historical idea of marketing that moves products in order to meet the market's demand moving to the idea that concerns the marketing project for consumers and then, up to now, toward the idea in which the consumer is a cocreative and participating resource. From the "*me*" era, we moved to the "*we*" one.

This last concept is the starting point of digital marketing: in recent years, with the frenetic growth of two-way communication, every new idea shares a formidable number of variables. Here is the magic driver of this epochal change: sharing. In short, the network is made up primarily of people and relationships, and it works involving them with a nonlinear dialectic. The great change of new marketing concern "the conversation", with a personal approach and a different ability of listening. To prove the importance of the ongoing change, the American Marketing Association is gradually revising the definition of "marketing."

### The Digital World Time Line

The digital world can be roughly divided into four stages:

1. The World Wide Web and networking websites, forums, e-commerce, online magazines, and blogs
2. Social environments - the great expansion of the global conversation through social networking platforms
3. Mobile, apps, and proximity marketing - the moving connection offers a high range of new paradigms, languages, and opportunities
4. Internet of Things - IoT - the technology that connects man to things is one of the innovations we will see in the coming years

---

[133] *The Cluetrain Manifesto*, written in 1999 by R. Levine, C. Locke, D. Searls, and D. Weinberger, is a set of ninety-five theses organized and put forward as a manifesto, or call to action, for all businesses operating within what is suggested to be a newly connected marketplace.

## 3.12.1 Web Marketing and Digital Marketing

The term "web marketing" defines the contribution of market knowledge concerning the first part of our limited time line. It is the branch of the marketing activities of a company that takes advantage of the online channel in order to study the market and to develop business relations (promotions/advertising, distribution, sales, customer support, etc.) across the web. The midpoint of a web marketing strategy is the implementation of a website and its promotion. With them, the relationship with the customer and the implementation of e-commerce strategies take place. Other activities that characterize web marketing are search engine optimization (SEO), which concerns the aspects of content, metadata, and code writing.

### 3.12.1.1 Digital Marketing

Web marketing becoming mature has accelerated new technologies, it is refined and became, first of all, the connector of the new market strategies, creating new opportunities for relationship, brand awareness, and new innovative ways often successfully combined with the offline world. In the past the web marketing role was quite near to the traditional marketing sector, but then, with the birth of the social environments, with connection portability, and finally with "IoT" opportunities, its role completely changed, and we started talking about digital marketing, a term used for the first time around 2006. That's way we are now beginning to operate in different digital environments and the marketing strategies must take into account at the same time dozens of new parameters, actors, and types of media.

These are the digital marketing activities: conversation analysis, online reputation analysis, definition of influencers concerning objectives and planning of digital PR activities, shares of search engine optimization (SEO), and search engine marketing (SEM). We have already met SEO and SEM within web marketing, and in our case, they enrich themselves through social media optimization (SMO It is important to remember, in order to develop contents, considering the knowledge of the three fundamentals mentioned above. They are essential.

There are platforms that have acquired a precise positioning within the ecosystem of a good digital marketing strategy: microblogging (twitter), for example, or the construction of a community, and of course, the implementation of brands in public social networks and social commerce. It is interesting to analyze the expansion projections of social commerce; it is estimated that in 2015 half of social-commerce will go through the Facebook platform.

### 3.12.1.2 Traceability and ROI

A great opportunity has been realized with the emergence of digital media: knowing the user through the use of this type of media. It is easy to understand how the information gleaned from statistics concerning the visits of a website (pages visited, time spent, internal path, etc.) can be extremely important to target the user. Beyond these techniques, we have to consider the ability to track other paths: for example, the click of a banner or the landing on a landing page. But, with the advent of social environments, we also have other parameters that add up to make even more precise user profiles: direct feedback (in addition, of course, to the contact e-mail, the "like," the "pins," and the shares that some content gets) and the more detailed analysis of the conversation.

A direct consequence is the ability to define exactly the cost of each contact toward traditional media, but, at the moment, the measure to quantify the ROI in social networks hasn't been identified. However, we identified methods that help us to better understand the value of a relation, for example, on a Facebook wall: the number of the "likes," and the number of "comments" and "share", shows how a page, a group, or a given post confers quality to a certain choice. It is important to underline how important is, in a successful marketing mix, to support the traditional methods of quantitative and qualitative analysis, a huge amount of data.

### 3.12.1.3 The Digital Marketer?

The digital marketer is a digital environments harmonizer, which includes new processes and unprecedented market mechanisms.

Let's explore the concept of digital marketing. On the web we can find numbers of interventions, but without a real definition - following the hypothetical actions of a digital marketer. You can start searching for new drivers that stimulate the emotional consumer, now turned into a "prosumer". Before this, however, we need to analyse network connections using the new technologies applied to logistics and also the time of evangelization - inside and outside the company - which becomes primary. Digital marketing will be able to design the architecture of a sales force that can go along with the company, using new technologies that can shorten the distance between it and the company: sales force connected through updated tools able to bring the necessary information in real time, creating a multi-channel marketing strategy that includes both traditional sales channels that those social digital.

Now we can delineate the roles and responsibilities of this young figure halfway between the trendsetters, the fluidizing, and the expert of the field in which he works - "integrating," "harmonizing," and "relating" seem to be the key words of the moment.

The CRM and its already tested tools, with the arrival of social thinking and its digital platforms, is the focus of a strategy in which relationships are fundamental and markets turn into conversations. A database molded according to the new social demands becomes the "soft machine" to promote sustainable development to the people, in which the degrees of separation between user and company, together with the emotional parameters, embody the true metric of the future. I conclude with the emergence of the central role played by the content, now considered only media (text, video, pictures); the content curator, dubbed the "hero of our time" by Steve Rosenbaum, has the task of guiding the Alchemy of multimedia content from various sources (editorial, RSS, aggregators, owners, sensors, etc.), in order to propose a new editorial product (if this term can still mean something) will be enjoyed in a new way and through new devices.

## 3.12.2 That Future! The best minds of the past twenty years

Some considerations and suggestions to better understand what is going on.

### 3.12.2.1 The Profiles

Before addressing a brief rundown of the insights that have built up a new way of thinking and being over the past twenty years a new way, it is good to ask yourself if there are, in digital marketing, great people able to leave a mark, as some individuals did in traditional marketing.

Any great charismatic figure was born in traditional marketing and something deeply new has happened as far as this particular aspect is concerned. People like Steve Jobs - who certainly did not come from the marketing sector but was able to match his technological abilities with his creative and commercial ones - have become inventors of technologies that figuratively contain their own DNA in a total and coherent marketing vision.

We can say that in addition to pioneering figures like Nicholas Negroponte, Kevin Kelly, and Chris Anderson, who have perceived and understood before others the upcoming innovations, many "technocreative" profiles tried to emerge in this sector. Similar to Leonardo da Vinci, they designed new technologies thanks to their extraordinary ability to move in a continuum from the . humanistic creativity to the technological reality At the same time, we can say, sometimes with a national breath, that many experts on the marketing sector have contributed to a better understanding of the potential and new opportunities coming from new ideas and devices.

## 3.12.2.2 A Twenty-Year Overview

Now I will list a series of characters and dates for various reasons, have marked the history and were the origin of the development of the digital world was unstoppable over the last twenty years.In the eighties, Steve Jobs and Bill Gates were the patriarchs of the digital world - two talented entrepreneurs who literally introduced the future with their new technologies. Without their insights, linked to their extraordinary creative ability, there would have been nothing that we know and we see today.

Along with Steve Jobs's Apple, we can speak of "brand religion": the dealers, so bare and minimal, making the purchase a unique experience. Create a line of products under the brand "Apple" to sell it in the apple store, it's definitely been a clever choice that surely helped build what is called a cult, with the exponential increase of notoriety is the result of the design of the latest devices so popular. Everyone knows that, in the 1980s, the few customers of Cupertino had to be very patient. Apple-branded products were wonderful and sexy with innovative design, but completely incompatible with systems more widespread; and repairs them were expensive in the case of malfunction. Today Apple is one of the few companies in the world to have fans rather than customers.The following sentence summarizes his philosophy: "Apple does not deliver to customers what they want, but what they will want."

It is easier now to better explain Bill Gates's approach: give your customers everything they want, quickly and cheaply, so as to make life easier, more normal, and more interconnected. A particular: while Cupertino has always tried innovative ways, primarily in the sector of communication, the Redmond company[134] has always followed the path of normality. Even in the recent advertising campaign that Microsoft launched, the central theme remains the family as a group of people but also as a family of products - a traditional scenario, in which the key words are "simplicity" and "normality."

In 1994, the Netscape browser was founded by Jim Clark and Marc Andreessen - the latter one of the developers of the Mosaic web browser. Netscape proposed a graphical interface and usability that were absolutely innovative for that period. The web started, and in the early years, until the "redemption" by Gates of network development, Netscape was the undisputed king, thanks to the intuition of free spread. In June, 1998, Microsoft published the new version of Internet Explorer deeply integrated into the operating system; the browser born in Redmond started, and, at the same time, the rapid decline of Netscape began.

Let's talk about more details about Marc Andreessen: he was among the developers of the Mosaic web browser, he also is the cofounder of the social platform

---

134 Redmond, Washington, best known as the home of Microsoft, for which it has become a metonym

# CHAPTER 3 — MARKETHINK

Ning[135] (2005) and has been CEO of Opsware[136], and was one of the investors of Digg[137] and of Plazes[138] and Twitter during their start-ups. We can affirm that new entrepreneurs are starting to grow in this scenario, thanks to Steve Jobs, Bill Gates, and Marc Andreessen, under a unique personality, from the technological, pioneering, and evangelizing perspective, toward the highly creative and at the same time sales-oriented one.

Levine, Locke, Searls, and Weinberger published the *Cluetrain Manifesto* in 1999, and through the "*95 Theses*" - similar to those of Martin Luther - they defined the era of interactivity as a turning point, especially (but not only) in the field of marketing; this change is well summarized in a quote that has become, in the course of time, one of the foundations of the new thought: "*markets are conversations.*" In the same year (1999), he contributed to the volume *New Rules for the New Economy: 10 Radical Strategies for a Connected World* by Kevin Kelley, cofounder of *Wired* magazine and visionary author of the book *Out of Control*.

Larry Page and Sergey Brin, founders of Google, did not stop after the creation of the most effective search engine in the world; they worked hard in order to realize entire worlds, all powerfully interconnected, creating finally "The Big G World": the search engine, online dealership, e-mail, chat, desktop products and organizing and editing technology, the Chromebook netbook, Google Chrome browser, the social network Google+, the Android System, Youtube, Nexus, Blogger, Motorola Mobility, Google Fiber, and much more.

One of their latest creations, which adapts well to smoother business that few others are able to identify completely, was to offer credit that can be used in the advertising schedule, starting in 2012. All this, after presenting a few months ago, the Google Glass project, which incorporates the technology of augmented reality. This latest project of this American group together with the auto-pilot project, which links Google Map, Street and places around the world with the mobile Android, is what currently shows the most potential for development.In our fast overview, we leave a place of honor also for Jeff Bezos, Amazon's father, who founded in 1995 (or rather in 1994, under the name of Cadabra), the first online library, which then expanded its range to selling DVDs, CD music, software, video games, electronics, clothes, furniture, food, toys, and much more. Amazon has adopted a strategy similar to the Google one, having announced the provision of microloans to independent sellers who use this portal as the main place for buying and selling. J. Bezos

---

135 Ning is an online platform for people and organizations to create custom social networks; it offers the ability to create a community website with a customized appearance and feel. For more details go to http://www.ning.com/

136 Opsware Inc. is the world's leading IT automation and utility computing software company.

137 Digg is a social news website that allows people to vote web content up or down, called digging and burying, respectively. See http://digg.com/

138 Plazes allows users to post their location and current activities and share this information with other Plazes users via computers or mobile telephones

was one of the first to understand and anticipate the real importance of the concept "the long tail."

The long tail[139] was a great insight from Chris Anderson, described for the first time in October, 2004, on *Wired*. The example from Jeff Bezos's company allows us to understand in brief this concept, by applying it to publishing: a library, even if large, can hold about fifteen thousand titles, which are constantly updated according to the demands. This is great for that percentage of books (very low) entering the charts, but what about the other hundreds of thousands of *niche* books that have few buyers? If in the past this part of the market used to disappear, now it plays a leading role: selling a few copies for a long time to *niche* readers can become more fruitful than selling many copies of hits in a short amount of time. This strategy is very profitable, because, thanks to digital media, there is more money circulating in the tail than in the head, and that gives niche products more of a chance to make profit. From a mass market, we move toward a mass of markets.

Jimmy Wales and Larry Sanger launched the open company Wikipedia on January 15, 2001, which is certainly a milestone in the history of the digital world. The challenge was to create free access to knowledge through the shared work of thousands of web surfers all over the world. So today, in 2014, Wikipedia is the largest and most popular reference work on the Internet: it has 285 language versions and about one hundred thousand active contributors with twenty-three million articles and 365 million readers around the world. It was one of the great historical revolution in recent years: there was nothing before that, in some way, could be compared to it.

### 3.12.3 Changing paradigms: Social Marketing

It is said that those who used to build carriages didn't build cars, and the same is happening today: those who made traditional marketing and communication didn't contribute to the development of the web, social networks, and mobile apps, and, on the contrary, tried almost always to stop the coming of the new. Today we are at a cognitive crossroads, with key words like relationship, listening, sharing, two-way communication, and social vision. New paradigms and assets arise in the daily practice of marketing, and sometimes they let us think that this term will be able to keep up with the ongoing change and will continue to be explicative and meaningful.

---

139 "Long tail" is a term coined by Chris Anderson, in a 2004 article in *Wired* magazine where he argued that "the availability of products online has changed the economy by allowing companies to make a profit selling small quantities of many products rather than large quantities of the same product." He later elaborated the concept in his book *The Long Tail: Why the Future of Business Is Selling Less of More*. For more info visit http://www.thelongtail.com/about.html

# CHAPTER 3 — MARKETHINK

Marketing takes a "circular" structure at whose center is the end user who creates around himself a number of social networks that intersect perfectly with the others. Finally come true the great insight dated 1999: "markets are conversations" and make up the area of intangibles assets.

## 3.12.3.1 The Social Network and the Network, or the Social Network is the Network?

There are more than one billion subscribers on Facebook in the world, QZone has 500 million subscribers in Asia (including recently also South Korea), VKontacte has a population of 190 million in the former USSR, Twitter has 200 million, LinkedIN has 150 million, and Google+ has 200 million (uncertain data). The trend that links these platforms, to the detriment of other little ones, it is evident and it is equally obvious that the Internet network - which has about 2.2 billion surfers - is now increasingly known as "social."

## 3.12.3.2 Social Network: a bit of history

LinkedIn was born on May 5, 2003, thanks to Reid Hoffman, Allen Blue, Konstantin Guericke, Eric Ly, and Jean-Luc Vaillant, and it is the largest professional social network in the world. LinkedIn was created in the same year as MySpace, a social platform created by Tom Anderson and Chris DeWolfe, which focused on the world of music. This website boasting one hundred million members, has been a milestone for the development of online music. It's interesting to note that the collapse of MySpace began (in 2008) due to something that made it, from a graphic and visual perspective, absolutely competitive and innovative: the ability to customize the look of your own page using HTML code. This characteristic on one hand gave us the opportunity to use new graphic expressions, even UCG visual design, which we'd never seen before; but on the other hand the website's decline was caused by the complexity of managing it and by the weight, which was too much at that time. In the October 2003, Mark Zuckerberg - a second-year student of Harvard University - launched Facemash, the predecessor of Facebook. This first experiment was closed for irregularities, but on February 4, 2004, supported by his university colleagues Eduardo Saverin, Dustin Moskovitz, and Chris Hughes, Facebook took off. Originally the project was restricted to Harvard University's students, but soon it was expanded to other universities in the Boston area and then, in 2006, to any individual over thirteen years old.

We can say that it is from this date that started the project of "social network" that has changed (and are still changing) our lives both personal and professional, But remember that, originally, the term "social network" referred to a physical network. Examples of social networks are the sports community, the community of workers who meet in their clubs, communities based on the common practice of a religion, and so on. This particularity is very important in order to correctly understand the digital development of social networks - the continuous transition between online and off-line will be one of the most important factors for an effective digital marketing strategy. Joichi "Joi" Ito, director of MIT's Media Lab, entrepreneur of many companies, venture capitalist, and web evangelist, focuses his attention on terms such as "emerging democracy" and "creative network."

As one last historical mention, in 1979 the first sharing program, Usenet (contraction of "user network" by Tom Truscott and Jim Ellis of Duke University), was released; the LiquidFeedback platform, which is spreading rapidly in politics and that came to prominence thanks to Pirates dl Berlin, was launched in Sweden five years earlier. Both of these solutions are characterized by an elementary simplicity, but at the same time they are clear and strong messages for which they were designed: to share. LiquidFeedback (and programs likeit) is having and will continue to have a strong impact on shared democracies, as they represent one of the fundamental aspects of the digital age. People propose ideas and programs, and at the same time, they can vote for them online and in real time. Simple!

### 3.12.3.4 There is a new Nation of over one billion people...

A new nation with more than one billion people has been born. It has no territoriality, but every inhabitant, taken individually, has it.

We have learned the language and customs of this nation, we have opened stores, and we elected ambassadors able to represent us successfully.

This new nation with 1.1 billion inhabitants (third in the world but not for long) has a name: Facebook. (Let's keep in mind that this is just the tip of the iceberg of many other social networks with hundreds of millions of people). This new country is different concerning political orientations, values, goals, and opinions for which, in a stream in real time, all day and all night, there is no distinction between a courtship, a picture of a party, and a recent event.

### 3.12.3.5 The portability of the connection allows it to become more then an extension of our body

In mobile marketing, the connection in movement opens another set of new paradigms, languages, opportunities, and connections within the territory. Digital marketing is oriented toward new experiences in which the geolocation is the most obvious; at the same time it paves the way for the advent of thousands of apps that, in some way, form an additional digital environment. Simultaneously, the apps, the web, and social environments are spreading, and they become a better opportunity to customize their own path in the network.

Once again, we are not talking about a new technical, specialized vision of marketing, but rather about a further reversal of paradigms so far acquired that leads to a reformulation of the marketing in its totality. The portability and the centrality (the smartphone is at the same time a telephone, computer, calculator, clock, a means to connect with the web and with one's surroundings, and a hundred other things) of mobile devices have introduced innovations that force us to rethink business models and marketing decisions. The geolocation and portability of mobile devices are archiving some insights that were the basis of new marketing: the customizing the relationship between consumer and brand. The concept of time and place through new values which lead us to say that "here, now" became a reality of marketing. Where geolocation has already become a digital reality, for example digital planning in Google AdWords and social advertising in Facebook, thanks to the user's geographic profile, here the possibility become also physical, and thanks to the device's portability, in this case, the relationship between consumer and brand is using major experiences that meet precise timed with General Geolocation.. We are ready for a big step, a kind of nervous system that connects the world, people, and objects.

## 3.12.3.6 And Today? Internet of Things and Near Field Communication

Now we will present the project "Digital Central Nervous System" signed "HP Cense," which implements a global connection that links the human and the so-called Internet of Things. Thanks to a series of sensors (RFID, NFC, and QRCode - Near Field Communication) we are associated with objects, flows, human thoughts, and human feelings, and in this new dimension, we will be easily connected with a variety of tools that will be driven by sensors but even more by our fickle emotions.

The possible geolocation is an absolute value. The spread of smartphones default on the latest generation of Near Field Communication that will opens the door to identity authentication, to augmented reality, to connection with the point-of-sale devices, and to the real revolution of mobile money.

## 3.12.4 What kind of Marketing will we use?

In conclusion, we should ask ourselves this question: in the next years the emerging nations of the African continent and BRICS (Brazil, Russia, India and China) - starting from nothing are going through the "comprehensive Omnia smartphone" - what will they want to come across in their social experience?

What kind of marketers will we be?

We have asked this to Marco Camisani Calzolari one of the most important Italian "digital Gurus":

Figure 81: Marco Camisani Calzolari

*Massimo Soriani Bellavista: What do you think will be the digital marketing scenario in the next 5 years?*

*Marco Camisani Calzolari:* Well, I think that the key word will be 'niche' – niche markets. Because all the vertical niche markets will be served: from the traditional ones – which are the existing niches, to the new niches that don't exist yet, such as the sharing/share economy - those that will put resources on the market that until recently couldn't be; because too small, with fast and/or specific exchange requirements thus making it hard to match offer and demand. Today, however you can do the matching of your couch to a person to sleep on in one hour; that is I decide that in one hour my couch will be available to anyone that needs it for the night and, that someone will give me money for it, or offer my free car seat to go across London.

Still there is a big cultural problem, there are many people that don't think (know) that they can offer their couch and be paid for it, and of course have no idea that it can be done in an only an hour. However, in the next 5 years, I believe there will be

# CHAPTER 3

# MARKETHINK

*a huge 'digital' diffusion due to the fact that most people have smart phones in their pockets that are able to handle these types of services and technologies.*

*Looking at the latest research carried out by Akamai, what clearly stands out is that 80% of mobile internet surfing is done through Safari, and therefore the i-Phone who we know holds a very small share of the smart phone market, meaning that there is an enormous amount of smart phones in people's hands that are not being used at all to navigate on internet and other. Little by little, with new offers and novelties, and from the cultural changes – today there is a tool rather than a 'culture of use' in people's pockets – where, as soon as this cultural wall start breaking down we will assist to an important growth in the digital world. At this point the successful ones will be those that will trade unused resources through macro-agreements from B2C to C2C and why not C2B.*

**M.S.B.:** *So you don't see an e-Bay or a Google cannibalize all markets but rather niche market opportunities. Is that correct?*

**M.C.C.:** *Well, these niches are surely going to be opened by the 'small', that will become leaders of their verticality to then, as we have already seen macro-economically, be sold to or bought by the 'big'. Think of Google that bought Uber. First comes Uber - with its niche market of connecting passengers to unused black cars and its driver for hire, and then comes Google. In depends on what you mean. If Google will be the one to invent the world of niche markets – No! On the other hand, if you mean that Google could decide, tomorrow, to buy everything – well, that could be.*

**M.S.B.:** *Aside from the previous, do you see other digital marketing opportunities?*

**M.C.C.:** *I stand behind what I have said up to now. There will obviously be, thanks to the increase of resources, the spread of technology and the greater access from a cultural point of view, a significant growth of what we have seen this far in the digital world. That is, I do not see a new marketing Facebook or strong changes, what I see is an evolution of what is already happening. I think that the least evolved aspect of digital marketing that has the most opportunities and the biggest growth margin is digital marketing in the share economy and geolocation.*

**M.S.B.:** *Again from a digital marketing point of view, what are the biggest criticalities?*

**M.C.C.:** *I definitely think Facebook is one of them. Because they continue to increase their monetization and can only use what they have to continue satisfying the market and pay dividends, but mainly because what is done on Facebook – which is almost everything – can now be and is starting to be done with vertical niche applications that serve that one specific purpose. Facebook is and will remain a great generalist aggregator of contents, but it will remain an aggregator of things that are happening 'outside'. I don't think there will be a new Facebook, even though Google with its plethora of tools can and is putting them together making their offer comparable to Facebook's.*

# MARKETHINK

### CHAPTER 3

*There is also an issue with the technologies, or the lack of, that should contribute to the development of those unexplored niche markets. Most of the technologies exist, but there are shortcomings - some improvements and refinements need to happen. Take for example indoor positioning and all the geolocation technologies that allows you to know where and exactly in front of which product the customer is at that precise moment to send promotions, share information, manage insights, etc., in different way; and not merely letting the customer know where you are in the shopping center. This new approach to indoor positioning could lead to interesting changes.*

*This is also true for the unification of the buying process that will become more structured thanks to the digital world. The level of profiling that exists today is invaluable and yet taken for granted. With my sensors and companies we are the proof: with 'live petition' I have a total of 3 million profiled users, I even know what's the color of their underwear - so you understand that I really know everything about them, and still there is no market for this type of insight. By this I mean that marketers continue to buy in bulk - they just want the numbers. They have the possibility to do many things, but rarely do or do it only because it's the trend. They are all interested in the numbers and pay little to no attention to profiling insights – they are still rudimentary and a bit behind.*

*M.S.B.: This is very interesting. It seems, by what you are saying, that there is a type of 'asymmetric interpretation of the opportunities' – you have the opportunities but you are not able to grasp them. Seth Godin said something similar and very interesting on the fact that there are many opportunities out there that marketing manager and decision makers don't manage to see and seize.*

*M.C.C.: This is certainly right. But it is also true, in this case, that the level of complexity involved in managing all these technologies is exponential and that the amount of extra resources needed is significant. Other reasons are that there are not only capable managers, that the organizational structure is inadequate and/or are not looking for change.*

*Currently in the digital world we are adapting everything to the structure available. We adapt to what there is because it is very rare to see organizational structures dedicated to and thought of at an operational level to manage what is new. Because of this complexity it is often the 'small' very specialized that are more successful.*

*The media centers and marketing departments are trying to get up to date, becoming or attempting to become digital, and adapting their practices to manage the digital age; although companies still use digital marketing as a gadget and in a unstructured manner. This is because they have no other choice; for them to behave differently would require to completely re-think their type of management, structure, practices and approaches, etc., which is realistically not feasible. And there are situations where it is better to go through the digital learning curve and follow its natural evolution.*

# CHAPTER 3 — MARKETHINK

*M.S.B.: You said that you have 3 million profiled users, a dream for segmentation and positioning, but have no demands in line with this. According to you, is it the same in the 'big data' world?*

M.C.C: No, I think that all of this will slowly shape up and there is no doubt that it's the future. Having access to all that information, to know what it is I do from the moment I wake up, will enable marketers to propose the best product for Me. Today though, this is still very rudimental – I am the one that looks for the plumber when I need it, go on the web and sort thing out. Imagine a future (that in reality already exists) where the sensor you have at home lets you and internet know that the temperature of your house dropped due to a problem with your heating system, you then get a text with a list of providers with solutions and propositions that would best solve your problem. This is something that already exists, and the matching is fairly simple, but still has an effect on people, and this is because there is still not a strong overall cultural preparation and penetration.

I do find it strange that they still haven't organized themselves – demand, offer, supply and all the other parst of the machine since we are definitely moving in that direction. I do think that little by little all the traditional bulk will disappear, and that the winners will be those that have access to data and know how to use it, those that will manage to coordinate and structure every level – technological, management, operational, information, and even the consumer. Once the various new niche players reach this point I do believe the whole marketing and digital scenario will face important evolutions.

*M.S.B.: Based on your experience and your clients behavior is there anything you would like to add.*

M.C.C.: Unfortunately the companies I work with follow the trends. They are always a little bit behind with their demands and what they should be doing simply because they want to see what is 'in vogue' and then follow or because they were told to and/or cannot do otherwise. Their approach is just a way to justify their actions and take no risks.

Those that recognize the trends and use new technologies, adapt them to their business in a serious and structured manner, and believe that the digital approach is the future will succeed in this digital era.

# Chapter 4
# Creativity and Innovation Thinking Models

## 4.1 Innovation in Management

We believe it is important to cover the matter of innovation at the management level because to be able to proceed with innovation within a particular department - the whole company, its structure, and its processes should be able to handle the changes and shift toward innovation and above all be capable of supporting the efforts and plans undertaken.

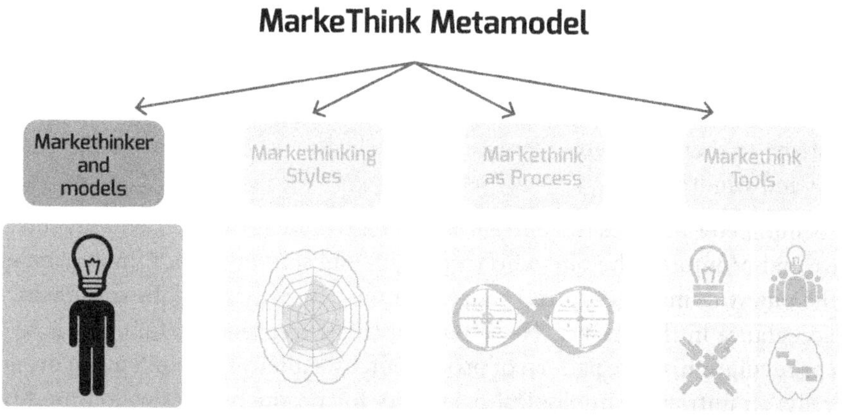

**MarkeThink Metamodel**

Figure 82: Marketing Models and Author

## 4.1.1 Joseph Schumpeter - Entrepreneurs and "Creative Destruction"

> *"The difficulty lies not in the new ideas, but in escaping from the old ones, which ramify, for those brought up as most of us have been, into every corner of our minds." - J. M. Keynes*
> *"Every act of creation is first an act of destruction." - P. Picasso*

J. Schumpeter is one of the first economists to evidence the key role innovation plays in changing the economic scenario and to state that the central innovator is the entrepreneur. He became famous by writing about the figure of the entrepreneur within an organization and, to a larger extent, society. He determined two major, intertwined, and codependent factors to succeed and grow in the free market: the key concept of "creative destruction," to define the "process of industrial mutation that incessantly revolutionizes the economic structure from within, incessantly destroying the old one, incessantly creating a new one."[140] It is the "necessary collateral damage that occurs when entrepreneurs breach established markets, and the entrepreneurial figure - who drives progress and creates wealth."[141] Basically it's when something existing is killed, rendered obsolete, by something new. J. Schumpeter wrote:

> *This process of creative destruction is the essential fact about capitalism. It is what capitalism consists in and what every capitalist enterprise has got to live in. Through destruction capitalism creates a new. The capitalist process not only destroys its own institutional framework but it also creates the conditions for another.*[142]

This logic of destruction being associated with creativity may seem like an oxymoron: how can you build and destroy at the same time? Well, it's simple; it's the basis of economic development. In the game of an organizations' economic success, the role of the entrepreneur is key, as he is to be the engine of this "creative destruction." By innovating, the entrepreneur changes the rules of the game; by innovating he destroys to then recreate - recreate, creatively, the way things are done within a market and win it over.

J. Schumpeter believes the entrepreneur/innovator is the one who invents, develops, and promotes; the one who recognizes and starts technical improvements; and the one who manages to introduce it in the company and gain consensus, but also acceptance in the market. He states that the entrepreneur's function is to "reform or revolutionize the pattern of production by exploiting an invention or, more generally, an untried technological possibility for producing a new commodity or

---

[140] He coined this term in his 1942 book: *Capitalism, Socialism and Democracy*. Harper & Brothers, New York
[141] From an article on P. Drucker on *Inc. Magazine*'s website, "The Wisdom of Peter Drucker from A to Z," retrieved from *http://www.inc.com/articles/2009/11/Drucker_pagen_3.html*
[142] J. Schumpeter, 1954. *History of Economic Analyses*, p. 81. Oxford University Press, New York

producing an old one in a new way, opening a new source of supply of materials or a new outlet for products, by reorganizing a new industry."[143] He considers entrepreneurs/innovators as the dynamic actors of capitalism who dominate the market at a profit for a short period of time - a day, as he puts it, to then see these profits nibbled by competitors who imitate them. Clearly, these innovations have the advantage of having no competitors unfortunately only until they look at the market.

## Killer Apps

"Killer Application" is the term, or metaphor, introduced by L. Dawnes and M. Chunka in their wonderful book, *Unleashing the Killer App: Digital Strategies for Market Dominance*[144], to tackle the issue of digital entrepreneurship and set the guidelines to become a company where "killer apps" are born. "When technologies, products, and services converge in radical, creative new ways, a killer app can emerge - a new application so powerful that it transforms industries, redefines markets, and annihilates the competition. Companies large and small are swiftly attempting to remake themselves into organizations that nurture killer apps and successfully translate their digital strategy into market dominance."[145]

A killer app, according to the authors, is a "product or service that winds up displacing unrelated older offerings, destroying and recreating industries far from their immediate use, and throwing into disarray the complex relationships between business partners, competitors, customers, and regulators of markets." But for our purposes, the most significant data that has emerged is that if a company does not undertake an internal action of "killer app", it will be forced to do it by the competition.

A wonderful example of this is the *Encyclopedia Britannica* and *Microsoft Encarta* case: Microsoft contacted the *Encyclopedia Britannica* to present them with the idea of a digital version of their famous encyclopedia. At the time, *Britannica*'s top management refused the proposal due to their understandable fear of cannibalizing their main, paper-based business. Failing to see the potential of such a venture, they managed to protect their business, but not for long. A new player came in taking up a large part of *Britannica*'s market share. In fact, since Microsoft really believed in the idea and the potential of associating an encyclopedia with digital media, they went forward with it, and they created *Encarta*, Microsoft digital multimedia encyclopedia. *Encarta* gained a large part of the market share because they saw an opportunity and managed, through an innovative concept, to satisfy in advance the market's needs and wants.

---

143 J. Schumpeter, 1952. *Can Capitalism Survive?* p. 63. Harper and Row, New York

144 L. Downes and M. Chunka, 1998. *Unleashing the Killer App: Digital Strategies for Market Dominance*, Harvard Business School Press.

145 From the book description given on Amazon UK, published in March, 2000, http://www.amazon.com/Unleashing-Killer-App-Strategies-Dominance/dp/1578512611

A similar thing happened in the music industry with the arrival of Napster.[146] With Napster allowing free downloading and music sharing, the whole industry made countermoves and took measures to stop, or at least stall, the introduction of music digitalization and free (and illegal) downloading of music files. The industry could only see the imminent dangers for their business, failing to see the potential and almost obvious opportunity this would and could bring. What happened then is that an outsider to the music world saw the huge opportunity and its business potential and took advantage of it, creating a billion-dollar market. This was S. Jobs with iTunes and the iTunes Store.

Therefore, the only way out, the strategy to follow to survive in the marketplace, is strongly linked to continuous innovation that creates and destroys all at the same time.

### 4.1.2 Peter Drucker - Management Theory and Practice

*"The business enterprise has two - and only two - basic functions: marketing and innovation. Marketing and innovation produce results; all the rest are costs." - P. Drucker*

"According to a recent book on management gurus, Peter Drucker is one of the few thinkers in any discipline who can claim to have changed the world: he is the inventor of privatization, the apostle of a new class of knowledge workers, the champion of management as a serious discipline. P. Drucker has been called everything from 'the father of management' to 'the man who changed the face of industrial America' to 'the one great thinker management theory has produced.'"[147]

As the father of modern management, he conceptualized and classified it has a discipline - which can be taught - to which he made invaluable contributions and even introduced essential management models:

- Self-governing communities of workers
- Importance of the person
- Self-managed work teams
- Concept of corporation
- Management theory combined with practice
- Management by objectives[148]

---

146 Napster is a name given to two music-focused online services. It was originally founded as a pioneering peer-to-peer file-sharing Internet service that emphasized sharing audio files, typically music, encoded in MP3 format.

147 J. Beatty, 1998, *The World According to Peter Drucker*. Simon & Schuster, New York.

148 P. Drucker's definition: "a principle of management that will give full scope to individual strength and responsibility, and at the same time give common direction of vision and effort, establish teamwork, and harmonize goals of the individual with the common weal." In *The Practice of Management*, Butterworth-Heinemann, 2007.

# CHAPTER 4 — MARKETHINK

- Knowledge workers[149]
- Strategic planning and corporate strategy
- Application of systems thinking to organization performance
- Systematic study of entrepreneurship
- Management's role in society
- Efficiency versus effectiveness [150]
- Strategic thinking versus operational planning
- Outsourcing
- Decentralization and simplification
- Privatization

In fact, out of his models, we are particularly interested in emphasizing the key concept of "knowledge management." P. Drucker differentiated knowledge management into two categories. The first is oriented to the use of technology to increase production and work potential, such as web-based knowledge management systems or CRM software, for example. The second one focuses on the humane side of things; unlike economists, he was "interested in the behavior of people" He went on to "explore how human beings organize themselves and interact," as well as the individual ability managers and executives to reflect on their own thinking, and on their managerial skills and abilities. He considers the organization's individuals as active and responsible, especially when they are well maintained and respected. "Central to this philosophy is the view that people are an organization's most valuable resource, and that a manager's job is both to prepare people to perform and give them freedom to do so."[151] A person's ability to learn, to grow, and to perform at his or her best; knowing oneself, how to self-motivate, and one's communication skills and strategies this is the model of knowledge management that P. Drucker deems most important. It's the one on which capitalize the future. "His books are filled with lessons on how organizations can bring out the best in people, and how workers can find a sense of community and dignity in a modern society organized around large institutions."[152]

Furthermore, "in his book *Innovation and Entrepreneurship*, P. Drucker took the ideas set forth by J. Schumpeter one step further. He argued that Schumpeter's type of innovation can be systematically undertaken by managers to revitalize business

---

p. 135

149 The idea of "knowledge worker" was first described in his 1959 book, *The Landmarks of Tomorrow*. The six factors determining knowledge-worker productivity were further described in *Management Challenges for the 21st Century*.
According to P. Drucker, they "work on the right things, manage themselves, are accountable for their performance, and continually develop themselves." In *Management Challenges for the 21st Century*, Butterworth-Heinemann, Oxford, 1999, p. 142

150 P. Drucker famously stated that "efficiency means doing things right, and effectiveness means doing the right things. It is far more important to do right things than to do things right."

151 P. Drucker, 2008, *The 5 Most Important Questions You Will Ever Ask About Your Organization*, Wiley, p. XIX

152 Drucker Institute, "Why Drucker Now?" found at http://druckerinstitute.com/WhyDruckerNow.asp

as well as nonbusiness organizations. By combining managerial practices with the acts of innovation, P. Drucker argued, businesses can create a methodology of entrepreneurship that will institutionalize entrepreneurial values and practices.

As we will see, the marketing model we propose called MarkeThink, is strongly influenced by the knowledge-management approach based on the individual, on self-actualization, and on working on oneself. P. Drucker is the father of a revolutionary movement, and this started when he stated that management is about human beings: "the task of management is to make people capable of joint performance, through common goals, common values, the right structure, and the training and development they need to perform and to respond to change"[153]. This, to enhance their strengths, minimize their weaknesses, and make the right team combinations to increase the company's productivity and results. Management is therefore the critical, determining factor for success.

### 4.1.3 Management Innovation by Gary Hamel

*"Two basic rules of life are:*
*1) Change is inevitable 2) Everybody resists change." - W. E. Deming*

*"Change is not merely necessary to life - It is life." - A. Toffler*

It seems evident that if innovation is not an integral part of a company's essence, the odds of being an innovative marketer are very low. That is why a company must undergo thorough and constant management innovation processes.

The core of a company is its vision, what it stands for; so how can it create innovation if its employees don't live it and breathe it every day? It has to be a fundamental.

Companies have an imperative to grow and prosper, or in worst-case scenarios, survive. Innovation, through creative thinking and imagination, has a great potential to generate growth: it alters the existing balance of the markets and allows for creating and developing new business opportunities.

G. Hamel wrote, "management innovation is anything that substantially alters the way in which the work of management is carried out, or significantly modifies customary organizational forms, and, by doing so, advances organizational goals" (Hamel 2007, p. 19). Further, he sustains that management innovation is "a marked departure from traditional management principles, processes, and practices, or a departure from customary organizational forms that significantly alters the way the work of management is performed."[154]

---

[153] P. Drucker, 1989, *The New Realities:Iin Government and Politics, in Economics and Business, in Society and World View*, in the 2003 revised and reprinted Transaction Publishers edition, p. 214

[154] From the Management Innovation Lab, *www.london.edu/managementinnovationlab.html*, an initiative led by G. Hamel and J. Birkinshow, based at the London Business School. The Management Lab works with lead-

# CHAPTER 4 — MARKETHINK

During an interview, he compares it to operational innovation by stating that "the management innovation is innovation in management principles and processes that ultimately changes the practice of what managers do, and how they do it. It is different from operational innovation, which is about how the work of transforming inputs into outputs actually gets done". Coordinate the work of transforming the inputs to outputs, however, is all the work managers do: pulling resources together, setting priorities, building teams, nurturing relationships, and forming partnerships. And it is innovation within this sphere that I'm interested in."[155]

## 4.1.3.1 The Ultimate Advantage

- A management innovation is anything that substantially alters the way in which management carries out its purpose or the way management becomes supportive to the whole company in achieving organizational goals. It means significantly modifying established organizational structures and processes, enabling organizational advances. Management innovation creates long-lasting advantages when it meets one or more of the following conditions.
- It must be a novel management principle that challenges long-standing business orthodoxies: "the innovation is based on a novel principle that challenges management orthodoxy."
- It has to be systemic, encompassing processes, procedures, and methods.
- It has to be an ongoing program, to continually enhance organizational performance and take it to the next level. "It is part of an ongoing program of invention where progress compounds over time.".[156]

*These are some examples of management innovations in the past century:*[157]

- GE's commitment to talent management
- DuPont's development of capital-budgeting
- P&G's brand management
- Visa's groundwork for industry consortiums
- Linux's open-source development and online collaboration
- Toyota's problem-solving contributions from front-line employees.

---

ing-edge firms to help them create new practices; their aim is to help pioneering companies create groundbreaking management innovation. The MLab is built around a collaborative research environment in which forward-thinking companies and distinguished scholars

155 An extract of Des Dearlove's interview with G. Hamel on May 23, 2003, at the London Business School. You can find the transcript at *http://www.management-issues.com/2006/5/24/mentors/gary-hamel-management-innovation.asp.*

156 From "The End of Management as We Know It" by Dr. Maynard Brusman, in the Working Resources Newsletter vol. 6, no. 1 - *http://www.workingresources.com/nss-folder/pdffolder/TheEndofManagementAsWeKnowIt.pdf*

157 From "The End of Management as We Know It" by Dr. Maynard Brusman, in the Working Resources Newsletter vol. 6, no. 1 - *http://www.workingresources.com/nss-folder/pdffolder/TheEndofManagementAsWeKnowIt.pdf*

Management innovation means coming up with new ways of managing a company - innovative management processes are the way a company carries out its tasks, such as the following:
- Setting and programming objectives
- Motivating and aligning efforts
- Coordinating and controlling activities
- Developing, assigning, and managing talent...

### 4.1.3.2 Why the New Mode?

In contrast to the laws of physics, the laws of management are neither foreordained nor eternal. Unfortunately management practices have been static for a long time now and the laws of management haven't been reconsidered - maybe because the need of adapting to the world's evolution and changes didn't seem so evident, but today companies are being violently forced to face twenty-first-century challenges, which are posing important limitations on the present/old management model. The old management model has very negative effects on the evolution and success of companies for two main reasons:

Opinionated and free-spirited human beings have to conform to standards and rules, squandering prodigious quantities of human imagination and initiative.

Established rigidity and discipline on the execution of operations limits organizational adaptability.

### 4.1.3.3 Why Will It Be So Hard?

G. Hamel uses a very clear and simple analogy to explain why it is so hard for companies to change their way of doing things and to innovate management: "Expecting large organizations to be strategically nimble, restlessly innovative, or highly engaging places to work (or anything else than merely efficient) is like expecting a dog to do a tango, dogs are quadrupeds, dancing is not in their DNA. Likewise, the managerial DNA of large companies makes some things easy, and others virtually impossible" (Hamel 2007, p. 11).

For T. Kuhn, management is based on a paradigm. And he defines a paradigm as a criterion for choosing problems that can be assumed to have solutions. To a great extent these are the only problems that the community will encourage its members to undertake. Other problems are rejected as metaphysica or sometimes as just too problematic to be worth the time. A paradigm can, for that matter, even insulate the community from those socially important problems that are not reducible to the *familiar* puzzle form because they cannot be stated in terms of the conceptual and instrumental tools which the paradigm provides.[158]

Management is captive of this paradigm, which places the pursuit of efficiency ahead of every other goal. We have witness of management progress but they have been constrained by our efficiency-centric, bureaucracy-based managerial paradigm. T. Kuhn's central thesis is incontestable: real progress demands a revolution. Just like Taylor's scientific approach to management required a mental revolution, management today needs a 'revolutionary imperative.' One can't shuffle his way onto the next S-curve, one has to reach for it. One has to go against and challenge preconceived notions, even over everyone else's best practices, over the advice of experts, over his doubts and mental patterns. (Hamel 2007, pp. 12–23)

## 4.1.3.4 The Fundamental Elements of Management Innovation

The concept of innovation has to be an essential component of the company's culture, mission statement, and values.

Innovation must be permanent and resonate throughout the whole organization, and cannot exclude any function, area, or business unit. All the members of the organization need to "live" innovation. When we speak of a culture of innovation, we also need strong propulsion toward change. The culture of change is an extremely important factor of innovation. Change has to be seen as positive; it needs to be understood and shared, perceived as natural and healthy, and viewed as an opportunity rather than a threat. An innovative company looks for change, responds to it, and approaches it as an opportunity.

*The organization's structure has to enable innovation to happen; it has to allow for the culture of innovation.*

An innovative company has a flexible, interconnected, and integrated structure that renders all needed resources available to all organization members and functions. Innovation is interdisciplinary; it arises through the exchange of knowledge, information, and technology between functions and from the combination of ideas and knowledge, which might not be related to one another but create value to the whole company. The company's structure and management needs to support and promote this.

*The key is human capital. In the innovation process, the human brain is crucial.*

A company needs a mix of attitudes among the ranks of its human resources. Special work teams, curious and ambitious, well prepared, professional, oriented to action, with minds out of the box, creative people, but at the same time, on Earth,

---

[158] T. S. Kuhn, 1996, "The Structure of Scientific Revolutions," 3rd Ed. University of Chicago. From the 2007 book, *The Future of Management* by G. Hamel and B. Breen. Harvard Business Press, p. 12

analytical and rational.

Top management is the driving force of decision making, the group in charge of the company's performance, and managers should therefore be the carriers and promoters of innovation throughout all levels of the organization. Management should be the representation of the company's culture of innovation and change; managers have to be truly willing to take chances and assume risks.

An example of a management innovation company is Google. Google has worked systematically to "distribute the responsibility for strategic innovation" throughout the company and its employees. Google is determined to have the most "at bats" than anyone else: they try out about five thousand new ideas per year. The way they achieve this is by dividing the organization into hundreds of teams composed of two to three people; each team has its own website to record the progress, and everyone throughout the company can provide feedback. The key point is that nobody controls the overall strategy, and the next innovation may come from anyone within the organization. Google has, as part of its DNA, adopted the following techniques to maximize management innovation: taking advantage of the power of Internet, encouraging constant and cross functional collaboration, reducing hierarchical boundaries, and dedicating 20 percent of employees' personal time to creating new ideas and developing them.[159]

## 4.1.3.5 Innovations Operating Systems

An innovating company is also characterized by having various operating systems, perfected through time to manage the company's resources.

*A market of ideas* is an established system developed to solicit, to gather, and to evaluate new ideas and then develop them. All ideas, valuable or not, are managed and kept as insight or starting points for the continual innovation process.

*A capital market* makes reference to the necessity to compensate individuals for the most attractive ideas, to assign funds for their development and investigation, and also to motivate and encourage proposals and creativity.

*A talent market* is the system that manages the talent within the organization: those people who are creative, inventive, and come up with the brilliant ideas.

Besides these three market systems, a company absolutely needs to have a solid but innovative process that supports the development and testing of ideas and concepts, financial analysis, development and testing of prototypes, testing the market and launching products, and implementing, controlling and monitoring the entire process.

---

[159] From "The End of Management as We Know It" by Dr. Maynard Brusman, in the *Working Resources Newsletter* vol. 6, no. 1 - *http://www.workingresources.com/nss-folder/pdffolder/TheEndofManagementAsWeKnowIt.pdf*

# Chapter 5
# Creativity Models and MarkeThinkers

## 5.1 Creativity Management

*"For everything related to creativity, I accept chaos.
I agree that people act out like kids." - N. Hayek Founder of Swatch group*

*"Creativity involves breaking out of established patterns in order to look at things
in a different way...We know very well that progress is due to creativity;
to looking at things in a different way; to doing things differently;
to putting things together to deliver new value." - Edward de Bono*

**MarkeThink Metamodel**

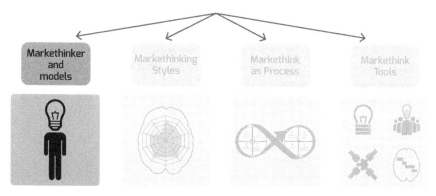

Figure 83: Marketing Models and Author

The English word "creativity" comes from the Latin term "*creare*," which means to create or make.

P. Kotler's insight on creativity is that "companies formerly won their marketing battles through superior efficiency or quality. Today they must win through superior creativity. Ones does not win through better sameness, one wins through uniqueness" (2003, p. 27). He advocates that to create uniqueness a company must develop a culture that "honors creativity." He suggests three things: "hire more naturally creative people and give them free rein," stimulate creativity with the use of effective and recognized creative techniques, and dare to ask for creativity help.

## 5.1.1 Approaches to the Creativity Process

Many models of the creative process have been developed, with more or fewer steps, focusing on more grounded or abstract concepts. The important facts are that creativity and thinking are processes that follow a sequence of events - episodes if you will - and that it is not about sitting around and waiting to be illuminated;it's about being active and stimulating your mind.

A. Osborn, in 1953, distinguished and expanded the list to seven well-defined stages that determine step by step how you are going to develop your thought process during the creative session. These steps allow for a better outcome:[160]

1. *Orientation,* pointing out and stating the problem
2. *Preparation,* gathering pertinent and necessary data
3. *Analysis,* "breaking down" relevant material
4. *Ideation,* generating ideas and alternatives
5. *Incubation,* letting go, giving it time, letting your mind work, and inviting illumination
6. *Synthesis,* putting things together
7. *Evaluation,* judging and value of the ideas

On the other hand, T. Amabile argues that for a company to enhance creativity in business it has to be in possession of three fundamental characteristics expertise - technical, procedural and intellectual knowledge, and creative thinking skills - flexible people with imagination, and motivation (extrinsic and especially intrinsic, which comes from within the individuals):[161]

---

[160] A. Osborn, *1953 Applied Imagination Principles and Procedures of Creative Problem Solving.* Charles Scribner, New York

[161] T. M. Amabile, 1998, "How to Kill Creativity," *Harvard Business Review* 76, no. 5 pp. 76–87

## 5.1.2 Some Creativity Techniques

This is a brief list of the many techniques and tools available to stimulate creativity. Each one serves a specific purpose; you can use one or a combination of these to gain more insight on the situation and deliver more creative ideas, leading to true, valuable innovations.

| Creativity Techniques | | |
|---|---|---|
| Fuzzy Thinking | Snowball technique | Disney Creativity Strategy |
| The Discontinuity Principle | Cognitive Acceleration | Think Tank |
| Force-Fit Game | Forced Field Analysis | Boundary Examination |
| Imitation | Chunking | Critical Path Diagram |
| Concept Fans and Concept Triangles | Advantages, Limitations and Unique Qualities | Observer and Merged Viewpoints |
| Metaphorical Thinking | Adaptive Reasoning | Method of Focal Objects |
| Lotus Blossom Technique | Divide-and-Conquer | Storyboarding |
| Assumption Smashing | Breakthrough Thinking | Problem Inventory Analysis |
| Morphological Analysis | In the Realm of the Senses | Hexagon Modeling |
| Forced Relationship/Analogy | Progressive Hurdles/Revelations | Backwards Forwards Planning |
| Kepner and Tregoe Method | Ishikawa Diagram | Algorithm of Inventive |
| Warizit | SCAMPER | Idea Lottery |
| Kaleidoscope Brainstorming | Starbursting | Reframing Matrix |
| Crawford Slip Method | Reverse Brainstorming | Brain Teasers and Riddles |

Figure 84: Various Creativity Thinking Methods, Tools, and Techniques

Each technique is like a tool in a toolbox, and they are all part of your workshop station. Each one has its specific purpose in the creative process. Some of these will be described in more detail in the following pages.

There are other very important techniques in their evolution, such as: CPS from Buffalo, the Herman Methods, and H. Jaoui with PAPSA. These, among many others, are very interesting models that, because of space issues, we will only briefly describe, though wet strongly recommend their books and works: The Herrmann Brain Dominance Instrument (HBDI) is a system to measure and describe thinking preferences in people, developed by William "Ned" Herrmann while leading management education at General Electric's Crotonville facility[162]

---
162 Wikipedia

"CPSB - Creative Problem Solving Buffalo - is the leader in services specializing in organizational creativity and innovation. They design, develop, and deliver corporate initiatives focusing on leadership, climate, culture, sustainability, creativity, innovation, strategy, and change. CPSB's methods and tools provide a framework for organizations to achieve higher levels of performance, innovation and growth," through the use of their "Proven Practical System and Tools." This system comprises, among other things, the GEMangination, the SOQ (situational outlook questionnaire), the VIEW (an assessment of Problem Solving Style, the Prioritizer (online and web-based Paired Comparison Analysis tool), and CPS101 (Creative Problem Solving course and tools). And all their service is supported by their worldwide network of researchers and creativity inquirers, the CRU - Creativity Research Unit. Its core is based on practical innovation, research in creativity, and real-life application."[163]

The PAPSA method was developed by H. Jaoui for finding new solutions based on a methodical and scientific approach, which embraces the whole process, from the invention to the innovation.[164] A creative process that consists of a five stages each consisting of a convergent and divergent phase of production.[165] The five stages, grouped under the acronym PAPSA, are perception, analysis, production, selection, and application. For each of them, various creative techniques have been developed, such as the "Devil's Advocate," "Magical Thinking," or "Catastrophe Strategy" to name a few. The key here is that they all respect the alternation between convergence and divergence; this is important because it enables people to welcome and accept new ideas without smothering them.

## 5.1.3 Creativity Umbrella and Definition

The word "creativity" is an umbrella concept under which we can find many meanings and approaches, all with different values and validations; each author has proposed his own definition of creativity. We strongly believe that it is not possible to unequivocally define the concept of creativity with a single definition. In fact, the umbrella covers everything from artistic, to musical, to literary, to cinematographic, and even scientific creativity.

In the following pages we will be presenting some of the most prominent au-

---

[163] Retrieved from their official website, where you can get more detail on their tools, practices, and their whole system at http://www.cpsb.com/

[164] Is an expert in the field of creativity since the seventies. Among his many contributions to the field are the PAPSA and the Total Creativity Management approach. He also created the GIMCA institute, which is an innovation source where senior consultants are at your service to increase and develop creativity, and help you reach high levels of innovation. For more information visit their website at http://www.gimca.net/.

[165] J. P. Guilford has the merit of being the first to have drawn a distinction between convergent (which measures the IQ) and divergent thinking or intelligence, which he considered as being synonymous to creativity. For further insight see J. P. Guilford, 1967, *The Nature of Human Intelligence*. New York, Mc Graw-Hill

thors in the field of creative thinking and the work we find most interesting in the field of creative thinking and most valuable to our MarkeThink concept.

## Approaches Discussed

- TRIZ by G. Altshuller
- Creativity Templates by D. Mazursky and J. Goldenberg
- Edward de Bono Technics
- Palo Alto School
- CreActivity model by M. Soriani Bellavista

Before we start, I believe the words of E. de Bono can be of great value: "Creative thinking is not a talent; it is a skill that can be learnt. It empowers people by adding strength to their natural abilities, which improves creativity and innovation, which leads to increased productivity and profits."[166]

# 5.2 "TRIZ" by Genrich Altshuller

> *"Somebody someplace has already solved this problem (or one very similar to it). Creativity is now finding that solution and adapting it to this particular problem." - K. Barry, E. Domb and M. S. Slocum*

TRIZ is the acronym for G. Altshuller's "Theory of Inventive Problem Solving." Since its creation fifty years ago, it has become a well-established system of tools used for problem solving, failure analysis and prevention, and idea generation. This model was developed based on the extensive analysis of thousands of patents and successful technical solutions, which led to the following affirmations:

- Technical systems are modeled on the natural evolution of the laws of nature.
- Models and tendencies can be used to develop and improve systems.

TRIZ is a powerful tool kit of problem-solving techniques that can help in many tasks, including inventing, improving, and designing. It is a creative method that doesn't rely solely on the brain, personal experience, and education. It shows how one can use the world's knowledge and combine it with personal thinking to resolve problems. Most problems aren't unique, and TRIZ describes how similar problems have been solved using the same basic concepts and solutions, and how you can apply these solutions to your own situation and create innovative solutions with low risk.

It is a methodology for finding solutions based on logic, data, and research, with past knowledge and experience to lead the team into finding creative solutions faster. It is a structured and algorithmic approach that brings repeatability, predictability, and reliability to problem solving. It is a worldwide scientific approach to cre-

---

166 De Bono Consulting the number one De Bono Thinking Systems distributor in North America. Available at *http://www.debonoconsulting.com/images/lateral-thinking-brochure.pdf*

ativity based on the analysis of patterns, its problems, and its solutions.

TRIZ helps the person or group focus their attention on specific areas that lead to the best possible solution. It is a method that enhances thinking capabilities: you think harder, faster, and smarter. You get to solutions you would have never found otherwise, but that are generally within your reach.

It is composed of four sets of problem-solving tools and four sets of problem-analysis tools. TRIZ is not just a problem-solving tool; it is a problem-definition tool too. It allows you to see the situation you are in clearly in regards to the product, your department, and the company. It helps improve the systems by eliminating useless processes or modifying them, reducing the costs and increasing the benefits. It can also help you see where your particular market is going and how you can get there in a clever way.

## 5.2.1   The TRIZ Problem Solving Method

You take your specific problem and determine which TRIZ general problem fits with it. From there you identify which TRIZ specific solution was used to solve the general problem. Once you have executed the three steps, you analyze how the specific solutions can be applied to your problem at hand.

Figure 85: The TRIZ Process

**Contradictions**

There is a fundamental concept behind TRIZ: many problems seem to arise from contradictions; for example, an umbrella has to be large to properly protect from the rain, but must be small enough to fit in women's bags when it's not raining. Contradictions are important, because every contradiction can be a valuable opportunity. Contradictions can either be technical or physical.

A *technical* contradiction means there is something in the system that prevents you from getting to the desired state. It is a classical trade-off, good versus bad: if something improves, something else automatically worsens. For example, beef has to be kept cool during transportation, so aircrafts need heavy AC machinery, the additional load of the machinery means that less beef can be loaded.

A *physical* (or *inherent*) contradiction, on the other hand, is one in which the contradiction is required to exist within the product or system, but the improvement of one characteristic results in the deterioration or destruction of another. To resolve the problem, you need to compromise. Physical contradictions are inherent: software has to be complex to contain its large amount of features, and at the same time simple for the user to learn and use. The characteristics must be contradictory: higher and lower, present and absent.

In 1969[167] he presented the thirty-nine characteristics of the contradiction matrix and the "forty universal inventive principles"[168] that can resolve almost all the complex technical contradictions without having to compromise. These principles together with the characteristics make the contradiction matrix has you can see below[169].

| PRINCIPLES | | | |
|---|---|---|---|
| Segmentation | Universality | Local Quality | Asymmetry |
| Skipping – Rushing Through | Taking Out – Extraction | Intermediary – Mediator | Spheroidality – Curvature |
| Cheap Short-Living Objects – Inexpensive Short Life | Nested Doll – Nesting Preliminary Action – Prior Action | Beforehand Cushioning – Cushion in Advance | Another Dimension – Moving to a new dimension |
| The Other Way Around – Inversion | Counterweight – Anti-weight | Continuity of Useful Action | Partial, Overdone or Excessive Action |
| Equipotentiality | Mechanical Vibration | Periodic Action | Dynamics – Dynamicity |
| Merging – Combination | Changing the Color | Feedback | Changing the Color |
| Parameter Changes – Transforming Physical or Chemical States | Discarding and Recovering – Rejecting and Regenerating Parts | 'Blessing in Disguise' – Convert Harm into Benefit | Mechanics Substitutions – Mechanical System Replacement |
| Use Pneumatic or Hydraulic Systems | Flexible Shells or Thin Films | Inert Atmosphere – Environment | Preliminary Anti-action – Prior Counter-action |
| Homogeneity | Copying | Self-service | Phase Transitions |
| Thermal Expansion | Strong Oxidizers | Porous Materials | Composite Materials |

Figure 86: The Forty Inventive Principles

---

167 In his book *Algorithm of Invention* (ARIZ)
168 These forty principles where further developed in 1974 in his book *'The 40 Principles*.
169 For more detailed information on the principles and contradictions it can help you solve please go tohttp://triz40.com/aff_Principles.htm.

| CHARACTERISTICS ||| 
|---|---|---|
| Weight of moving object | Weight of nonmoving object | Length of moving object |
| Length of nonmoving object | Area of moving object | Area of nonmoving object |
| Volume of moving object | Volume of nonmoving object | Speed |
| Force | Tension, pressure | Shape |
| Stability of object | Strength | Durability of moving object |
| Durability of nonmoving object | Temperature | Brightness |
| Energy spent by moving object | Energy spent by nonmoving object | Power |
| Waste of energy | Waste of substance | Loss of information |
| Waste of time | Amount of substance | Reliability |
| Accuracy of measurement | Accuracy of manufacturing | Harmful factors acting on object |
| Harmful side effects | Manufacturability | Convenience of use |
| Repairability | Adaptability | Complexity of device |
| Complexity of control | Level of automation | Productivity |

Figure 87: The Thirty-Nine Characteristics for Contradiction

## 5.2.3 The Inventive Process Based on TRIZ

G. Altshuller determined that there are different stages undertaken during the inventive process: choosing the task and the search concept, gathering data, searching for the idea, and finding the idea and its practical implementation. Associated with these stages are his five complexity levels and the characteristics of the inventive process, as seen below:[170]

| | |
|---|---|
| Level one: | Utilization of one existing object without consideration of other object |
| Level Two: | Choosing one object out of several |
| Level Three: | Making partial changes to the selected object |
| Level Four: | Development of a new object, or complete modification of a chosen one |
| Level Five: | Development of a completely new complex of systems |

Figure 88: The Five Levels Characteristics

---

[170] From *The Innovation Algorithm: TRIZ, Systematic Innovation and Technical Creativity* by Genrich Altshuller, translated in 1999 by Steven Rodman and Lev Shulyak. p. 43

In the table below, which represents a structured diagram[171] of the creative process, you can see how these two variables - stages and levels - relate to each other:

| Levels | Chosing the task | Choosing search concept | Gathering data | Searching for idea | Idea found | Pratical implemantation |
|---|---|---|---|---|---|---|
| | A | B | C | D | E | F |
| 1 | Utilize an existing task | Utilize an existing search concept | Utilize existing data | Utilize an existing solution | Utilize ready design | Manufacture an existing design |
| 2 | Choose one task out of several | Choose one search concept out of several | Gather data from several resources | Choose one idea out of several | Choose one design out of several | Manufacture a modification of an existing design |
| 3 | Change origina task | Modify search concept suitable to new task | Modifly gathered data suitable to new task | Change existing solution | Change existing design | Manufacture new design |
| 4 | Find new task | Find new search concept | Gather new data relative to new task | Find new solution | Develop new design | Utilize design in a new way |
| 5 | Find new problem | Find new method | Gather new data relative to new problem | Find new concept (principle) | Develop new constructive concepts | Modifly all systems in which new concept is implemented |

Figure 89: A Structured Diagram of the Creative Process

Altshuller then analyzed "fourteen classes of inventions from 1965 to 1969" to establish the difference between the outcomes of first-level inventions and those from the fifth level. This revealed the following interesting dispersal:[172]

| | |
|---|---|
| Level one: | 32.0% |
| Level Two: | 45.0% |
| Level Three: | 19.0% |
| Level Four: | Below 4.0% |
| Level Five: | Below 4.0% |

Figure 90: Dispersal between the Levels

---

171 From *The Innovation Algorithm: TRIZ, Systematic Innovation and Technical Creativity* by Genrich Altshuller, translated in 1999 by Steven Rodman and Lev Shulyak. p. 44
172 From *The Innovation Algorithm: TRIZ, Systematic Innovation and Technical Creativity* by Genrich Altshuller, translated in 1999 by Steven Rodman and Lev Shulyak. p. 47

The result of his analysis further shows that, today, the real inventive creativity takes place between the third and fifth levels. The first two levels are only about new design, yet these amount to 77 percent of all inventions. This also supported G. Altshuller's belief that problem solving is based on "trial and error," as seen in the image below.[173] The "differences between the levels in stage D can be characterized by the number of trials and errors made by the average engineer while searching for a solution."[174]

| Level one:   | 1 to 1                     |
|--------------|----------------------------|
| Level Two:   | 10 to 10                   |
| Level Three: | 100 to 100                 |
| Level Four:  | 1000 to 1000               |
| Level Five:  | 10,000 to 100,000 and more |

Figure 91: Number of Trials and Errors per Level

You can see that as the complexity level of a problem increases, so does the amount of trials and errors required in solving the inventive problem.

It is clear that the more variables and elements a problem has, the harder it is to control them and find a solution easily, leading to more trials and failures. For a better understanding of this, Altshuller made a differentiation between level one and level four problems:[175]

| 1st Level | 4th Level |
|---|---|
| 1. Small number of elements<br>2. No unknown elements<br>3. Simple Analysis: elements that need to be modified are easy to separate from those that should remain unchanged under the problems conditions.<br>4. Interrelationships between the elements are easy to trace.<br>5. Little time is given to solve the problem | 1. Large number of elements<br>2. Significant amount of unknown elements<br>3. Difficult to analyze, it is hard to separate the known from the unknown.<br>4. Almost impossible to establish a complete model that takes into consideration all the relationships between elements.<br>5. Long time is given to solve the problem |

Figure 92: First versus Fourth Level Creativity Process Problems

---

173 From *The Innovation Algorithm: TRIZ, Systematic Innovation and Technical Creativity* by Genrich Altshuller, and translated in 1999 by Steven Rodman and Lev Shulyak. p. 47
174 From *The Innovation Algorithm: TRIZ, Systematic Innovation and Technical Creativity* by Genrich Altshuller, and translated in 1999 by Steven Rodman and Lev Shulyak. p. 47
175 Elaborated from *The Innovation Algorithm: TRIZ, Systematic Innovation and Technical Creativity* by Genrich Altshuller, and translated in 1999 by Steven Rodman and Lev Shulyak. p. 55

## 5.3 "Creativity Templates" by David Mazursky and Jacob Goldenberg

D. Mazursky and J. Goldenberg, in collaboration with S. Solomon, developed an innovative process for the ideation of new products and processes through the stimulation of our ability to think creatively, to see things differently, and to dissociate ourselves from established schemes and patterns. They suggest we examine the products or attributes through the systematic use of their four "creativity templates."[176] These templates, the four ideative schemes, serve as a framework that can and will lead to the most successful new product or process idea.

Innovators should consider these creative templates first instead of just developing new products in an attempt to meet the ever-changing and complex needs of consumers. Once the analysis of the product and process attributes has been done through the creativity template lenses, one can create and redefine the products according to the outcome of the analysis.

The creativity templates are clearly defined operations that attempt to manipulate the knowledge encoded in the product, process, or its attributes in order to uncover and/or discover innovative approaches, functionality, use of components, and so forth.

The first step when using the creativity templates is to identify the internal and external determinant attributes. The second step is to manipulate the determinant attributes according to each template operational approach. The third, and final, step is to follow a systemic approach in the search for new patterns through the use of the authors' forecasting matrix.

### 5.3.1 The Templates

Attribute dependency template, the goal here is to find the functional dependencies between two independent variable attributes. There is an imposed interaction that provides a creative solution to a design challenge or a creative new product concept.

The replacement template is about removing an essential component of a product and replacing it with another one found in the near environment to perform the previous component's function. The function remains, but it is performed by another component.

The displacement template is all about removing an intrinsic element as well as the function it performs, causing a qualitative functional change. The component

---

[176] From our point of view the model of "creativity template " is a good example of a practical synthesis of the model of TRIZ applied to marketing.

and its performed function are completely removed, creating a new product for a different and new market.

The component control template is used to identify and create new connections between internal components and external ones, even if connections are not evident or seem too provocative.

As an example, Domino's Pizza was successful because they established a relationship between the price of the pizza and time of delivery. If the pizza were to be delivered after half an hour, then the price of the pizza would be cut in half, giving them a strong differentiation advantage compared to competitors. The innovation here is that the price of the pizza is not constant anymore; it depends on delivery time.

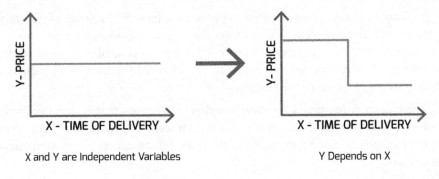

Figure 93: Time of Delivery Variable

They established a new relationship between price and a service characteristic.

But you can also consider establishing other relationships, such as between the pizza price and its temperature, where you pay full price as long as the pizza is over a certain temperature when its delivered to your house. The delivery variable is out of the picture, and the new message is that pizza taste depends on its temperature and not the time of delivery.

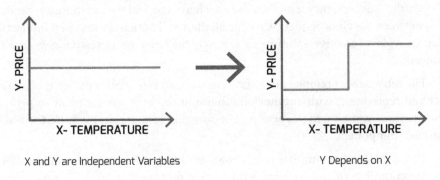

Figure 94: Temperature Variable

## 5.3.2 The Forecasting Matrix

The systemic application of the templates is provided by a two-dimensional forecasting matrix. The columns are labeled with the important internal attributes. The rows are labeled with the internal and external attributes. Every cell is then marked by a one if there is an existing dependency between the important and not important attributes, or by a zero if no dependency exists.

|  |  | \multicolumn{5}{c}{INTERNAL VARIABLES} | | | | |
|---|---|---|---|---|---|---|
|  |  | Price | Colour | Weight | Power | Decorations |
| INTERNAL VARIABLES | Price | X | 0 | 1 | 1 | 0 |
| | Colour | 0 | X | 0 | 0 | 1 |
| | Weigth | 0 | 0 | X | 1 | 0 |
| | Power | 1 | 0 | 1 | X | 0 |
| | Decorations | 1 | 1 | 0 | 0 | X |
| EXTERNAL VARIABLES | External Temperature | 0 | 0 | 0 | 1 | 0 |
| | Visibility | 0 | 0 | 0 | 0 | 0 |
| | Users Age | 0 | 0 | 0 | 1 | 0 |

Figure 95: Forecasting Matrix

# 5.4 Edward de Bono The Guru of Creativity: Past, Present, and Future

Whereas R. Descartes propounded "cogito ergo sum" (I think, therefore I am), E. de Bono proposes "ago ergo erigo" (I act, therefore I construct/act). It is not enough to sit, talk, and think; action, together with an intentional design of the thought process, is required to constructively advance toward results and change.

## 5.4.1 About Dr. Edward de Bono

Dr. Edward de Bono is regarded by many as the leading international authority on creative thinking and the direct teaching of thinking skills. He has written over seventy books which we highly recommend, with translations in more than thirty-eight languages. He has consulted with major corporations and governments in more than fifty countries over the last thirty years. He has taught thinking skills to corporate executives, four-year-olds, and Nobel Prize laureates.[177]

In his book *The Mechanism of Mind*, Dr.de Bono first described how the nerve networks in the brain behave as a self-organizing system. It was from this base that Dr. de Bono designed his thinking methodologies. He is the inventor of the term "lateral thinking" and the designer of the CoRT Thinking Program for schools, which is the most widely used program internationally for teaching thinking skills.

In 1991, Dr. de Bono arranged for the corporation that is now de Bono Thinking Systems to publish his training materials and certify instructors to teach his thinking methods. Now more than six hundred thousand people have learned to use his tools at work.

Dr. de Bono has worked internationally with leading corporations such as IBM, Siemens, Motorola, Mars Inc., AstraZeneca, British Telecom, and Merck, to name a few.

For enquiries relating to the use of the de Bono IP (including any licences or copyright permissions) and publishing enquiries relating to the licensing of the de Bono trade books please contact: www.debono.com

## 5.4.2 Power of Perception

> *"The real voyage of discovery consists not in seeking new landscapes but in having new eyes instead."* M. Proust

> *"Many problems require a different perspective to solve them successfully."* - E. de Bono

Perception is "the way in which something is regarded, understood, or interpreted."[178]

"Godel's Theorem proves that from within a system you can never logically prove the starting points - no matter how logical you might be. The starting points are arbitrary perceptions and assumptions that cannot be proved logically. So no matter how logical you think you are your conclusion will be determined by your starting points, not the excellence of your logic" (de Bono 2009, p. 137).

"The way we see the world - our perception of it - determines the decisions we make and what we do. Perception is probably the most important part of our thinking, but unfortunately, most mistakes in thinking are mistakes in perception."[179]

---

[177] You can find the extensive list of the books he has written at *http://www.ranker.com/list/edward-de-bono-books-and-stories-and-written-works/reference*

[178] Retrieved from the Oxford Dictionary online at *http://www.oxforddictionaries.com/view/entry/m_en_gb0618760#m_en_gb0618760*

[179] de Bono Consulting, the number one de Bono Thinking Systems distributor in North America. Available at *http://*

To overcome the barriers raised by our perception, E. de Bono emphasizes the importance of improving our "perceptual thinking." He suggests that we use perceptual tools and maps, but more importantly that we change our attitudes toward thinking. By changing our attitudes, he means that we need to understand that logic alone is not sufficient and to acknowledge that our logical thinking starting point is our perception; by looking for and accepting alternatives, opening up to different possibilities, avoiding judgments, and moving away from our patterns.

With his "Power of Perception" (POP) tools, E. de Bono gives us a "framework for defining a situation, to improve your ability to consider consequences before you take action." They are "ten simple strategies" for sharpening your perception and focusing your thinking in a more comprehensive, effective, and efficient way. These are the ten POP tools:[180]

Tool 1. Consequences and sequels - look ahead to see the consequences of an action, plan, decision, or rule.

Tool 2. Plus, minus, interesting - ensure that all sides of a matter have been considered before a decision or commitment is made.

Tool 3. Recognize, analyze, and divide - break a larger concept into smaller, more manageable parts.

Tool 4. Consider all factors - explore all factors related to an action, decision, plan, judgment, or conclusion.

Tool 5. Aims, goals, objectives - focus directly and deliberately on the intentions behind actions.

Tool 6. Alternatives, possibilities, choices - deliberately try to find other ways.

Tool 7. Other people's views - put yourself in others shoes.

Tool 8. Key values involved - ensure that your thinking serves your values.

Tool 9. First important priorities - select the most important ideas, factors, objectives, consequences, etc.

Tool 10. Design/decision, outcome, channels, action - direct attention to the outcome of the thinking and action that follows.

The way we see things represents reality, our own personal reality, based on our education, social background, experiences, and so on. Perception is reality, but one's individual reality!

---

www.debonoconsulting.com/power-of-perception.asp

[180] de Bono Consulting, the number one de Bono Thinking Systems distributor in North America. Available at http://www.debonoconsulting.com/power-of-perception.asp

## 5.4.3 "Parallel Thinking" and the "Six Thinking Hats"

"Imagine a rather ornate building of a square shape. There are four people, each of whom is facing one aspect of this building. Through a mobile phone or walkie-talkie, each person is insisting and arguing that he, or she, is facing the most beautiful aspect of the building" (de Bono 2009, p. 92).

Parallel thinking, explained by E. de Bono, "means that they change how they go about this argument. All four people move around to the south side of the building together. Then all of them move on to the west side, then the north and finally to the east side. So, all of them, in parallel, are looking at the same side of the building at any one moment" (2009, p. 92).

"Instead of argument, where A is adversarially attacking B, we have a system where A and B are both looking and thinking in the same direction - but the direction changes as they move around. That is parallel thinking" (E. de Bono 2009, p.92).

We have seen that it is important to think by looking in the same direction, but thinking in the same direction that is not all. He argues that there is also the need to have the same "mode of thinking," the same state of mind, when looking at something, to avoid the confusion of tackling every aspect at once. Parallel thinking means that all statements, ideas, and opinions, even if contradictory, are not put in discussion, but rather "laid down in parallel," which will lead to generating ideas "*to explore a subject in a constructive and not adversarial way!*"

### 3.7.3.1 Six Thinking Hats[181]

E. de Bono's Six Thinking Hats" is a powerful technique, a tool that helps teams look at important decisions from different perspectives. It helps us make better decisions by pushing team members to move outside their usual modes of thinking, understand the full complexity of a decision, and uncover issues and opportunities that have a tendency to go unnoticed. It is a technique for changing the way you are thinking about a particular problem, channeling thoughts, emotions, and approaches. It's all about looking at decisions from all points of view.

This method is basically a structure that can include more than one approach of thought, including lateral thinking. A valuable critical thinking and judgment that is systemic but, somehow, is not a dominant variable. Edward de Bono defines the Six Thinking Hats as a method that *"separates ego from performance."*

---

[181] From E. de Bono's 1985 book *Six Thinking Hats: An Essential Approach to Business Management*, published by Little, Brown & Company

# CHAPTER 5 — MARKETHINK

## The Tool

Each "thinking hat" is a different style of thinking. Each hat represents one of six modes of thinking, to be interpreted as "directions to think" rather than "labels for thinking, meaning that each hat needs to be used proactively, and not reactively. When looking at a problem using the Six Thinking Hats technique, every approach needs to be elaborated on in order to find and develop the best solution. The result of using this method is that all decisions and plans will be composed of an adequate mix of perception, dimensions, ambition, sensitivity, creativity, skill in execution, and contingency planning.

*White Hat - facts and objectivity.* The white hat is all about looking at the information available: facts, figures, information needs, and gaps. Past trends are analyzed, and historical data is extrapolated to see what can be learned. It is looking for gaps in your knowledge, filling them, or taking them into account. "I think we need some white hat thinking at this point..." means drop the arguments and proposals, and look at the data base. This hat implies that you are neutral in your thinking; you are only information seeking. What are the facts? What information is available? Is it relevant?

*Red Hat - intuition, feelings, and emotions.* With the red hat, the decision is being analyzed using intuition, feelings, gut reactions, and emotions. The red hat allows the thinker to put forward an opinion without any need to justify it: "Putting on my red hat, I think this is a terrible proposal." It gives full permission to a thinker to put forward their feelings on the subject. What do you feel? What are your gut reactions? What's your intuition?

*Black Hat - judgmental and cautious.* Using the black hat, one looks at things negatively, cautiously, and defensively. You attempt to see and understand why ideas and approaches might not work. It highlights the weak points, dangers, and difficulties in a plan or course of action, providing the possibility of eliminating them, altering the approach, and preparing contingency plans to counter possible problems. Black hat thinking provides the real benefits of this technique: it helps detect problems in advance and prepare for difficulties, but it cannot be overused. This "hat" must always be logical. What are the risks or dangers involved? What are the possible pitfalls, problems, and difficulties?

*Yellow Hat - positivism, brightness, and optimism.* The yellow hat is the positive, constructive, and optimistic approach to identify the benefits and values of a decision and spot the opportunities that arise from such a decision. It is also a useful tool to use when everything looks gloomy and difficult, and can be used to find value in things that have already occurred. It's about getting the job done effectively. What are the benefits and advantages?

*Green Hat - creativity, new ideas, alternatives.* The green hat stands for creativity, alternatives, proposals, provocations, and changes. This is the moment to develop creative, out-of-the-ordinary solutions to a problem. It's the freewheeling approach to thinking, where there is no criticism or judgment.

*Blue Hat - control and reflection.* Applying the blue hat controls and organizes the thinking process itself. It looks not at the subject discussed but at the thinking process. It's worn by the person chairing the meeting and used when faced with a difficulty to redirect the group to the most appropriate approach: "Putting on my blue hat, I feel we should do some green hat thinking at this point."

## 5.4.4   Lateral Thinking

*"Lateral thinking is a new way of thinking that opens a door they didn't even know existed. A way of thinking that seeks a solution to an intractable problem through unorthodox methods or elements that would normally be ignored by logical thinking." - E. de Bono*

"Lateral thinking" is a term developed by E. de Bono in 1967 in his book of the same name, in which he shows us how we can be more creative and gives us the power to create ideas on demand, by pushing us to break out of our patterned ways of thinking.

### Idea Creativity

"If doors are normally rectangular and you suggest a triangular door, that is not creativity unless you can show value for the new shape" (de Bono 2009, p.23).

E. de Bono sustains that there are strong barriers to understanding the word "creativity." In his book *Think! Before It's Too Late*, he suggests that we need to see and understand the distinction between "artistic creativity," as we commonly understand it, and "idea creativity," which is our ability to think. This belief led E. de Bono to create the term "lateral thinking" to refer to the process of "idea creativity," indicating changes, newness, and value. He says, "Lateral thinking involves disrupting an apparent thinking sequence and arriving at the solution from another angle."[182]

### The Logic of Lateral Thinking

Lateral thinking is based on the logic of perception, i.e., how the brain handles information. Starting from the logic of perception, it is possible to develop a set of practical tools used to trigger creativity. The human brain operates as a system that is organized in an autonomous way, like a system that receives information and organizes it into predetermined patterns. E. de Bono wrote, "The brain as a self-organizing information system that forms asymmetric patterns. In such systems there is a mathematical need for moving across patterns. The tools and processes of lateral thinking are designed to achieve such 'lateral' movement. The tools are based on an

---

182 E. de Bono from the E. de Bono Thinking System global community website, available at *http://www.debonothinkingsystems.com/tools/lateral.htm*

understanding of self-organizing information systems."[183]

In essence, the brain reorganizes the new information into default binaries, and only by coming out of these patterns can we identify and recognize new ideas.

According to de Bono is there is a need to find alternative routes for the flow of attention and thoughts identified through different entry points. The interesting thing is that if perspectives don't change, every effort in an attempt to find a solution will be done in vain. Our thoughts and thinking processes cannot move simultaneously in different directions: once on a path, it stays on it all the way through.

The subsequent and repeated use of the logical methods tends to "mechanize" the process, preventing them from seeing the possibilities and existence of alternative routes. E. de Bono's lateral thinking approach "implies moving sideways and changing perceptions, concepts, starting point, et cetera, instead of just working harder with the existing ones." "It implies moving across patterns instead of just along them" (2009, p. 40). Lateral thinking is done through the application of a set of provocation and movement tools that enable us to get value from "apparently unworkable ideas."

There are four critical factors associated with lateral thinking: recognizing the dominant ideas that polarize perceptions, promoting different ways of looking at things, relaxing rigid thinking, and encouraging other ideas.

Lateral thinking is the opposite of vertical thinking, similar to what we saw in the lateral marketing section. E. de Bono uses a good analogy to describe the "why" of such a difference: "you cannot dig a hole in a different place by digging the same hole deeper."[184] This simply means that concentrating all your efforts into the same ineffective activity, constantly, in the same direction, might not be the solution to your complex problem or situation. Instead, changing direction and taking on a different approach could be the way to success. You need to take a different direction, follow a new approach, and start something else instead of doing the same thing over and over, because it will only make your problems bigger.

Lateral thinking has a specific meaning in the context of heuristically creative thinking attempts to modify concepts and perceptions. It's based on the behavior of self-organizing systems and teaches us how to use creativity in a deliberate and systematic manner instead of making it a question of talent, temperament, or pure luck.

E. de Bono coined the two terms for convenience and differentiation: vertical thinking indicates the logical method, while lateral thinking refers to this alternative method of handling and organizing information. The following table compares the main features of the two types of thought.

---

[183] E. de Bono, "Lateral Thinking and Parallel Thinking." From Edward de Bono's authorized website, 2009, available at http://www.edwdebono.com/debono/lateral.htm

[184] E. de Bono, "Lateral Thinking and Parallel Thinking." From Edward de Bono's authorized website, 2009, available at http://www.edwdebono.com/debono/lateral.htm

| LATERAL THINKING | VERTICAL THINKING |
|---|---|
| Richness | Rightness |
| A probabilistic process | A finite process |
| Generative and Provocative | Selective and analytical |
| Unstructured: makes deliberate jumps | Structured: one thing must follow another |
| Looks for what is different – for as many approaches as possible | Looks for what is right – for the one right approach |
| Welcomes chance intrusions and imagination | Focuses on relevance |
| Explores the least likely directions/paths | Explores only the most obvious directions/paths |
| Proceeds to generate new different directions and patterns | Proceeds only if there is a direction, within established patterns |
| Flows in a non-sequential and free manner | Moves forward by sequential and justified steps |
| 'One moves for the sake of moving'* | One moves for 'a clearly defined direction, towards the solution of a problem'* |

Figure 96: Lateral versus Vertical Thinking Defined by E. de Bono

The contrast that emerges is a theoretical aid to ease the explanation and understanding of these two concepts. In reality, the two types of thinking are complementary and belong to a single continuum of human thought.

Lateral thinking is about finding new ways of seeing things, about moving away from established patterns and changing preconceived ideas, conceptions, and assumptions. It looks for what is different rather than right or "wrong," good or bad, positive or negative, and it analyzes ideas and thoughts to generate new ones. In contrast to vertical marketing, which looks for absolutes, always seeking justifications and faults, only concerned with continuity and what is right.

## 5.4.5 "Sur/petition"

The concept of "sur/petition," was developed by E. de Bono in 1993 to emphasize that just being able to compete in your market is no longer enough. There is definitely a need to keep up with the marketplace and competition, but that will not suffice. Companies will (if they do not already) have to deliver more "integrated value" to their overall offer, increase differentiation and uniqueness in all aspects, and develop new creative marketing initiatives. To better understand the concept, let's define it and compare it to competition.

# CHAPTER 5 — MARKETHINK

Competition is for survival. Competition is the key ingredient in free-market economics, and its purpose is to benefit the consumer: keeping prices down and quality up, but also increasing the quantity of goods and services, giving consumers more choices to fit their needs. Competition puts pressure on the whole organization because being competitive is essential for maintenance and for ensuring the baseline of survival.

Sur/petition, on the other hand, is for success. Sur/petition is concerned with how you move upward from the baseline. Physical monopolies are illegal in many countries, but value monopolies are not. Value's monopolies are for the benefit of the producers, and are also in the interests of consumers. In today's value-based economics, sur/petition and "integrated value monopolies" are very much in the general economic interest.

In his book *Sur/petition*, E. de Bono discusses "how competition will no longer be enough in the future and why there will be a need to shift to sur/petition. The word competition means 'seeking together.' This means accepting that you are running in the same race as your competitors. Your behavior is quite largely determined by the behavior of the competitors. Sur/petition means 'seeking above' or creating your own race. It means creating new 'value's monopolies, based on 'integrated values.' For example, a car is no longer just a lump of engineering. The integrated values include the ability to buy, sell, and insure the car. They include safety and security against theft. Integrated values also include the ability to park in cities."[185]

"Competing is joining everybody's race, it's like being trapped in a rats' race. Sur/peting means creating your own racing track".[186]

Sur/petition is all about entering the "third phase of business." Business started by being a product or a service, then it became all about competition (being and staying competitive). Today it must be more than that: it must be about "integrated values."[187]

As we have mentioned, E. de Bono is the author of over seventy books, each with valuable insights, but for the purpose of our MarkeThink process, we suggest the following selection, other than the ones previously covered:

- *Serious Creativity*
- *The Mechanism of Mind*
- *The Six Action Shoes*
- *The Six Value Medals*
- *I Am Right, You Are Wrong: From This to the New Renaissance: From Rock Logic to Water Logic*
- *Atlas of Management Thinking*

---

185 From a 1992 passage of *Serious Creativity*, by Edward de Bono. Found at http://www.edwarddebono.com/PassageDetail.php?passage_id=72&

186 By Carlo Scodanibbio on his World Class (Lean) Performance in the SME website. Retrieved from http://www.scodanibbio.com/site/access/homeaccess/31.html

187 From a 1992 passage of *Serious Creativity*, by Edward de Bono. Found at http://www.edwarddebono.com/PassageDetail.php?passage_id=72&

## 5.6 Palo Alto School: From Palo Alto to Arezzo

*"Good practice does not exist without good theory."* - Leonardo da Vinci

*A special thank you goes to Professor Giorgio Nardone and Roberta Milanese for the following article.*

The art of changing problematic situations through strategic interventions that generate virtuous circles where vicious circles were in place has existed since the dawn of time; therefore, it goes without saying that *strategic problem solving* interventions are certainly not a novelty. At this point we have to emphasize that the use of the term *"strategic problem solving,"* here, refers to a particular model of problem solving that is based on a specific, highly advanced epistemology and logic that distinguishes it from other models. There is a well-known Islamic story that helps understanding the premises of *strategic logic* and the role a *strategic problem solver* should cover.

It is told that, at his death, Ali Baba left an inheritance of 39 camels to his four sons, with the stipulation that: half go to his eldest son, a quarter to his second son, an eighth to his third son, and a tenth to his youngest son. The four sons immediately started an intense argument: how could it be possible to divide 39 camels in that manner? While the sons were animatedly discussing how to solve their dilemma, a Sufi - wandering sage - happened to pass by on his camel. He listened to their problem, and decided to help them, so he got off his camel and added it to the 39 others. Then, as the brothers looked in astonishment, he started to divide the camels: 20 to the eldest, 10 to the second, 5 to the third, and 4 to the youngest. He, then, got back on his camel and rode away, leaving the brothers bewildered.

You might be left wondering, just like the four brothers, if the division of the camels was made possible by magical intervention. The fact is that the wise man did not perform any kind of magic, he simply applied rigorous mathematical logic by adding a *variable:* "X" (as is in mathematical equations) in order to make, an otherwise, impossible operation possible. At the end of this operation, all he did was to take the "X" variable back (his camel).

This rigorous type of logic makes it possible to provide a simple solution to an apparently complicated problem that would otherwise seem impossible to solve, especially from the traditional perspective of Aristotelian logic, which relies on the premises of "true or false" or "no third value."

We think that the story of the 39 camels is a great metaphor to illustrate what the attitude of a strategic problem solver should be; just like the wandering sage in the story, a modern *technician of change* sets out to reach an objective, applies his tools and professional skills and then, having started the change process that will lead the system to evolve, he takes them back. However, the problem solver's strategies are not the product of a sudden spur of creativity, but rather based on applying a precise and rigorous logical model of intervention.

One of the features that distinguishes strategic logic from the traditional types of logic is that it provides the possibility to develop models of intervention based on preset objectives and the specific characteristics of the problem at hand, rather than on rigid, pre-constituted theories. In other words, they do not blindly follow some rigid, deterministic perspectives that dictate how to proceed and [intend] to provide, a priori, an exhaustive description of the phenomena at hand.

Their approach has its roots in modern constructivist epistemology, according to which there is no ontologically "true" reality, but many subjective realities that vary according to the point of view that is adopted. They, therefore, avoid defining the nature of things, or determining a definitive, universal mode of intervention: it is always the solution that adapts to the problem and not the other way around, as in most traditional models of clinical psychology and psychotherapy. In short, strategic logic wants to be flexible and [strives] to adapt to its object of study.

We can compare the strategic problem solver to an experienced seafarer in the middle of the ocean, who tries to predict and plan his actions based on the current conditions of the sea. He needs to plan for the unexpected, and be prepared to deal with it, relying on his own "operative awareness," and not on having absolute control over events. Moreover, the seafarer does not and cannot know the deep truths contained in the sea, nor the reasons for its changes; and yet, with the limited know-how knowledge that he does have he crosses the oceans and rides out storms, constantly adapting his actions to the current developments.[188]

## 5.6.1 Strategic Therapy Model

Based on what we have said so far, the strategic therapy model is based all on the desired objectives that have to be reached. Therefore solution strategies are not the logical consequence of a normative theory about sanity or insanity, nor are they the logical consequence of a process that defines reality in light of previous knowledge; but the take into account the characteristics of the problem to be solved and goal to reach.

The strategic problem solver possesses a series of flexible tactics and tools that can be adjusted to the different cases at hand; they do not invent the model of intervention from scratch every time, but are able, based on experience, to select the strategies they consider most adequate for solving the type of problem and reaching the specific objective presented. It is important to note that although the strategic

---

[188] G. Nardone, 1991, "Suggestione + Ristrutturazione = Cambiamento. L'approccio strategico e costruttivista alla terapia breve." Giuffrè, Milan

therapy model is rigorous and systematic, it also has the essential characteristic of being flexible and self-correcting. It can be modified and adapted throughout its interaction with the reality to which it is applied.[189] The possibility of correcting the intervention model, according to the observed effects, takes place at every phase of the problem-solving process. This means that its effectiveness is not only measured at the beginning and the end of the process, but is evaluated after each single move and maneuver, so that the model of intervention constantly corrects itself during its application.

Just as in a game of chess, the strategy is continuously corrected and adapted based on the adversary's moves and the variations of each specific game, which makes every game unique and original. Despite the fact that the possible number of moves is limited, the combinations of moves produce an infinite number of possibilities. To understand the fundamental difference between ordinary logic and strategic logic interventions, let us imagine that we need to guess which one of the sixty-four squares of a chessboard a person is thinking about by asking the least possible number of questions.

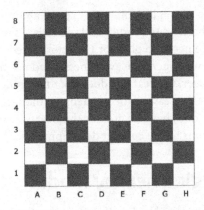

Figure 97: Chess Game Board (G. Nardone - R. Milanese)

With ordinary logic, we might have to ask up to 63 questions, since we would have to rule out every single square by asking one question at a time. If we follow strategic logic, we can guess the square by asking six questions: we start by tracing a hypothetical line along the middle of the chessboard, and ask whether the square to be guessed is on the left or right side of the board, allowing us to rule out thirty-two squares; then we trace a horizontal line and ask whether the square is on the

---

[189] G. Nardone and P. Watzlawick, 1990, "L'arte del cambiamento: manuale di terapia strategica e ipnoterapia senza trance," Ponte alle Grazie, Firenze (En. Tr. The Art of Change. Strategic Therapy and Hypnotherapy Without Trance, Jossey-Bass, San Francisco) /G. Nardon, and A. Fiorenza, 1995, "L'intervento strategico nei contesti educativi. Comunicazione e problem-solving per i problemi scolastici." Giuffrè, Milan / G. Nardone and P. Watzlawick, 1997, "Terapia breve strategica." Raffaello Cortina, Milan / G. Nardone, T. Verbitz, and R. Milanese, 1999, "Le prigioni del cibo - Vomiting Anoressia Bulimia: la terapia in tempi brevi." Ponte alle Grazie, Milan

higher or lower half of the chessboard, ruling out sixteen more squares. By proceeding this way, we eventually divide the chessboard into eight, four, and finally two squares, until we can tell exactly which square the person was thinking about. We have been able to guess correctly with only six questions.

This is a great example to illustrate a strategic intervention. Based on the belief that it is impossible to know a priori the right path to take to reach an objective, the only way is to move along that path and adapt as functionally as possible to what is perceived.

As a consequence, we can only achieve knowledge of how a problematic situation persists by intervening actively and trying to solve it. The only variable of knowledge that a researcher can control is his own strategy. If the strategy works, it enables the researcher to show the functioning of the reality that is being studied.

The concept of strategic problem solving, which is at the basis of brief therapy, is guided by this apparently simple logic. In clinical practice, this is often expressed by using stratagems, behavioral tricks, beneficial deception, and forms of refined suggestion in order to guide the subject's experiences in the direction of alternative perceptions of reality.

This type of intervention is made possible by the adoption, in the construction of strategies, of new models of logic that go beyond the Aristotelian logical principles of "true or false" and "noncontradiction."

The essential characteristics of strategic problem solving make the model logical and rigorous, but also flexible and creative, which has made it possible to successfully apply it in many different contexts, from the clinical to the educational, from interpersonal relationships to the corporate/organizational world.

The models of intervention are constructed based on objectives rather than on the instructions of a strong a priori theory.

The logic used in the construction of strategies is constitutive-deductive - not hypothetical-deductive. The solution is adapted to the problem - not the problem to the solution.

Instead of performing interventions based on the investigation of the causes of the phenomenon, they induce change through the use of stratagems.

Constant self-correction is built into the model, which allows them to avoid the continuation of attempted solutions that produce no positive results and often exacerbate the problem that they are meant to resolve.

## 5.6.2 CTS Arezzo: therapy as research, research as therapy

At this point, after having simply summarized the development of brief therapy, from its first Ericksonian rough formulations to the building of real theoretical-applied models and their following evolutions, we can go deeply into the topic of the model of advanced brief strategic-solution therapy, developed by an author at CTS in Arezzo. This work was carried out first under P. Watzlawick's supervision and then oriented by a specific methodology of research toward the formation of an advanced approach characterized by the setting up of specific protocols of treatment for particular pathologies. Since 1985, evolving by means of the empirical-experimental method, the Centro di Terapia Strategica (Strategic Therapy Center) in Arezzo, Italy, has conducted research for the development of advanced models of strategic solution-oriented brief therapy.

The key idea was to get general models of therapy developed toward specific protocols of treatment for particular pathologies, that is, fixed sequences of therapeutic maneuvers with heuristic and predictive power, capable to guide the therapist to the breaking, through particular therapeutic stratagems, the specific pathological rigidity. After this first big change, the protocols lead the perceptive-reactive system to reorganization in a functional balance. In other words, the strategy adapts itself tactic by tactic to the answers deriving from the interventions acted: as in a chess game, we proceed with an opening followed by moves that depend on how our adversary plays.

Finally, it is important to note that this model is not only effectively and efficiently, but predictive; the latter feature allows a developing practice therapeutic arts and crafts to the advanced technology, without reducing or losing that rate of artistic creativity needed in its process of constant innovation, which in this case takes place in accordance with the criterion of scientific rigor, producing a truly reliable therapy.

Once you note the peculiarities of the persistence of the problem, it will be able to use the problem-solving logic that seems most suitable, followed by applying it to the related model, adapting it to the logic and the language of the costumer. In this way, the therapeutic intervention truly keeps its capacity to adapt to every new person's peculiarities and situation, and keeps even the strategic rigor to the level of the intervention structure. To further clarify this important concept, it is useful to underline all that it is possible to rearrange is the strategy, to the level of intervention structure, which adapts to the structure of the problem and to its persistence, what always changes is the therapeutic interaction, the relationship with the patient and the type of communication used. Every maneuver is always different, but it always remains the same, because this one changes in its communicative way, but it remains the same maneuver at the level of the strategic procedure of problem solving. So we are claiming rigor but not rigidity.

## 5.6.3 Introduction to Stratagems: Strategic Therapy Advanced techniques

As the reader may have noticed earlier in this chapter, this strategy has many things in common with the ancient Chinese art of stratagems, as well as with techniques of rhetorical persuasion. Both these technical fields of knowledge are based on the idea that, in order to obtain a quick and effective change, people must be led to change their attitudes of perception and reaction without realizing it. Any tricks employed are not revealed until after the change has occurred. To produce this unconscious "leap," these ancient arts (like our own approach to brief therapy) make use of existing resources already contained within the reality to be changed, by applying specific maneuvers that mobilize these resources into a process that inevitably leads to change.

The innovative work carried out at the School of Palo Alto in Arezzo, guided by Professor G. Nardone, has led to the successful application of the strategic problem solving model in many corporations as well as profit and nonprofit organizations.[190] The application of strategic problem solving allows unblocking and enhancing teamwork and resulting outcomes. Of all the well-known contributions of the school of Palo Alto, we are most interested in the strategic model for our MarkeThink process (discussed in the last part of the book) is the use of strategies and stratagems that allow to approach problems differently and to see and generate new successful ideas and solutions or opportunities.

The use of strategies and stratagems:
a. To unlock people and allow them to get into a performance state of mind
b. To stop the recurring "attempted solutions" that worsen the problem and its persistence
c. To sell products or persuade and motivate people to achieve their personal or professional goals, for the good of everyone concerned

---

190 For further infomation on the subject, see G. Nardone, R. Milanese, R. Mariotti, and A. Fiorenza, 2000, "La terapia dell'azienda malata," Ponte alle Grazie, Milan, and R. Prato Previde, R. Milanese, and M. C. Nardone, 2012, "L'azienda vincente: Migliorare il presente, inventare il futuro: problem solving per le organizzzioni," Ponte alle Grazie

## 5.7 "CreActivity" by Massimo Soriani Bellavista

*"The creative creates a lot, but carries out little: he thinks a hundred things, but carries out only one (when all goes well). If we talk about creActivity, with a 'C', things change completely. The creActive thinks a hundred things, and carries out a hundred things. The 'creActive' ideas, since their birth, have a high chance of success. In order to be 'creActive' you cannot limit yourself to just having good ideas. Ideas need to be extraordinary, exceptional." - Claudio Ciaravolo*

*"Creativity is 1 percent inspiration, 99 percent perspiration" - Thomas Edison*

### Creativity is not enough... CreActivity is

In the wonderful article of 1963, "Creativity Is Not Enough," the great Theodore Levitt wrote: "'Creativity' is not the miraculous road to business growth and affluence that is so abundantly claimed these days...This is because they tend to confuse the getting of ideas with their implementation - that is, confuse creativity in the abstract with practical innovation; not understand the operating executive's day-to-day problems and underestimate the intricate complexity of business organizations."[191]

Having worked for more than twenty years in consulting and training in business creativity, I found myself in full agreement with the reflection of Theodore Levitt: to survive and thrive, companies cannot be based just on creativity; in order to make extraordinary products/services, companies must gather funds, look for the right people, make some prototypes to be tested in the market, and sell the ideas with their implementation.

I have called this ability to implement ideas "CreActvity." Here, I will present a summary of the model, which is analyzed in the book that I'm about to publish in Italian: *La CreAttività (CreActivity)*.

### 5.7.1 CreActivity

CreActivity is based on two constructs:

a) Phases and types
b) The process

### a) Phases and Types

The different phases that Theodore Levitt developed are "creativity" an "innovation"; I extended my model to three steps:

---

[191] Levitt, T. 1963 article, "Creativity Is Not Enough," published in the *Harvard Business Review*, republished in the August 2002 issue

1. Inventiveness: the creative phase, having the idea
2. Innovation: the implementation of the idea
3. Entrepreneurship: turning the innovation into corporate success (both profit and nonprofit entrepreneurship)

The inventiveness phase is focused on the business idea; the innovation phase is concerned with the implementation of the idea; while the entrepreneurship phase is linked to the creation of value. The three phases are very important, and they require the application of different ways of thinking and different techniques.

In brief, in order to assess whether an organization is more CreActive than another, I will analyze the three phases with these parameters:

1. Inventiveness
2. Number of ideas
3. Quality of ideas
4. Innovation
5. Number of ideas implemented
6. Quality of the ideas implemented
7. Entrepreneurship
8. Economic impact (profit sector) or social impact (nonprofit sector)
9. Strategic impact

## b) CreActivity as a process

In the figure below we can see what the process of CreActvity looks like.

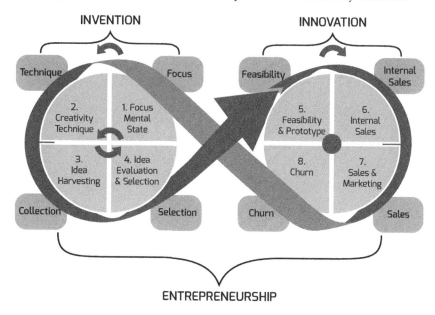

Figure 98: The CreActivity Process and the Three Phases by Massimo Soriani Bellavista

# MARKETHINK — CHAPTER 5

The process is divided in eight phases, which are not always in sequential order and sometimes vary based on the situation or sector, or on the type of creative production. The first four concern the invention phase, the last four represent the innovation phase, and all eight are part of the entrepreneurial process. We will describe in detail the eight phases in the next chapter, where we will illustrate the process of "Markethink" (as you will see, the process of Markethink is based on the model of Creactivity by M. Soriani Bellavista).

# CHAPTER 6 — MARKETHINK

# MarkeThinking Styles

**PART TWO**

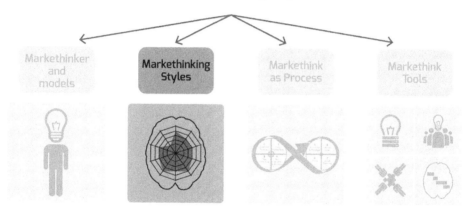

MarkeThinking Style

# Chapter 6
# MarkeThinking Styles

## 6.1 The Seven (Plus Three) Brains-Pearls of a MarkeThinker: 10 CommandMents

> *"These are the actions that count. Our thoughts, however good they may be, are false pearls until they are turned into actions. Be the change you wish to see in the world."* - Mahatma Gandhi

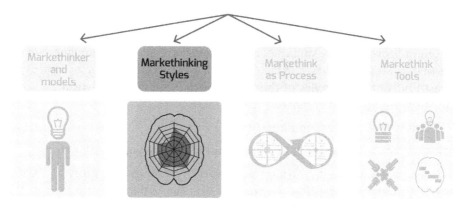

Figure 99: MarkeThinking Style - The Ten Commandments

It is recognized, in the field of marketing, that the SWOT analysis is a concrete and practical tool for marketing analysis; the SWOT analysis premise is to analyze a business or a market through the use of different thinking styles sequentially:

Strengths = Value
Weakness = Risk
Opportunities = Opportunities
Threats = Risk

It is essential for many methods to reach their full potential to create a link, or a connection, between the thinking styles, the phases, and the goals.

MarkeThink is a broad conceptual framework; each one of the 10 tools focuses on the MarkeThink thinking style profile. The MarkeThink thinking styles are inspired by various conceptual models; these include the model developed by Cicero, more than two thousand years ago, on the rules of rhetoric; the psychological model of the Hermann Method, which is based on the differentiation of thinking styles (starting from a different setting); from brainstorming, which divided the creative phase by phase evaluation; from the TRIZ model by Altshuller to the early work on brainstorming and Tony Buzan's mind mapping and the lateral thinking developed by Edward de Bono. Massimo Soriani Bellavista wants to state that there is a big difference between the MarkeThink and the great tool that is the six thinking hats. The "MarkeThink thinking style" profile developed by Massimo Soriani Bellavista is a psychometric measurement of the differences of thought. A process very similar method to Hermann's brain dominance; a classification of thinking styles; the "six thinking hats" method is a general tool, where it is not expressly stated that a person wear a "Green Hat" (creative) or a "Black Hat" (negative risks and dangers), but rather in every person there is each of the six types of thought. From our point of view, the "six thinking hats" method is a complementary tool to strengthen the thinking styles in a "brain gym" logic. In fact, if according to the styles of thought MarkeThink test there is a predominance of organizational thinking rather than creative, thanks to the 6 hats to think with you can improve creative thinking, as well as all other types of thought. We believe that "six thinking hats" and lateral thinking are excellent tools for improving at least four of the ten styles of thinking: creative thinking, analytical thinking, evaluation thinking and organizational thinking.

How it works 10 Markethinking Styles:

We would like to explain how Markethinking styles works with a story:

"In Polynesia, the oyster farmers use a special technique for growing natural pearls within the oysters; after they have caught the oysters they tie them all together:

# CHAPTER 6　　　　　　　　　　　　　　　　　　　　MARKETHINK

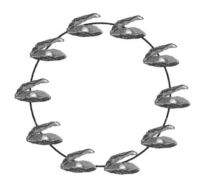

Figure 100: Tying the oysters together technique

This technique consists of tying ten oysters together and throwing them back into the sea; in the tropics the coral reef is about two to three meters deep with calm waters. Assuming that an oyster is able to move a meter per day, they could potentially move three hundred to four hundred meters away from where they were dropped. But, when the oystermen return, after one year, the oysters are two to three meters away from where they had left them. Why do you think that is? The reason is very easy to understand; in fact, if nothing keeps them together, every oyster goes about its business, which leads to the situation we can see below. They scatter:

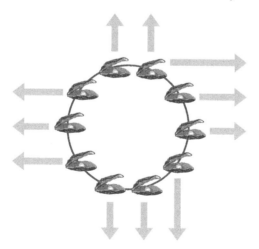

Figure 101: The Oysters' Energies Are Cancelled

More specifically, each one goes its own way, cancelling the energies and remaining stationary (we call this the locked state). How could the oysters save their pearls?

They could all go in the same direction for three months, then in another direction for two and so on:

217

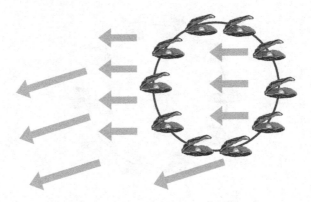

Figure 102: If the Oysters Go in the Same Direction, They Will Go Farther

By doing this, the distance they would cover in a year would definitely be much higher than two to three meters.

The same thing happens to our brains when we try to do everything simultaneously - we create the idea, but at the same time, we try to assess the risks and benefits, understand how to put it into practice, and even express the emotions evoked by the idea. In short, we seek to pursue too many goals at the same time. This way of proceeding *blocks* our creativity; instead of bringing us to the solution, we remain still, just like the oysters that remain stuck in the same place for months.

For cultural reasons, we are used to discussing and focusing on the discordant aspects of things, ideas, or situations. The predominant logic of "I'm right, you're wrong" remains strong at the expense of creativity (searching for solutions) - antagonistic thinking versus parallel thinking.

The concept of parallel thinking was a very important discovery in the field of human thought (in this logic there is a big difference between a discovery and an invention; in fact a discovery presumes that there is a know-how that hasn't been revealed or conceptualized by someone). The early theories of parallel thinking can be referred to the tools of rhetoric developed by Cicerone; this method, in fact, divides the use of thought in the various stages of speech into phases: inventio, *dispositio*, *elocutio*, *actio*, memoria (inventio=creation, *dispositio*=organization and evaluation, etc.). In the field of creativity, the first major contribution came from Osborn, the father of brainstorming. With his technique, he separates the creative phase from the evaluation phase; in the field of creativity many others have separated and differentiated the thinking phases. In the marketing field, as we have already mentioned, the SWOT Analysis (strengths, weaknesses, etc.) segments the thinking types functional to marketing. Perhaps one of the most important works that formalized this concept is the work that established the fundamentals of the six thinking hats method parallel thinking developed and presented by E. de Bono in 1985.

# CHAPTER 6 — MARKETHINK

Parallel thinking is the model at the center of the six thinking hats method, and despite its extreme simplicity, it's one of the most important conceptual contributions in the field of managerial thinking. Working in recent years with marketing managers and entrepreneurs, M. Soriani Bellavista has noticed that the parallel thinking model can be expanded to the various types of thinking that are essential to excel as a marketer (communications, speed reading, memory, creativity , etc.). In addition to this reflection, there are other ways of thinking that in our opinion need to be separated - namely the addition of motivation and its importance, as well as the ability to learn and self-teach the skills on how to best communicate and sell your idea, solution, or project (see other models presented in this book such as TRIZ, etc.).

So here are the seven (plus three) brains explained, or as we also like to call them "The Ten Command*ments* of MarkeThink." Why Commandments? There's no action to be done, rather principles, concepts, topics, and "key words" that open the doors of Markethink!

**M**otivation
**A**nalysis
Oppo**R**tunities
Ris**K**
Valu**E**
Crea**T**ivity
**H**igh Organization
Learn**I**ng
Commu**N**ication
Practical Thin**K**ing

We are all able to use the ten commandments, or thinking styles. Generally we tend to have a preference for two to three thinking styles, and we typically have two or three styles that are our weak points. In the representation below, this MarkeThinker is strong in seizing the value, with a strong sense of organization - he could therefore be a person who plans and works countless hours on his project but rarely puts things into action; he is a well-organized and motivated dreamer.

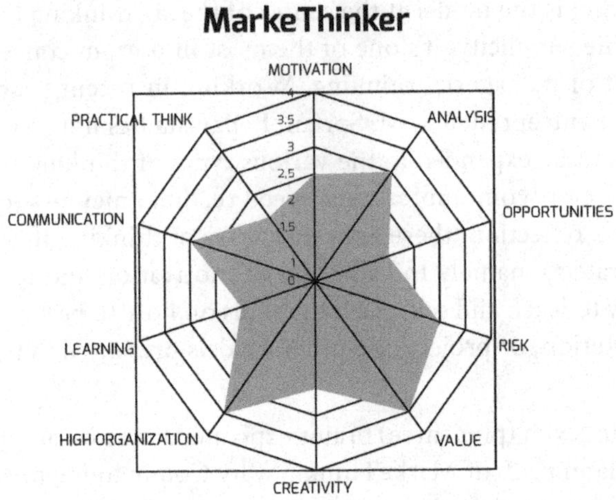

# MARKETHINK — CHAPTER 6

**MarkeThinker**

Figure 103: The Analysis of a MarkeThinker - Rainbow Thinking (10 commandments?)

A growth or development plan will be elaborated on based on the gap that exists between the strong-dominant and the weak-critical thinking styles.

The results of the dominance of thought test will generally show that there is a gap, that there are shortcomings in a person's or team's thinking process. At this point there are two possible paths to follow to become a great MarkeThinker (there is also a third one that integrates the two other paths that will be covered later on).

The first path is concerned with the development of the person as an individual. It is about adopting a thinking-style development plan that integrates training, coaching, and in-the-field professional experience, with the clear objective of strengthening the various thinking styles, paying particular attention to the weaker areas, and aligning one's skills to the actual position or the desired role one wants to cover workwise.

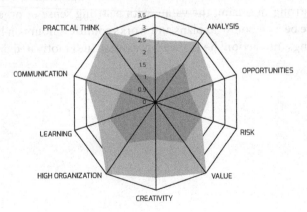

Figure 104: Gap of Thinking Styles

# CHAPTER 6　　　　　　　　　　　　　　　　　　　MARKETHINK

In fact, in the example above, we can see that there is a clear gap in the person's thinking styles to successfully cover the role of chief of direct marketing. Based on the results and the individual's specific needs, we would choose to enhance a maximum of two thinking styles; in fact, to try to enhance all of them would be extremely expensive and time consuming. We would proceed by strengthening and developing the critical skills aggressively - the person's weakest styles that are needed for that specific position, and possibly approach another specific area in a defensive manner. For example, based on the graph above, we could choose to strengthen communication and/or creativity, and maybe proceed to compensate the gap in practical thinking.

The second path focuses on strengthening the team as a whole, specifically its thinking ability and power - the MasterThink Mind Group. In his wonderful book *Think and Grow Rich*, Napoleon Hill presented the "power of the master mind,"[192] a brilliant principle that he considers to be central to a person's success. He defines the "master mind" as the "coordination of knowledge and effort, in a spirit of harmony, between two or more people, for the achievement of an established purpose" (N. Hill 2013, p. 154). In this power chapter what is key is to create a team and surround oneself with people who have commonalities - shared values and interests - and who have complementary skills and competences. In fact, N. Hill understood that it is much easier to enhance one's power as a MarkeThinker by joining forces with others instead of developing and boosting every single thinking area alone. We obviously completely adhere to this idea since it is the starting point to the second path, where we will work hard on the creation of MarkeThinker Mind Groups.

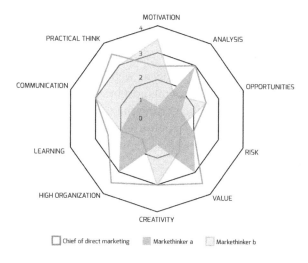

Figure 105: The Master Mind MarkeThinker

---

192　In chapter 10 "The Power of the Master Mind: The Driving Force," pp. 153–159

Consider the following: you are a very creative MarkeThinker but have significant organizational shortcomings. The energy and resources that have to be invested for you to reach a satisfactory level of organization are considerably high. Instead, we would integrate a person with the team who is a strong organizer to create a winning team of MarkeThinkers. The goal is to create the "dream team" of MarkeThinkers with different thinking styles that can and will work in winning combinations and will combine with and compensate for each other perfectly. In the example above we have two MarkeThinkers, each with their strong and weak areas, who together manage to compensate for and *heighten their richness of thought*.

The story of successful companies, particularly those with an entrepreneurial array and in their initial phase, is often made up of two individuals; take, for example, Apple, which was founded by two very complementary characters, S. Jobs and S. Wozniak, or Microsoft by B. Gates and P. Allen, Google by S. Brin and L. Page, Hewlett-Packard (well, the name says it all). This "alliance of the brains" (masterminds) has given way to the creation of some of the most important and influential entrepreneurial business empires.

Figure 106: Successful Duos - S. Brin and L. Page, B. Gates and P. Allen and S. Wozniak and S. Jobs

The evaluation of one's thinking style, as well as the team's, can be carried out with the use of various tools. The first and most basic one is our online test, whereas the advanced version involves integrating the test with evolved methodologies, typical of assessment centers, such as one-on-one interviews, and group dynamics. You will find a more detailed description of our different approaches in the MarkeThink Tools chapter.

Now let's take a look at thinking styles, one at a time.

## 6.2 First Commandment - Motivation: "Stay Hungry"

> *"Everyone needs something to aim for. You can call it a challenge, or you can call it a goal. It is what makes us human. It was challenges that took us from being cavemen to reaching for the stars." - R. Branson*

> *"Stay Hungry, Stay Foolish"*[193]

In his historic UCLA commencement ceremony speech, which we strongly recommend, S. Jobs said many very important things, and spoke about one in particular: passion and the love for what you do. "You've got to find what you love. And that is as true for your work as it is for your lovers. Your work is going to fill a large part of your life, and the only way to be truly satisfied is to do what you believe is great work. And the only way to do great work is to love what you do."[194]

To truly love what you do, passion and motivation are essential, because they will both particularly affect and influence one's state of mind with which we will deal with and approach problems and solutions. It's the motivation that drives us to overcome our failures and turn them into successes.

In the *I-Ching* the first hexagram is "Ch'ien," the Creative Principle, which is described as follows:[195] "*Judgment:* The Creative works sublime success, furthering through perseverance."

Figure 107: The Ch'ien "creative" *I Ching* Hexagram

According to Confucius, "Great indeed is the generating power of the Creative; all beings owe their beginning to it. This power permeates all heaven". He further

---

193 From the prepared text, "You've Got to Find What You Love," of the commencement address delivered by Steve Jobs, CEO of Apple Computer and of Pixar Animation Studios, on June 12, 2005. *Stanford Report*, June 14, 2005. You can find it at http://news.stanford.edu/news/2005/june15/jobs-061505.html

194 From the commencement address by Steve Jobs, on June 12, 2005, at Stanford University. *Stanford Report*, June 14, 2005.

195 R. Wilhelm and C. Baynes, 1950, *I Ching or Book of Changes (Arkana)*, translation. Princeton, NJ: Princeton University Press. All the information regarding the *I Ching* is available at http://deoxy.org/iching/1

explains, "The beginning of all things lays still in the beyond in the form of ideas that have yet to become real."[196]

The stories of many creative entrepreneurs and marketing managers are primarily linked to their personal motivations.

## 6.2.2 Second Commandment - Learning

> *"Learn as though you would never be able to master it;*
> *hold it as though you would be in fear of losing it." - Confucius*

Right now, while reading this book, you are putting into practice the "learning "thinking strategy. In other words you are reading to learn something for your professional or personal dreams and desires. Every year, thousands of marketing books and tens of thousands of articles are published each year in print and on the web. Learning is essential for a creative marketer (or any other professional); a marketer's success is strongly linked to his learning ability and his disposition to self-teaching.

It is this *self*-learning concept that we want to dig a little dipper into. It is true that the systems of formal education and other institutions - primary and secondary, undergraduate, and graduate school are a few examples - are essential (in fact, two of the three authors have taught in these institutions). But it is equally true that self-learning is the key that allows you to turn your knowledge into opportunities; in fact most successful marketers have strong entrepreneurial roots (Steve Jobs, Bill Gates, Benetton, etc.) and don't have any kind of degree, or just an *honoris causa*. The reason behind this phenomenon is brought up by the self-learning component, which is structured on two levels:

a) Motivation toward self-teaching
b) Strategies to enhance the quality and quantity of learning

Motivation toward self-teaching is closely tied to the motivational component previously mentioned. We will not go in depth, but we will quote a passage from S. Jobs's speech that says it all:[197]

"And much of what I stumbled into by following my curiosity and intuition turned out to be priceless later on. Let me give you one example:

Reed College at that time offered perhaps the best calligraphy instruction in the country. Throughout the campus every poster, every label on every drawer, was beautifully hand calligraphed. Because I had dropped out and didn't have to take the normal classes, I decided to take a calligraphy class to learn how to do this. I learned about serif and sans serif typefaces, about varying the amount of space between dif-

---

[196] R. Wilhelm and C. Baynes, 1950, *I Ching* or *Book of Changes (Arkana)*, translation. Princeton, NJ: Princeton University Press. All the information regarding the *I Ching* is available at http://deoxy.org/iching/1

[197] From the commencement address by Steve Jobs, on June 12, 2005, at Stanford University. *Stanford Report*, June 14, 2005. You can find it at http://news.stanford.edu/news/2005/june15/jobs-061505.html

ferent letter combinations, about what makes great typography. It was beautiful, historical, artistically subtle in a way that science can't capture, and I found it fascinating.

None of this had even a hope of any practical application in my life. But ten years later, when we were designing the first Macintosh computer, it all came back to me. And we designed it all into the Mac. It was the first computer with beautiful typography. If I had never dropped in on that single course in college, the Mac would have never had multiple typefaces or proportionally spaced fonts. And since Windows just copied the Mac, it's likely that no personal computer would have them. If I had never dropped out, I would have never dropped in on this calligraphy class, and personal computers might not have the wonderful typography that they do. Of course it was impossible to connect the dots looking forward when I was in college. But it was very, very clear looking backward ten years later."

## Strategies to Enhance One's Self-learning Ability

M. Soriani Bellavista has taught for the past twenty years the strategies for fast learning, and particularly the best self-learning strategies for reading and memorization.

## Reading Strategies

Quantity intended as speed: a good reader reads about two hundred words per minute; with a quick training course (a few days), one can learn to double or even triple their reading speed and get to four hundred to six hundred words per minute; through advanced techniques such as speed and fluidity, and others, one can also reach higher speeds, and therefore a higher quantity of material.

Quality intended as understanding: Massimo Soriani Bellavista said: "I'm still amazed that in these twenty years the vast majority of people asked me for speed reading course, and very few on how to increase the level of comprehension." Our view is that understanding is more important than speed; consider that the level of understanding of a good reader is on average 30 percent. Therefore, to efficiently read and effectively understand a text, a good reader should dedicate to it more or less three times the duration he would normally spend reading. With speed reading courses, you can increase your understanding of a text by 80 to 90 percent.

### Quantity x Quality = Performance

|  | Speed | Comprehension | Coefficient (Speed x comprehension/ 100) |
|---|---|---|---|
| Good reader | Average 200 word per minute | 30 % | 60 |
| After a good course | Average 500 word per minute | 70 % | 350 |
| Increase | 200-300 % | 100 % | 500-600 % |

Figure 108: In summary, a well-executed course can lead to a significant increase in the rate of coefficient of reading from 500 percent to 1000 percent.

What advantage does all this give a MarkeThinker? Well, consider that being creative and reading only one book in the course of the year will be very different from being creative and reading hundreds of books of marketing a year.

## Memorization Strategies

Sadly, in a year, you will be left with only a 2 to 5 percent of memory recall of what you are now reading in this book - your memory will have declined by about 95 percent during this time, unless you are proactive and dedicate time to reviewing the material and to specific memory-training exercises. In fact, even those who have had the opportunity to read P. Kotler's *Marketing Management* manual (or any other manual) will remember, in the following years, on average only 2 to 5 percent of the text.[198]

Through training, in only a few days, it is possible to learn the strategies used by rhetoricians of ancient Greece more than two thousand years ago, and integrate them with modern techniques to potentially reach up to 60 to 70 percent greater memory recall performance. "Reading Like Leonardo" is a reading method invented by M. Soriani Bellavista that allows for the integration and combination of speed reading, increased comprehension, higher memory performance, and a more creative interpretation.[199]

## Self-Learning and Social Learning: Internet and Marketing

A revolution in self-learning is being led by the World Wide Web. Just think of all the search engines and online databases. You can watch almost anything on YouTube: speeches, visual explanations (try searching for Edward de Bono's or Philip Kotler's speeches). You can even build your own personal newspaper based on your specific interests through RSS feeds, and not least all developments led by the e-learning platforms integrated with social media. This revolution will ultimately force all universities involved in marketing training and education to transform their ways of teaching. This is and will always be the revolution of self-teaching and social learning for a marketer.

The learning opportunities today are nothing short of groundbreaking. Today you can structure, after assessing an individual's skills and interests, a personalized plan to develop and enhance his or her knowledge. On this book's website - www.markethink.guru - you will be able to discover the contents of this book through films, testimonies, e-learning platforms, and tutorials, and you will have access to our database of marketing innovations.

---

198 This is a spur made by P. Kotler, where he suggests that one should always read the latest edition of his famous *Marketing Management* manual in order to stay up to date and not fall behind the evolutions and innovations in the marketing field. It fits perfectly with the fact that people remember little of what they have read only a month ago...now imagine after a few years have gone by!

199 For more information concerning Reading like Leonardo, please visit Creattività's website at: *www.creattivita.it*

## 6.2.3. Third Commandment - Communication

> *"The biggest problem is not to let people accept new ideas, but to let them forget the old one." - J. M. Keynes*

The power to communicate and sell your marketing idea within and outside your organization is essential - the key for a marketer to succeed. There are two communication skills that marketers must master:

a. Clear communication - to be understood, by all, not a few
b. Persuasive communication - to change the auditor's mind, to convince the non-believers

### Clear Communication

Very often people underestimate the power of being able to speak in a simple and straight-to-the-point manner. *Speaking in* specialized terms (brand, positioning, segmentation, market share, impression, etc.) *will allow professionals from the same background to understand you, but might hinder the comprehension of* other professional backgrounds (consider that the CEO or CFO might not have marketing knowledge). In fact, the marketer has to know how to "translate" the message they want to communicate based on who the decision maker is, and not to expect them to be the ones to adapt. Knowing how to make a PowerPoint presentation in ten slides to explain marketing strategy in a simple and understandable manner is very rare, but is fundamental for the success of an idea or the reach of a message.

It is important to speak the public's language, to relate to them by using simple accessible words, to listen to them - what they ask, what their body language says - and to put yourself in their shoes.

### Persuasive Communication

Having and dominating persuasive communication is crucial for a marketer. Usually how something is being said is much more important than what is being said. The power of persuasion will allow the marketer, or any other person for that matter, to do the following:

1. Convince decision makers of the marketing budget
2. Negotiate with suppliers to get the best and most innovative solutions possible
3. Negotiate the purchase prices of spaces, media, distribution, etc.
4. Motivate employees to give their best at all times
5. Collaborate with those in sales and other departments
6. Convince the headhunter that you are the right person for that company and for that specific project
7. Convince an audience of investors to go with your idea, or convince them of its viability (venture capitalists or private equity firms or a bank)

8. Convince a publisher to publish your own book about marketing

History is full of stories of successful people who had this ability, as well as people who did not have this capability. Steve Jobs has devoted a great deal of time to presentations of his products, even months. He spent whole days to do the tests before the launch of its innovations. He knew the importance of communication and this shows that he knew perfectly how to communicate and how to approach people. When the founder of Swatch, Nicolas Hayek, had to convince Swiss Bankers to finance his entrepreneurial initiative in the field of watchmaking (of which he had no experience) he made use exclusively of his ability to communicate. Internal sales, as we will later see, are very important for marketers because they need to convince decision makers, leaders, teams, and even whole departments of their idea's value. The fundamental competencies required for sales are as follows:

- Verbal
- Nonverbal
- Static
- Dynamic
- Paraverbal

Borrowing from the ancient rhetoric of Cicero, in the last few years, M. Soriani Bellavista has developed a model to sell and communicate ideas called IDEAM™.[200]

- *Inventio* - knowing what to say. The creativity/invention phase is the brainstorming phase, where we find ideas on what we want to communicate, keeping in mind the goal and target to convince.
- *Dispositio* - the actual lineup of your speech.
- *Elocutio* - the style and metaphors used to communicate the concept, selecting what image to use, determining the colors and key points for the presentation or PowerPoint or whatever else. When S. Jobs wanted to communicate the lightness of the new laptop during its presentation, he put it in an envelope and opened it in front of everyone; this also added some drama to the message.
- *Actio* - Nonverbal communication, considering and focusing on the use of space during the speech as well as all body movement, eye contact, and control the voice (its pitch and level).
- *Memoria* - memorizing the highlights and key points of a speech (with a mind map or mnemonics) so that you can focus your attention on your audience and not have to read your notes.

M. Soriani Bellavista and his team at Creattività have taught hundreds of people this method of persuasive communication, always achieving great results due to the simplicity and effectiveness of the instrument (if it has been used for the past two thousand years, there must be a reason).

---

[200] For more information concerning the IDEAM Framework, please visit Creattività's website at *www.creattivita.it*

## 6.2.4 Fourth Commandment - Creativity

### Lateral Thinking

Thanks to E. de Bono's studies we know that our brain works schematically and is oriented to search for patterns. Creative thinking, on the other hand, is a type of asymmetrical thinking; in fact, in order to better stimulate creative thinking, we need to follow patterns that are seemingly paradoxical that can lead to logical solutions. For this we will use lateral thinking as a strategy that pushes us outside our mental schemes and allows us to break boundaries and create new, logical, and valuable patterns.

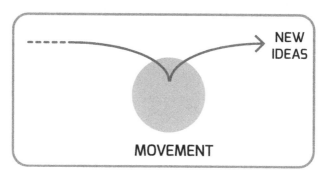

Figure 109: PO Lateral Movement Dislocation

### Lateral Marketing

Creative thinking is definitely a skill - a skill essential to create the "new": new markets and products and services. Strangely, though, despite the recognized importance of creativity for a marketer, the academic world gives it little consideration: the only area where structured creativity techniques, such as brainstorming, are used is in the advertisement world.

### Our Definition of Creativity in Marketing

For the past fifteen years, M. Soriani Bellavista has been teaching strategies and techniques to increase individuals' creativity; in recent years, though, he has stopped trying to give a clear-cut definition of creativity, and shifted his focus to the actual output of creativity. In a nutshell, we believe that the purpose of these techniques and tools that focus on enhancing creativity can be summarized in two key points:

a) Have more marketing ideas (quantity).
b) Have higher-quality marketing ideas (quality).

## More Marketing Ideas

*"Nothing is more dangerous than an idea, when it's the only one you have." - E. A. - Chartier*

On average, a team of five to six good managers working on solving a marketing problem in thirty minutes can find about eight to fifteen ideas. Using specific techniques, such as the six thinking hats, lateral thinking, or with other techniques or Markethinking styles you can, in the same time with the same people and focus, generate between sixty and eighty new ideas, therefore increasing idea production by 400 to 1000 percent.

### Quantity is the key to finding the right idea!

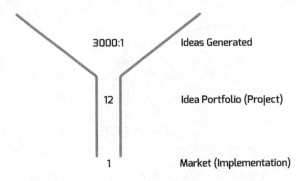

Figure 110: The Funnel of Ideas of the Du Pont Process

The Funnel of Ideas diagram above, which the interpretation of the Du Pont process extrapolated from David Tanner's "Total Creativity in Business and Industry," helps us understand the importance of having a lot of ideas from the start. To have truly innovative marketing strategies come to light, you have to start with a large number of ideas, possibilities, options, etc.

## Higher-Quality Marketing Ideas

*"The best way to get a good idea is to have lots of ideas." - L. Pauling*

We have already anticipated that quantity increases the quality of the output. But quantity alone doesn't guarantee the best quality of ideas, therefore, one can and should be stimulated by advanced creativity techniques (or through elaborate techniques such as TRIZ by Altshuller, or even the Ideabase™ of marketing innovations that we will see below).

# CHAPTER 6 — MARKETHINK

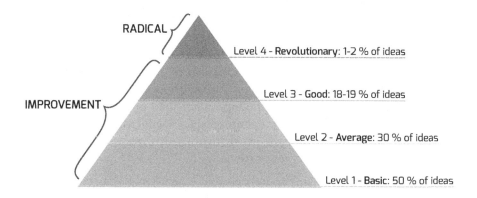

Figure 111: Value of Ideas - From Improvement to Radical Innovation

In summary, the aim of generating more ideas of higher quality is of crucial importance to its success. To help you better understand the pyramid, let us explain: If the ideas you have belong in the lower level of the pyramid, level one or two, we are talking about continuous improvement - if you change the color of a car, or use a different channel, etc. - it's for nothing that we find most of marketing improvements at this level in a mature market within the traditional marketing-mix strategies, for example.

If we look at the pyramid classification, the iPod is, according to us, a level-two innovation, since the patent already existed and they focus on its design; a level-three innovation is the rechargeable SIM card, as it modified the market by opening a new market category and satisfying new needs (Telecom market). And finally, a revolutionary (level four) innovation is the iPhone, which radically modified the world we live in.

This is even more true for ideas concerning the marketing mix (product, price, promotions, and place) and the different basic level needs; for example, at the pricing level, a discount based on the quantity purchased (if you buy ten pieces you get an x-percent discount) would be considered a level-one, maybe level-two, innovation.

An another interesting example is given by J. Welch, ex-CEO of GE, who developed the "strategic breakthrough model" to stimulate the generation of higher-level revolutionary ideas. A whole day was assigned to the "breakthrough" session, where twenty managers formed four teams with a specific mandate. In the morning the teams had a brainstorming session, and during the afternoon the ideas where presented to the whole group. At this point the managers began to criticize each one of the twelve ideas that emerged, dropping them one after the other because they were deemed "inappropriate or infeasible," except for two of them. The two ideas that showed valuable potential where carried out with great success (Kotler 2001, pp. 44-46).

As a creativity professional, my view on creativity strongly differs from that of "lateral marketing," even if I might struggle to express it here, P. Kotler and F. Trias de Bes see creativity as being differentiated between: taking place within a market (Vertical Marketing) and outside the market (Lateral Marketing), to the point that the lateral marketing allows you to create a totally new market. My vision, on the other hand, comes more from the actual practice and application of creative interventions and strategies to improve thinking, rather than pure marketing know-how where the two gurus are, for me, unreachable. My focus towards creativity relies on generating ideas at different levels that allow, even within the present market, to produce revolutionary innovations.

For example, when ING Bank in Italy created *"Conto Arancio"* it revolutionized the savings-account market in Italy with three innovations:

1. Using of most direct channels - the web and call centers
2. Offering only deposit accounts (at the beginning)
3. Differentiating itself from the standards of traditional banking advertising strategies with a very nice ad campaign

Figure 112: "Conto Arancio" - Human Billboard Campaign (ING Direct)

When an Italian follower, CheBanca (Mediobanca Group), entered the Italian market, it proposed a simple but ingenious innovation focusing on the marketing mix, with particular attention given to the price element and the associated benefits linked to it. Their innovation consisted of anticipating the interest (we will see later that this concept is based on "do it in reverse," focused on price).

1. As soon as you make a deposit, and as long as you do not withdraw any of it for a year, you immediately get the interest.
2. It created engaging and accessible spaces to accommodate clients in public spaces. Therefore it accomplished a higher level of innovation; we would say at least a level two or three, with a focus on price and place (we consider these to be two good improvement innovations).

Another example of a revolutionary innovation within the insurance sector is what Ron Barbaro[201] from Prudential Insurance created through the use of an advanced lateral thinking technique by E. de Bono called "PO - Provocative Operation." "You die before you die" is the stimulus that led him to "the hugely successful idea of 'living benefits' - if you contract a terminal illness, you benefit from 75 percent of the insurance money before you die. It resulted in a valuable innovation providing a real advantage for both the customer and the supplier: On the one hand, it made income available to the customer/patient in a critical phase of his life, allowing him to live with dignity. On the other hand, the insurance company sees a significant decrease of its premium cost. This idea was revolutionary when it was introduced, given that it didn't create a real product category (though some might say it did).

## 6.2.5 Fifth Commandment - Organization

*"The secret of all victory lies in the organization of the non-obvious." - O. Spengler*

*"Order or disorder depends on organization." - Sun Tzu*

*"Plans are of little importance, but planning is essential." - Winston Churchill*

Planning and organizing are two very important skills for a marketer to possess and master. Primarily, the ability to write a well-structured marketing plan is not something as trivial as one may think. Through the years, M. Soriani Bellavista has seen that many marketing graduates, MBAs, and professionals are having great difficulty, even to a point that they burn themselves out, when they are required to write a marketing plan. Therefore, organizational and planning capacities are essential. Furthermore, in planning, the ability to structure the implementation phases, as well as the harmonization of resources, is important to achieve the marketing plan's objectives.

"I will never forget, the marketing manager of a major multinational company that had planned an ad campaign on TV, with a toll free number but failed to consider that their call center was understaffed in the evening; the result was that almost 90 percent of prospect were lost rendering absolutely useless most of his in-

---

[201] R. Barbaro is the mind behind a great invention "Living Benefit," which refers to getting part of your life insurance premium while still alive. He invented the practice at Prudential, and it has become a worldwide industry standard. More information at *http://www.academyofachievement.org/honorees/ron_barbaro.htm*

vestment. With this type of thinking having the adequate skills in project and process management are of great support."

There are three aspects of planning that we want to recall and emphasize, because they are important to our MarkeThink process:

*Project marketing management* - when you create a marketing plan, make sure that it comprises the project management process of the implementation of said plan: who does what, when, with what resources, etc. This will make the plan more realistic, achievable, and controllable.

*Marketing process* - arrange your own marketing department, paying attention to the design of processes and the creation of KPI (key performance indicators) to measure results effectively.

*Plan for marketing innovation* - in the logic of planning and organizing, the marketing plan should allocate some time, resources, and a budget to strategies for rethinking the marketing strategy. "For me it's always been a big surprise to discover that million dollar marketing plans, there is usually NO budget for marketing innovation; whether with 'Lateral marketing', 'Markethink', 'Lovemarks' or any other, there is no consideration to innovation in marketing. If there is NO budget for marketing innovation, things will be the same as in the past years. The only difference: they will be repainted...modernized."

We will conclude by saying that an organization should allocate somewhere between 2 to 5 percent of their total marketing budget to marketing innovation.

## 6.2.6   Sixth Commandment - Data Analysis and Evaluation

*"The analysis of data will not by itself produce new ideas." - E. de Bono*

Please answer the following question, and then read on:

How were your company's/business's results last year?

If you answered by writing a number, such as income or a percentage, you used data, therefore, analytical thinking. If, on the other hand, you answered "good" or "bad" or even "the best ever," you used some other ways of thinking that we'll cover later.

When we use an analytical thinking mind-set, we speak only of numbers and facts; here our thinking is similar to Mr. Spock, the Vulcan-human hybrid of the Starship Enterprise.[202] In the world of marketing, analytical thinking focuses mainly on the following areas:

---

202 Mr. Spock is a fictional character in the world-famous *Star Trek* media franchise. He is one of the central characters in the original *Star Trek* series and movies, in which he served as the science officer and later commanding officer of the vessel.

a) Market research, both qualitative and quantitative
b) Marketing measurements and metrics: conversion rate, market share, ROS, ROI, etc.
c) Economics of the marketing plan
d) Analytical marketing tools and instruments such as data mining

Too often has M. Soriani Bellavista met marketing managers and entrepreneurs who developed their business or marketing plan using little objective data. In addition, he also found that they had a strong tendency toward mixing and confusing an objective fact with its interpretation. In other words, when we use analytic thinking, we are dealing with the following:

a) What data, facts, and information do we need, such as number of prospects, market share, percentage of loyalty, etc.? You need to know exactly what information is critical to make a decision.
b) Where do you find it, or how do you get it? It might seem to be an extremely trivial question, but is often a big problem marketers have to face.
c) How do you keep and manage the collected data? How do you add value to them or get value from them?

"Analytical intelligence involves the conscious direction of our mental processes to find a thoughtful solution to a problem. It is the ability to overcome obstacles to find a solution. Being analytically intelligent is having the ability to solve problems effectively." [203]

## 6.2.7 Seventh Commandment - Risk Assessment

*"You don't learn to walk by following rules. You learn by doing and by falling over." - R. Branson*

Being able to analyze and calculate the risks and dangers of one's actions is crucial. To illustrate this, here are the words of some great marketers:

### Bill Gates

On the topic of problems, Bill Gates says, "I believe that if you show people the problems and you show them the solutions they will be moved to act."

### Alfred Sloan

If we are all in agreement on the decision - then I propose we postpone further discussion of this matter until our next meeting to give ourselves time to develop disagreement and perhaps gain some understanding of what the decision is all

---
[203] Definition retrieved from *http://www.quintcareers.com/intelligence_quiz.html*

about. The greatest real thrill that life offers is to create, to construct, to develop something useful. Too often we fail to recognize and pay tribute to the creative spirit. It is that spirit that creates our jobs.

There has to be this pioneer, the individual who has the courage, the ambition to overcome the obstacles that always develop when one tries to do something worthwhile, especially when it is new and different. Some have an idea that the reason we in this country discard things so readily is because we have so much. The facts are exactly opposite - the reason we have so much is simply because we discard things so readily. We replace the old in return for something that will serve us better.

## Richard Branson

*"If you don't take risks you won't achieve anything."*

*"You don't learn to walk by following rules. You learn by doing and by falling over."*

One of the reasons Virgin's enterprises have been successful over the years is that we empower the staff to make mistakes and then learn from them. This ability to bounce back after a setback is the single most important trait an entrepreneurial venture can possess. If innovation is at the heart of your business, obstacles come with the territory. How you react to and navigate those hurdles will make the difference between failure and success.

## Nicolas Hayek

I never follow advice; that's because whenever I wanted to take a risk and create something new, I was advised not to do it. But I always went ahead and did it anyway.[204]

Lots of people in this company told me, "I cannot do this job of creating things." And I asked them, "When you were 6 years old and you were on vacation with your parents, playing on the beach, you had lots of fantasy. Didn't you believe in Santa Claus? Didn't you believe in fairy tales? Well, continue like this." You lose this capacity to believe in many fantastic, unreal things because of school, society, the army for men. You must motivate the people around you to overcome obstacles, to believe that they can create things.[205]

As artists, the real entrepreneurs do not opt out, they simply change function.[206]

If you are studying medicine at a big university, you will be a physician once you have finished your studies. Unhappily, it is not the same with entrepreneurs. If you send a donkey to the music school in Salzburg, you are not going to make a Mozart out of him. The same thing if you send a camel to Harvard Business School - he is

---

204 Retrieved from *http://www.jayonline.co.uk/news/best-piece-of-advice-nicolas-hayek/*
205 Retrieved from *http://magazine.wsj.com/features/behind-the-brand/time-bandit/3/*
206 Translated from a French quote he gave to "Le Nouveau Quotidien" in 1997

not going to be a genius, a Henry Ford, unless he is a born Henry Ford, and if you send him to Harvard, he will be a better Henry Ford.[207]

During an interview with William Taylor for the *Harvard Business Review*, N. Hayek shared his two most important lessons:[208]

First, it is possible to build high-quality, high-value, mass-market consumer products in high-wage countries at low cost. Notice I said *build*, not just design and sell.

We do this all the time. We agree on the performance specifications of a new product - a watch, a pager, a telephone. Then we assemble a project team. We present the team with some target economics: this is how much the product can sell for, not one penny more; this is the margin we need to support advertising, promotion, and so on. Thus these are the costs we can afford. Now go design a product and a production system that allows us to build it at those costs - in Switzerland.

The second is related to the first. You can build mass-market products in countries like Switzerland or the United States only if you embrace the fantasy and imagination of your childhood and youth. Everywhere children believe in dreams. And they ask the same question: Why? Why does something work a certain way? Why do we behave in certain ways? We ask ourselves those questions every day.

Too many of Europe's large institutions - companies, governments, unions - are as rigid as prisons. They are all steel and cement and rules. We kill too many good ideas by rejecting them without thinking about them, by laughing at them.

The Swatch is based on radical innovations in design, automation, and assembly, as well as in marketing and communications. One of our plants in Grenchen makes up to 35,000 Swatches and millions of components a day. From midnight until 8 a.m., it runs practically without human intervention. Swatch is a triumph of engineering. But it is really a triumph of imagination. If you combine powerful technology with fantasy, you create something very distinct.

And now for a marketing lesson - during the same interview, he shares how it is that they launched Swatch in Germany:

## The Giant Plastic Swatch

Did we saturate the airwaves with paid advertisements? No. Anyone can do that. We built a giant Swatch. It was 500 feet high, weighed 13 tons, and actually worked. We suspended that giant Swatch outside the tallest skyscraper in Frankfurt, the headquarters of Commerzbank. It was really something to see!

I remember asking the chairman of the bank for permission. He thought we were crazy. We were crazy, but we had already gotten authorization from the city

---

[207] Retrieved from *http://magazine.wsj.com/features/behind-the-brand/time-bandit/3/*

[208] Taken from a 1993 interview of Nicolas Hayek by William Taylor "Message and Muscle: An Interview with Swatch Titan Nicolas Hayek" for the *Harvard Business Review*. You can find the full article at *http://hbr.org/1993/03/message-and-muscle-an-interview-with-swatch-titan-nicolas-hayek/ar/pr* and we strongly recommend it.

engineers and the local government. And we persuaded him that this giant Swatch would show his customers that his bank had heart and emotion. So there it hung. And all it said was: Swatch. Swiss. DM60.

Figure 113: The Giant Plastic Swatch (Commerzbank)

## Steve Jobs

A lot of people in our industry haven't had very diverse experiences. So they don't have enough dots to connect, and they end up with very linear solutions without a broad perspective on the problem. The broader one's understanding of the human experience, the better design we will have.

Again, you can't connect the dots looking forward; you can only connect them looking backwards. So you have to trust that the dots will somehow connect in your future. You have to trust in something - your gut, destiny, life, karma, whatever. This approach has never let me down, and it has made all the difference in my life.

But innovation comes from people meeting up in the hallways or calling each other at 10:30 at night with a new idea, or because they realized something that shoots holes in how we've been thinking about a problem.

Creativity is just connecting things. When you ask creative people how they did something, they feel a little guilty because they didn't really do it, they just saw something. It seemed obvious to them after a while. That's because they were able to connect experiences they've had and synthesize new things.

I didn't see it then, but it turned out that getting fired from Apple was the best thing that could have ever happened to me. The heaviness of being successful was replaced by the lightness of being a beginner again, less sure about everything. It freed me to enter one of the most creative periods of my life.

I have a great respect for incremental improvement, and I've done that sort of thing in my life, but I've always been attracted to the more revolutionary changes. I don't know why. Because they're harder. They're much more stressful emotionally. And you usually go through a period where everybody tells you that you've completely failed.

If you haven't found it yet, keep looking. Don't settle. As with all matters of the heart, you'll know when you find it. And, like any great relationship, it just gets better and better as the years roll on.

Innovation has nothing to do with how many R&D dollars you have. When Apple came up with the Mac, IBM was spending at least 100 times more on R&D. It's not about money. It's about the people you have, how you're led, and how much you get it.

It took us three years to build the NeXT computer. If we'd given customers what they said they wanted, we'd have built a computer they'd have been happy with a year after we spoke to them.

Sometimes when you innovate, you make mistakes. It is best to admit them quickly, and get on with improving your other innovations.

That's been one of my mantras - focus and simplicity. Simple can be harder than complex: You have to work hard to get your thinking clean to make it simple. But it's worth it in the end because once you get there, you can move mountains.

The people who are doing the work are the moving force behind the Macintosh. My job is to create a space for them, to clear out the rest of the organization and keep it at bay.

What we want to do is make a leapfrog product that is way smarter than any mobile device has ever been, and super-easy to use. This is what iPhone is. OK? So, we're going to reinvent the phone.

Your time is limited, so don't waste it living someone else's life. Don't be trapped by dogma - which is living with the results of other people's thinking. Don't let the noise of others' opinions drown out your own inner voice. And most important, have the courage to follow your heart and intuition.

## 6.2.8 Eighth and Ninth CommandMents - Value and Opportunity Evaluation

*"The question is not what you look at, but what you see." - H. D. Thoreau*

*"Take the obvious, add a cupful of brains, a generous pinch of imagination, a bucketful of courage and daring, stir well and bring to a boil." - B. M. Baruch*

*"Opportunity is missed by most people because it is dressed in overalls and looks like work." - T. A. Edison*

### Value

The ability to recognize the "value" of a marketing idea is a very important thinking skill because it presents two aspects. In fact, as we will see shortly, the concept of "value" of a marketing idea can be divided into two different topics. The first refers to the value expressed in the past, in this case, we call it simply the value; the second one is concerned with the future value tied to an idea - in this case, we will define it as an opportunity.

Knowing how to recognize positive value is a crucial advantage in identifying, confirming, and endorsing marketing strategies that have worked in the past and significantly contributed to the success of the business or company. Too often we see newly appointed marketing managers who, instead of assessing the value of what has been done in the past by the previous marketing manager, simply scratch everything and start from nothing (usually to legitimize their role more than anything else). They create paradoxical situations where in the short to medium term they are faced with a situation where the performance results are worse - compromising their role as the new marketing manager.

### Opportunity Defined

Edward de Bono says that we are not able to recognize opportunities; he further sustains that if we found an idea or one were staring at us in the eyes, we would not understand the opportunity and we would miss it.

An opportunity is an "exploitable set of circumstances with uncertain outcome, requiring commitment of resources and involving exposure to risk."[209] It is anything that gives you the possibility to change things for the better, but it is not without its challenges and hard work; it is an opportunity to change, to improve, to gain experience, to learn, to make progress, and so on.

There are two important things to note. One, an idea, no matter how good it

---

[209] *The Business Dictionary*, retrieved July, 2012, http://www.businessdictionary.com/definition/opportunity.html#ixzz20zH76f9U

sounds, is not necessarily a good opportunity to go after. Two, opportunities are just as dependent on external factors and circumstances as they are on personal views, beliefs, attitudes, perceptions, and perspectives.

People who understand how to seize and evaluate an opportunity possess five key convictions. They know what they want and why they desire it, and they understand what drives them. They strongly believe in the possibility and how to make it happen. They possess abilities, competencies, and skills, and they trust them. They believe they are worth it, that they deserve it. Finally, they are convinced it is their responsibility - that they and only they need to do it. Overall, they are confident, they don't doubt themselves, and they trust their skills, strengths, abilities, and resources.

They see opportunity where no one else does, take risks where no one would, and therefore experience success where no one else ever could.

## Key Behaviors of Opportunity

People who seek opportunities and find their value are usually hard workers with determined behaviors that allow them to see these opportunities and actually go for them.

*They are prepared.* They possess a strong knowledge of the business, the market intricacies, and environmental and social factors. And they continually strive to learn more. They don't wait around for an opportunity to knock on their door but take responsibility by continually preparing and strengthening their ability to recognize them; they work on developing their skills, capabilities, and knowledge. They prepare to be able to identify changes that can lead to great opportunities by reading as much as possible on subjects of interest, taking interest in the changes of the business landscape and new and emerging developments. They also work on gaining as many different experiences as possible, which leads them to see similar patterns across apparently unrelated fields. To be able to seize an opportunity, know how to set the time to think about the opportunities and get out of their daily routine to broaden their vision and to recognize those that are just around the corner. To further enhance their ability to spot and seize opportunities, they know to broaden their reach by learning new skills, gaining more experiences, and digging deeper into different and unrelated fields. When they are interested in something, they educate themselves on the subject, even if there isn't an immediate use for it; they know they are preparing for the future.

*They are avid goal setters.* They know what they want to accomplish and set specific, time-framed goals that are motivational and challenging yet realistic and achievable. They have a clear picture of what they want and how they intend to reach it - they have outlined every step of the way, but they are flexible and willing to reconsider it according to new circumstances.

*They observe trends, search for clues, and find gaps.* They are constantly on the lookout for "newness" - new trends, problems to solve, opportunities, unusual patterns, events, or circumstances to exploit. They ask quality questions to everyone around them to uncover hidden desires, patterns, needs, and so on. And they also listen to the answers attentively and without prejudice. They closely follow economic, social, and political trends, new technologies, and developments. They search for clues and attempt to understand the changes taking place, changes that impact the marketplace and influence its trends. Therefore, they find gaps, which are, as we know, needs that are not satisfied or problems still to be resolved. Observing the world and finding clues gives them the ability to do something different, new, or out of the ordinary. It allows them to see things from a unique perspective, giving them the insight on what needs to occur to better things. These trends, clues, and gaps lead them down new paths, open new doors, and may even present the necessary unthought-of resources, tools, and support needed to succeed. They are aware of their environment and surroundings, since they know that new opportunities are intrinsically dependent on what is happening today.

*They are problem solvers and individual thinkers.* They look at problems through new and different lenses because they know problems can turn into good opportunities, no matter how small they are. One can say that they look at problems as opportunities - the opportunity is to find a solution to that problem, become the solution.

*They take action and risks.* When they truly believe in the success of an opportunity, they go for it, even if the timing is not perfect or not all doubts have been cleared. They know the perfect time doesn't exist! But they are also well aware that the opportunity is there for anyone to seize and it's only a matter of time before someone else beats them to the punch. Just because they are risk takers does not mean they are reckless. On the contrary, they are strong risk analyzers who actively weigh the pros and cons, dangers, costs, and potential downfalls of going forward. The difference, ultimately, is that they take action.

*They learn from failure.* They don't let failure or adversity defeat them. They understand that an opportunity rarely becomes a successful reality at the first go. But rather it builds up and evolves from past trials and errors. Therefore they carefully analyze, whether successful or not, what they did, what it went wrong and where it happened, and how they can improve or take advantage of circumstances in the future to continue pushing and bettering themselves. They see failure as a source of learning and believe it is key for their success.

*They have a good network.* They know that is important to be well connected; they are willing to get inspired by others. They understand how important it is to share information with many diverse people, from the very creative, to the extremely academic, to the professionals, to the common person. The creative person sees opportunities everywhere; he or she enjoys thinking of possibilities, talking, and sharing his or her creative insights and ideas. The academic is up to date with the latest advancements. Professionals know what is happening now in the market; they understand the needs and difficulties and might see solutions. The common people, well, they are who need to be satisfied. Opportunity seekers also understand that people have themselves the solution and have the answers to finding opportunities - the problems to solve. They therefore continuously build, strengthen, and maintain relationships with key individuals across all fields and with people who challenge their thinking and push them to think outside the box.

*They have a decision making system.* They depend on a trustworthy system for evaluating the risk factors when making critical decisions. Not only does the system scientifically evaluate the risk and validity of an opportunity, but it takes the emotional factor out of the equation.

## Obstacles to Seizing Opportunities

History and the many successful stories of hard work have shown us that spotting a good opportunity when it arises and going for it are actually very challenging. There are two main reasons for this. The first one is that we don't know what a good opportunity looks like; we are not ready and have a narrow vision of what that opportunity is supposed to be. The second is that we are afraid to take action; we have a fear of failure, ridicule, or rejection, or anther fear blocks us from taking the leap and going for it.

Other factors that can hold us back when an opportunity presents itself are personal beliefs, one's strengths and weaknesses, risk and uncertainty intolerance, the efforts required, following the crowd, seeking security and comfort, procrastination, pessimism, and skepticism.

This is the style of thought, which is usually less implemented, although this is perhaps the most important thought for a creative marketing and a marketing plan In other words, Carpe IDEAM...seize the day, the opportunity.

The following example is a very interesting story of an editor who sees the value of an idea but asks for an adaptation of it:

## The Hotmail Story[210] - Venture Capital

The Hotmail story started in 1995, when two young men from Silicon Valley, Sabeer Bhatia and Jack Smith, decided to start a company that would develop Java programming tools to help publish databases on the Internet. *They both worked at different companies at the time* and didn't want to use the companies' e-mail accounts for their start-up. This gave them an idea that sounded much more interesting than Java tools - a free e-mail service that could be accessed through the web.

Bhatia and Smith started making the routine rounds among venture capitalists,

---

[210] "The Story of Hotmail," posted in the Management Paradise Forum by Sunanda K. Chavan, on September 16, 2010. To read the full story go to *http://www.managementparadise.com/forums/marketing-management-rm-im/201572-hotmail-story.html*

trying to raise money. After about twenty rejections, they came to the venture capital firm of Draper Fisher Jurvetson. Venture capitalists are used to hearing inflated numbers, but Steve Jurvetson remembers Bhatia's as giving "the most hallucinogenically optimistic forecasts that you could imagine." Still, DFJ liked the idea and gave the men $300,000 in seed money.

In the course of their meetings, Tim Draper of DFJ suggested that they add a line at the bottom of each e-mail message sent by a subscriber of the service: "Get your free e-mail message at Hotmail.com." This, he thought, would help spread the word as people used the service. Bhatia and Smith were concerned initially that this might turn people off. "It took a meeting or two before they agreed," Jurvetson recalls.

The word started to spread both electronically and as a result of face-to-face conversations. It was good old word-of-mouth marketing, at Internet speed. One person would adopt the service, and others would follow in just days. "We would notice the first user from a university town or from India, and then the number of subscribers would rapidly proliferate," Jurvetson and Draper wrote.

Students were one early group to adopt the service. Before Hotmail was available, they juggled e-mail addresses between school, home, and summer jobs. Now they had one e-mail address that was accessible from any computer with web access.

Within two months of its launch, Hotmail had more than one hundred thousand registered users. Bhatia and Smith went around Silicon Valley with beepers hooked to the server that buzzed whenever they reached a certain benchmark. This buzz was very helpful as they were going through their second round of financing. On November 11, the company announced that it had more than half a million subscribers; eighteen months after its launch, Hotmail had twelve million subscribers. Looking back at Bhatia's "hallucinogenically optimistic forecasts" of subscriber growth, Jurvetson comments, "He more or less hit them or beat them."

Hotmail piggybacked on personal e-mails, from one person to another, to publicize their free e-mail service. At a time when few people had e-mail, the first and only free e-mail service in the marketplace was appealing and novel - hence the rapid adoption and spread.

## Harry Potter

This is the amazing story of a manuscript that was *considered not valuable to many, but of enormous value to one*. This teaches us an important lesson: use the actual target and look for the true value to them, not your presumed target.

What was once rejected many, many times has sold four hundred million copies. We are talking about JK Rowling's Harry Potter.[211]

---

[211] In John Lawless's article, "Revealed - The Eight-Year-Old Girl Who Saved Harry Potter," which appeared in *The Independent*, July 3, 2005. You can read the full article at http://www.nzherald.co.nz/lifestyle/news/article.cfm?c_id=6&objectid=10333960.

# CHAPTER 6

# MARKETHINK

As Nigel Newton, the chairman of Bloomsbury Publishing, reveals today, the first Harry Potter manuscript was rejected by all of his major rivals. And it was only the pester-power of his daughter, Alice, an eight-year-old girl - who read a chapter and demanded more - that finally convinced the publisher he had a winner on his hands.

Her agent, Christopher Little, called at Bloomsbury Publishing's cramped offices in Soho Square and gave Newton a sample to read. He took it home but, instead of settling down with it himself, handed it to Alice, then eight years old.

"She came down from her room an hour later glowing," Newton recalls, "saying, 'Dad, this is so much better than anything else.'"

She nagged and nagged me in the following months, wanting to see what came next.

He says, "eight others turned J K Rowling down; i.e. the whole lot."

The not-knowing-what-comes-next factor has created 260 million sales for successive books.

But Rowling became a dollar billionaire. Forbes magazine estimated her wealth last year at (pounds sterling) 562M, reporting that she is "one of only five self-made female billionaires and the first billion-dollar author."

"To demonstrate how it can sometimes be difficult to grasp or even recognize a new and useful idea, we have put together a rather amusing series of errors of judgment - that is, opinions and forecasts about the future, as authoritative when they were made as they have proven to be entirely baseless now with the benefit of hindsight."[212]

"Television is technically feasible, but commercially it is a waste of time."
Lee De Forest, inventor- 1926
"I think there is a world market for about five computers."
Thomas Watson, president of IBM - 1943
"The concept is interesting and well-formed, but in order to earn better than a 'C', the idea must be feasible."
A Yale University management professor in response to Fred Smith's paper proposing reliable overnight delivery service. (Smith went on to found Federal Express Corp.)
"We don't like their sound, and guitar music is on the way out."
Decca Recording Co. rejecting the Beatles, 1962.
"Britain will never have a female prime minister." Margaret Thatcher - 1969
"There have been 17 films made about the *Titanic*, almost all of them failures. It

---

[212] This is the best explanation of what we are attempting to do with the following examples; it comes from "Nuovo e Utile," a creativity training provider that aims to convey a view of creativity as a style of thought oriented toward the production of effective results. It seeks to make available quality information and tools that are useful for thinking in innovative ways. You can get more information by visiting their website at http://www.nuovoeutile.com/

is likely that this one will share that fate."*Los Angeles Times* - 1997

And now, here are some examples of errors where editors were definitely wrong when they rejected certain manuscripts (but still were not fired...).[213]

*Chicken Soup for the Soul* by Jack Canfield and Mark Victor Hansen. Within a month of submitting the first manuscript to publishing houses, the creative team behind this multimillion-dollar series got turned down 33 consecutive times. Publishers claimed that 'anthologies don't sell' and the book was 'too positive.' Total number of rejections? 140. Then, in 1993, the president of Health Communications took a chance on the collection of poems, stories, and tidbits of encouragement. Today, the 65-title series has sold more than 80 million copies in 37 languages.

*Carrie* by Stephen King. If it hadn't been for Stephen King's wife, Tabitha, the iconic image of a young girl in a prom dress covered in pig's blood would not exist. King received thirty rejections for his story of a tormented girl with telekinetic powers, and then he threw it in the trash. Tabitha fished it out. King sent his story around again, and eventually, Carrie was published. The novel became a classic in the horror genre and has enjoyed film and TV adaptations as well. Sometimes all it takes is a little encouragement from someone who believes in you.

*The Alchemist* by Paulo Coelho is an international bestseller that was first published in 1988 and is the most famous work of author Paulo Coelho. This symbolic story, that urges its readers to follow their dreams, sold only 800 or so copies in its first release and was dropped by its first publisher as a result. It has now been translated into more than 60 languages, and has sold more than 75 million copies in more than 150 countries, and is one of the best-selling books in history.

## 6.2.9 Tenth Commandment - Practical Thinking: ThinkACT

> *"The theory of marketing is solid but the practice of marketing leaves much to be desired."* - Philip Kotler

The great marketing innovators have very developed practical thinking abilities, and almost all entrepreneurs are very practical people.

The practical thinker will mainly care about functionality and getting things done, however this may be achieved, without procrastinating and by putting aside all unimportant and superfluous details. His main concern is getting things moving

---

[213] We have used more than one source to compile this list of entertaining error of judgment statements. You can see other examples at *http://www.rickwalton.com/pbclass/miscstuf.htm*, *http://socyberty.com/history/having-second-thoughts-sometimes-the-less-said-the-better/*, *http://www.readnsurf.com/inside.php?id=82*, *http://entertainment.howstuffworks.com/arts/literature/14-best-selling-books-repeatedly-rejected-by-publishers3.htm*.

# CHAPTER 6 — MARKETHINK

with no consideration for theoretical practices and possibilities; he goes for the actual application and the change of things in practice - to see things in action even if this means not succeeding, and he would rather fail than speculate.

A practical person is the following:

- Guided by acquired practice, general experience, and observation.
- Devoted to action, to seeing things moving forward, and ultimately reaching his big goal.
- Driven by common sense and efficiency; has a very simple yet calculated approach to problems and life in general. This gives him or her the capacity to put things to use, to combine his or her knowledge and imagination, and to put it all into motion, even when they are unconventional ways of doing things.
- Down to earth and open minded - he or she accepts that there are various possibilities and is willing to try them out.
- Definitely a "hands on" type of person - willing to get his or her hands dirty as long as he or she can see things in practice.
- Not afraid of failure as long as things get done, and moves on to the next possibility fast with no ruminating.
- Able to foresee and anticipate roadblocks and problems, but is also able to see a way out of almost all problems and complicated situations by simplifying the matter to its core concept and eliminating the complications one by one.

Practical thinking captures the strengths of how we think for everyday problems, calling on experience more than formal models. Practical thinking includes creative and critical elements. Creative thinking techniques help to generate new information. Critical thinking brings out differences that would normally not be obvious. Both types of thinking help to fill in gaps in knowledge and resolve uncertainty. Signs of a practical thinker include a willingness to try alternate approaches to thinking, being open to others' positions, being prepared to think about issues instead of ignoring or dismissing them, and asking insightful questions.[214]

If we consider that being practical is making things work, making life easier, and getting things done, there is an interesting theory called "Successful Intelligence." We believe that understanding this simple but complete concept will make your thinking and approach to life and problems that much easier and more effective.

Successful Intelligence is an approach to intelligence that stems from the 1984[215] "Triarchic Theory" proposed by R. Sternberg.[216] In this theory he states that there

---

[214] Definition retrieved from the US Air Force's "Guidelines for Leaders to Consider When Making Decisions," found at http://www.au.af.mil/au/awc/awcgate/army/ari_ldr_guidelines.htm

[215] Proposed in his 1984 book, *Beyond IQ: A Triarchic Theory of Intelligence*. He further developed the definition of successful intelligence with his 1996 book, *Successful Intelligence: How Practical and Creative Intelligence Determine Success in Life*.

[216] R. J. Sternberg is an American _psychologist, psychometrician_, and researcher (in collaboration with the PACE Center) in the fields of creativity, leadership, thinking and cognitive styles, all of which relate to his major interest, which is the higher mental functions of human beings.

are three fundamental types of thinking that will determine how well a person will cope with life and succeed in his career. He categorizes intelligence into analytical, creative, and practical thinking skills. In R. Stenberg's words, "the theory suggests that successfully intelligent people are those who have the ability to achieve success according to their own definition of success, within their socio-cultural context. They do so by identifying and capitalizing on their strengths, and identifying and correcting or compensating for their weaknesses in order to adapt to, shape and select environments. Such attunement to the environment uses a balance of analytical, creative and practical skills. The theory views intelligence as a form of developing competencies, and competencies as forms of developing expertise. In other words intelligence is modifiable rather than fixed."[217]

Successful Intelligence is the type of intelligence one needs to make it in the real world, because it's the conversion of underlying skills and abilities into innate routines that lead to high-quality performances in every aspect of your life: job, relationships, private life, etc.

---

[217] Retrieved from *http://dis.ijs.si/mitjal/genre/online/data/file1353.htm*

# MarkeThink as a Process

**PART THREE**

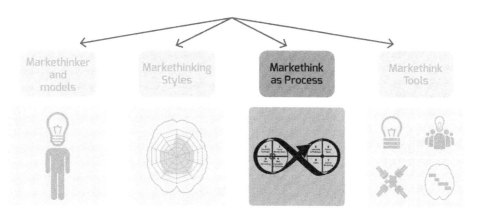

MarkeThink as a Process

# Chapter 7
# MarkeThink as a Process

## 7.1 MarkeThink as a Process

### MarkeThink Metamodel

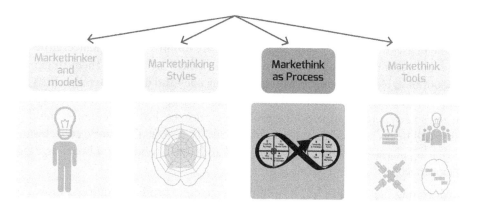

Figure 114: MarkeThink as a Process - Eight Phases

### 7.1.1 The Endless Cycle of MarkeThink

Here we face the creation and the execution of ideas as a process, the MarkeThink process. The process is divided into two main phases.

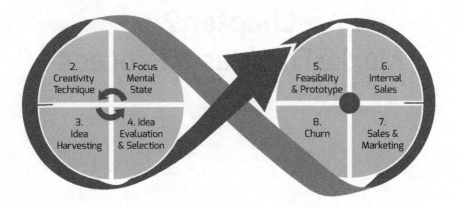

Figure 115: MarkeThink as a Process

*Thinking*, the creative phase, understood as the idea generation process, a subprocess of innovation. In brief, the objective of this phase is to find lots of ideas of high value. The process of "think," the inventive part, can and should be used at each stage of the MarkeThink process, and it's more than recommended in the "market" phase.

*Market*, the second phase, is the execution of the think output, the subprocess of implementing the invention or idea.

The phases of the process and subprocesses are not in a fixed sequence, although we would recommend you follow the order in which we present them to get the most out of it. Nothing impedes you from going back and doing a step that fits your current dilemma or situation and gaining more insight based on what you have learned so far, getting unstuck or simply going deeper. For convenience, the processes will be presented in sequence, but in reality it's often a chaotic collection of alternating phases that will then be analyzed and understood with a linear and logical approach.

Morphing the "bright idea" into the final concrete product requires a thorough process of thinking through issues, working out details, and defining specificities: how to make it, what exact materials to use, what the possible failures and barriers to its success and making all the needed adaptations are. This is what we are trying to simplify and what we wish to establish as a high result-generation process.

Very often the focus is on the inventive side of a new product or service - we want to have the brilliant idea. This is what is generally called creativity, and little time and effort is devoted to getting news ideas, implementing these ideas, selling them to the market, finding the money to finance them, finding the "right people" to realize them, or quickly incorporating market feedback to adapt an idea and all the other details.

## 7.1.2 State of Mind

People tend to believe that ideas are flashes of brilliance, or pure intuitive creativity. They're not. Generating, designing, and developing new ideas requires researching things, finding inspiration in the arts, trying out different alternatives, making educated guesses, and using different creative techniques. But it also requires failing, making mistakes, and learning from them

Additionally, it requires being open and ready to let your thoughts go free, free from all inhibitions. You need to be less judgmental, less controlling, and open to the possibilities. You have to question and challenge yourself and your perceptions and assumptions willingly; you have to be ready to let go and be confronted by yourself and others. Be ready to accept contradictory thoughts and different points of view and approaches. Be in a receptive, creative, and intuitive state of mind. Be open minded!

## 7.1.3 Challenging Oneself

A challenge is a "call to prove or justify something, dispute the truth or validity of assumptions."[218]

"Challenging is breaking free from the limits of accepted ways of operating. Challenge involves examining our current thinking against the following checklist: dominant idea, borders, essential factors, assumptions, avoidance factor."[219]

Challenging is about questioning the uniqueness of the status quo to see if other options or possibilities are available. This is certainly the most basic creative technique out there, and most of us use it daily, more than once. Progress has been possible because we have always wanted more, and through time, we have challenged assumptions, ideas, statements, etc. Challenging things is a defining element of humanity.

We challenge most things because we tend to never be content with the way things are. Challenging is all about changing, improving, and evolving. If it hadn't been done since the beginning of time, things wouldn't be the way they are today. (I personally believe that more challenging should be undertaken on everything, every day, and by everybody - it would certainly change things in the world for the best.) Challenging things allows us to improve things even when they work just fine; remember, you can always do and find better, or different. This is not just to look for ideas on a topic but a specific poll. It's asking the "why" of things.

---

218 Retrieved from the Oxford Dictionaries online at *http://oxforddictionaries.com/definition/challenge*

219 From the Selangor Human Resource Development Center, "Creativity & Innovation: Lateral Marketing Applications," course outline, found at *http://www.shrdc.org.my/downloadcourse.asp?no=9*

It is, as with most creative techniques, essential to define a focus to challenge, which can be one or all the parts of an object or situation or process, a system, or a concept, or even the way you think about an issue or assumption, or anything for that matter.

Challenging our way of thinking isn't easy - it's challenging! A good way to challenge something, according to E. de Bono, is by determining the five essential criteria on which you base your thinking process and logic on a specific subject. These criteria are as follows:

- *Define the dominating ideas.* Broadly define the general ideas controlling your thinking and the opinions you have on them, even if these are different.
- *What are the boundaries you face?* Since we usually stay within our boundaries, you need to be aware of their existence and what they are in order to challenge them.
- *State the prevailing assumptions.* Assumptions are necessary elements of the thinking process, but, as with boundaries, you have to know what they are in order to challenge them.
- *Determine the essential factors.* What is and what is not essential to the matter at hand?

*Clarify the avoidance factors.* We usually tend to avoid certain things. Which ones are they, and do you still need to avoid them?

This approach is extremely useful to challenge long-standing traditions, approaches, standards and beliefs, and assumptions, in order to improve something that actually exists.

## 7.2 Think: The Process

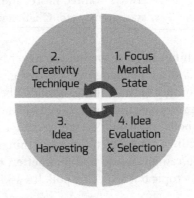

Figure 116: Think: The Process

The steps of *think* - the steps to generating ideas through creativity and invention - are as follows:

# CHAPTER 7 — MARKETHINK

1. Focus
2. Idea Generation
3. Idea Harvesting
4. Evaluate and Select

Earlier we saw that the creative process was approached from many points of view: some are down to earth and methodical, others balance imagination with analysis, and others see it as purely mysterious and spontaneous. But the spontaneity of the idea still remains very strong; they do not confirm the concrete use of creative tools and techniques. They rely on thinking wildly with no clear guidelines or direction. It is true that there are a lot of examples of ideas that have been born spontaneously, but if we stopped to analyze only spontaneous phenomena and believed that ideas cannot be stimulated or developed, the world would be different. Since the world we live in is always becoming more and more complex, we are in constant need of new, bright, and innovative ideas and solutions to become a reality. This is what we want to give you: a process for "systematic" creativity that covers the whole cycle, increasing your chances of success and creating value for all your creative effort.

We can divide the process of deliberate creativity in four phases: focus, application of creative thinking techniques, harvesting all kinds of material produced in and outside the creativity sessions, and evaluation and selection of ideas. Each stage must be addressed separately for best results.

## 7.2.1 Focus

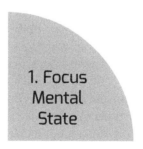

Figure 117: Focus - The First Step

*"We wanted Nike to be the world's best sports and fitness company. Once you say that, you have a focus. You don't end up making wing tips or sponsoring the next Rolling Stones world tour." - P. Knight*

*"People think focus means saying yes to the thing you've got to focus on. But that's not what it means at all. It means saying no to the hundred other good ideas that there are. You have to pick carefully. I'm actually as proud of the things we haven't done as the things I have done. Innovation is saying "no" to 1,000 things." - Steve Jobs*

Before putting in motion the creative idea generation phase, it is key to have determined the focus point, the root of the problem, on which to work. We are not saying that there is no creative thinking in this phase; we are just saying that it isn't the main purpose of this phase. Using creative approaches to determine the focus is always an advantage; it gives you more chances to find the best possible solution, idea, or opportunity.

By focus we mean being very clear and concise on what it is you want to think about, what result you want to achieve, and what the required output will be. It's having a clear understanding as to where you want to direct your creative processes and energies and what it is that you want to achieve. Choose a topic, area of interest, or problem to solve, and analyze it from all angles in order to decide which one will be your actual focus statement: the starting point of your creative process.

So, before deciding what your focus point will be, it is key to analyze various probable focuses from different angles, perspectives, and points of view. A good approach is to generate more than one statement for each probable focus and develop the most interesting ones. By having multiple focus statements, your creative thinking can take new directions and increase the quality of its outputs.

Focus is all about ensuring that the thinking process is directed toward the needed or desired results. Focus has to be the first step because it determines the best possible starting point.

### Unconscious Focus or Serendipity

Now we want to give particular attention to the unconscious activities that are unattended and of which we are unaware. For example, we find a solution to a problem while under the shower - here our brain has continued to work independently and at the right time came up with the solution. We must consider the fact that our mind perceives and recognizes a particular stimulus or a collection of them, unknowingly, due to ongoing desire to find a solution, it has never ceased to develop and work on the problem and at the right time, lighting occurs.Serendipity is the innate ability to make fortunate or desirable discoveries accidentally - while looking for something else, while you are not looking for it, or even just like that! To illustrate this, we will use two well-known cases.

The first one is the case of Viagra. Sildenafil citrate was being studied as a cure for hypertension and angina, but clinical trials lead to interesting results: the component had no effect on angina or hypertension, but had an interesting effect on men - it induced erections. This is how Viagra came to be.

The second case is Canon's ink-jet printer. A canon engineer accidentally put his hot soldering iron on top of his pen, which started ejecting ink from its tip. This led him to develop the ink-jet principle.

## 7.2.2 The Lateral Thinking Point of View

With this approach, two types of focus are available: the general area focus and the specific purpose.

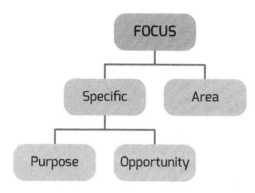

Figure 118: Focus Dimensions

### General Area

The general area focus defines the *where*. We know where we want new ideas but not why we need these new ideas. With this type of focus you can think about anything at all; it is more than just finding solutions to a problem - it is broadening your vision, uncovering underlying events, and finding opportunities. If the area of focus is properly determined, it can be a very powerful approach to thinking that leads to opening new paths that no one saw or paid attention to before.

### Specific Purpose

The specific purpose focus spells out the *reason* for undertaking the thinking process: there is a problem to solve, a task to accomplish, and/or an improvement to make. These statements are usually very clear and concise, composed of a verb that specifically spells out what it is that you want to do about a given problem or situation. An example could be, "How do we simplify the website?" or, "How do we reduce the waste of white paper." This enables you to be extremely clear and precise as to what you want to do.

This type of focus has two different orientations.

The focus can be identified through solving a problem or by focusing on creativity. "Problem setting" is an important area of focus for finding problem solving ideas, but the truly generative area of creative value is to focus on possibilities and opportunities.

To better understand these concepts, just think, for example, about finding ideas to solve an actual problem in your company that will enable you to perform your task better; or focus on creative ways to uncover new ways of doing things that create new opportunities.

*Problem setting* if there is a problem to solve! Here you need to list all the features that constitute the problem; that will be the landmark for its solution. For example, one might describe a problem in this way:

We would like to build a shoe that allows the foot to breathe.
1. The shoe perspires, but will get wet inside when it rains.
2. We would need a type of membrane that allows water to go outward but not inward.
3. The material must be cheap.

The bulk of work developed by G. Altshuller with TRIZ in the process of problem setting is quite interesting; instead of identifying the characteristics of the problem, it attempts to bring the difficulties to light within a matrix to identify the "type" of problem. Once the type is identified, it provides the problem solving tool(s) based on the collection, analysis, and organization of forty creative solutions. Based on A. Maslow's comment that "if the only tool you have is a hammer, you will see every problem as a nail," the metaphor of TRIZ is that there are now forty "hammers" for forty types of nails.

*Focus on creativity*, not to find solutions to a problem, but to invent ideas and seize opportunities. This can be divided into two approaches. With the problem solving approach, you have a purpose, where creativity is oriented to the problem. With the creativity approach, you are searching for opportunities and improvements.

## 7.2.3 The MarkeThink Point of View

There is another way to look for the focus statement - through the MarkeThink[220] lenses: the market, the product, and the rest of the marketing mix.

### At the Market Level

The market level, it's about focusing on changing one of the "dimensions." By this we mean substituting one of the dimensions of the market, such as a need or occasion, with another one that has been discarded or unattended. Lateral displacement can be done on any one of the following dimensions:

- Need - covering another need or selecting an uncovered one and thinking about how the product or service should be in order to meet said untapped needs
- Target - identifying the potential groups not targeted, and who are the nonpotential targets; substituting a target group by choosing a target that is considered nonpotential.

---
220 This point of view is based on "Lateral Marketing" work of P. Kotler and F. Trias de Bes

- Time - finding new moments in which the product can be embedded or associated; find new moments for the purchasing act or usage of the product, for example
- Place - changing the setting of your product; placing the usage or consumption or purchase in place that is different and in which the product or type of product is not present yet
- Occasion - linking the product to an occasion: popcorn at the movies or in front of a movie on the couch; finding an event (holiday) previously not considered with which you can incorporate your product, or even creating one
  Situation - placing the product into experiences

## At the Product/Service Level

At the product/service level you are focusing on changing something within the product or service. You are seeing if and for what it can be used - what situation, by whom. It's about finding out the utility, the target, and the setting for the altered product.

It is about deconstructing the existing product into its components, parts, pieces, and/or elements. These deconstructed components can be classified into the product's main steps: tangibles, packaging, brand attributes, or usage.

Once the product or service has been dissected into its different parts, it's time to change or remove one or some of them to create a new product. This is done by applying lateral displacement to the chosen elements.

## At the Marketing Mix Level

The marketing mix level is all about finding an innovative commercial or communication approach for the product or market, instead of creating a completely new product category or business line. Lateral displacement at this level means moving inside the given category through innovation at the distribution level without altering the existing service, for example. This leads to the use of alternative marketing mix strategies or to the creation of a new marketing mix formula.

## 7.2.4  The Criteria

There are some important criteria to consider in order to have a clear, synthesized, and refined focus point.

- Address one and only one topic, issue, problem, or area per focus statement.
- Don't accept he first focus statement that pops out: challenge it, look at it from different angles, and talk about it.
- Be absolutely sure that everybody involved in the creative process has the same understanding of the terms used, of the actual problem or area considered, and of what you are trying to achieve through the process. To think together in the same direction, speak the same "language."

- Consider all the implications the focus has, the important contributing factors, and the different perspectives, assumptions, and positions of the stakeholders. Be clear on who and what will be affected by the changes that will follow from developing the thinking process. Avoid surprises!

## 7.2.5 Idea Generation

Figure 119: Idea Generation - The Second Step

*"The best way to get a good idea is to get a lot of ideas." - L. Pauling the only man in the world who has won two undivided Nobel Prizes*

*"The only sure way to avoid making mistakes is to have no new ideas." - A. Einstein*

*"It is better to have enough ideas and for some of them to be wrong, than to be always right by having no ideas at all." - E. de Bono*

Ideas are generally of four types. There are the basic or average ideas, good ideas, and revolutionary ideas. The aim of this phase is to generate as many ideas as possible - the more the better. This increases the chance of getting good and revolutionary ideas with the highest possible value. More choices you have, the higher are the chances of giving birth the best idea. What you want to do is have an idea that reaches the top 20 percent of the pyramid, those that really matter and create value.

Once you have established your focus, it is time to unleash your creativity. Based on your starting point, you have to choose which technique or combination of techniques is most appropriate to channel your imagination and creativity. There have been many techniques developed in recent years, each with its own validity and importance as well as downfalls and limitations. The essential thing to be successful is to know the techniques well: know how to use them and when to use which one, considering individual styles and how it all fits together. What we recommend is to experiment as much as possible with each technique until you become truly competent in each, then select the one that best suits you and the problem at hand. The aim is to contextualize them to get the greatest benefit.

# CHAPTER 7 — MARKETHINK

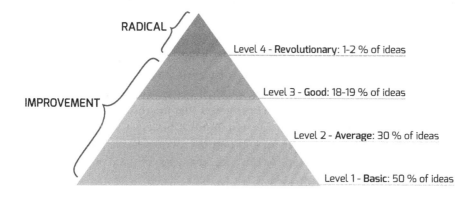

Figure 120: The Qualitative Aspect of Ideas

The main goal to keep in mind when choosing to apply these techniques of creativity is to generate a greater number of high-level ideas. Know and apply these techniques is a key skill, leading to competitive advantages, but never forget that you have to get out of your comfort zone, you have to really be willing to go beyond your limits and you'll be ready to dig deep and face yourself and others.

You have to be, above all, in the right state of mind, no matter how well you can apply these techniques.

Knowing these tools and how to execute them will lead to the deliberate use of these techniques, and will therefore formalize your creative thinking process. This means that you can activate the creative thinking process when required. They are powerful, deliberate, and systemic tools for thinking outside of our mental frames.

If they are put into motion correctly and for the right purpose, they enable you to break away and distance yourself from your normal thinking habits, challenging the patterned system that is your brain.

## MarkeThink Ideabase

E. de Bono used the term "concept R&D"[221] to differentiate the research and the development of concepts from "technical R&D." But his main goal was to highlight the importance of concepts for the future success of organizations. He strongly believes that for companies to survive in the future economy and markets, the key will be having the ability to develop concepts and knowing how to apply and gain value from them, hence the term "concept R&D."

If you think about it, the concept is what lies behind everything: a business, a process, a theory, technology, scientific research, and so on. Knowing how to rec-

---

[221] In a blog posted by E. de Bono, in 2006, "Concepts Department: How About a New Department for Concept R&D?" found at *http://www.thinkingmanagers.com/management/concepts-strategy.php*, Edward de Bono and Robert Heller's Thinking Managers website.

ognize them, find them, develop them, and uncover applications for them has to be taken seriously.

Technology is becoming a commodity. Concepts are more volatile and dependent on personal mental capabilities and experiences. Different people have different approaches, perspectives, and opinions on a certain topic or concept, matches with other people thought the outcome is "x." If some of these people mix with other people, the outcome will be "y." Don't forget that the resources available - humans, information, capabilities - vary as well. Innovation, creativity, and new ideas based on concepts are hard to get to, and become a competitive advantage since not everybody sees the connections or can take advantage of them or even imagine them, making them hard to copy.

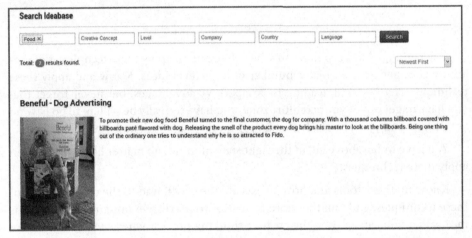

Figure 121: MarkeThink Ideabase

The "Ideabase" is the marketing concepts R&D tool that we have developed to give marketing managers and business owners the access to the most powerful marketing concepts, ideas, and practices from around the world in all sectors, industries, and fields. We invite you to go to the next chapter to see the Ideabase in more detail.

## 7.2.6 Harvesting

Figure 122: Idea Harvesting - The Third Step

*"Verba Volant, Scripta Manent."* - Latin proverb

Harvesting, in agriculture, is the process of gathering the mature crops from fields after cultivation and the growing period, and then storing them. For our purpose, it needs to be understood as gathering results - the product of your effort and creative activity - collecting, accumulating, and storing all the output. We believe there are two types of idea-harvesting approaches:

The first is harvesting the solutions from creative sessions for immediate use to solve a concrete problem at hand - collecting and organizing them to find a final solution.

The second consists in gathering, accumulating, collecting, and organizing these outputs for future use, to have the necessary Ideabase, to be prepared for what tomorrow holds. Have enough knowledge on what has been done, what worked and what didn't, what can be connected, which are the opportunities, and so on.

The harvesting step is extremely useful and valuable, for the present but also for the future. Unfortunately, little attention is paid to it; no time is dedicated to creating a warehouse of possibilities, insight, ideas, and creativity. This is mainly because it is not a very creative step but rather a meticulous organizational task. It is a task that aims at optimizing the output produced during the idea generation sessions (and all other input from your company's idea collection systems), for immediate and future use. Just because little attention is paid to it, though, does not mean that it's not essential. It will be even more so for a company's survival. Be careful not to dismiss it; is an extremely important and valuable source of insight, data, ideas, possibilities, and opportunities. It's a big mistake not to give it the right attention and value.

It would be as if a surgeon, after a delicate and hard brain operation, dedicated very little time and attention to mending and cleaning the wound just because it is not as "creative" as the surgery itself. This will automatically lead to complications for the patient, and maybe even his or her death. This is just a way to illustrate the importance of every step of the process. The real success of anything one ever starts comes from executing, methodically and systematically, all the steps of your action plan from beginning to end, no matter what, and following through! Value what you create, no matter how irrelevant you might find it, and don't take shortcuts. All the steps can be the key to your future success, so make good use of it; you never know!

We have said it many times, but we cannot understate how fundamental it is to carry out this step with immense dedication. This step of the creative MarkeThink process assures that you get the most of the creativity outcome, the resources and efforts invested in it. It is here that you get the real value independently from your creativity, whether it is now or in the future. One thing is for sure: it is an asset and will be your most valuable asset in the future idea-based economy. This will be your competitive advantage.

Once the creative step has been executed and a large and broad amount of new ideas and concepts have emerged, it is time to gather and organize them. This is also the moment when you take time to look at the output you generated, seeing what you got, what is missing, and what the key points are. This step of collecting and organizing all ideas in your "idea warehouse" also gives you the ability to extract new and interesting concepts and establish possible interdependencies and connections. Consider that once you categorize and upload it to your idea warehouse, adding it to your previously generated ideas, you might just come up with the most incredible solution or amazing new idea.

The first step of the harvesting is to gather and organize the inputs and outputs from the creative session as well as the out-of-session inputs. Look for the concepts that lie behind the ideas proposed and see how they can be linked to one another - what new concepts emerged, and do we see any other ideas or solutions? Once ideas have been matched to concepts, it is useful to determine which ones are specific enough to be immediately actionable and which ones need further development. The second step is to increase the reach and value of the outputs by adding and combining more ideas and concepts. The third step is to examine these outcomes, see what changed and how it did so, and what changed in your thinking approach. The fourth step involves taking your recently acquired insights, developing your idea, implementing it, and then starting again!

## 7.2.7   The "Idea Brokering" Concept

We know that we are entering a new era, we are slowly moving toward an economy of ideas, and therefore new ideas will become the currency of the future. Don't forget that ideas are the key to innovation. The generation of ideas, as we have seen, is not only about sitting around waiting for a genius idea; it requires time, effort, knowledge, and dedication, and a company needs to catalyze its ideas systematically through very structured methods. In "Building an Innovation Factory," A. Hargadon and R. Sutton describe the process of "knowledge brokering," which is how a company fosters its ideas and innovations. The authors state that the "knowledge brokering cycle" has four phases:

*Capture ideas* - use as many resources as possible to generate ideas. Create an environment that stimulates the mind, imagination, and creativity. Give people the opportunity to experiment, to play with things, to share information, and to collaborate.

*Keeping ideas alive* - create a system that enables people from different corporate and geographical areas to share information and knowledge, give them the necessary incentives to collaborate in finding the best solutions. Having the right information, at the right time, is key, and when there is enough information you have to make sure you have a dynamic system that allows you to use others' knowledge.

*Imagining new uses for old ideas* - once the ideas have been captured and kept alive, you should see how you can apply those ideas in different situations. Create an environment prone to questioning and challenging.

*Putting promising concepts to the test* - a good idea becomes valuable only once it has been developed, and the execution of it is paramount. For our authors, "a good idea for a new product or business practice isn't worth much by itself. It needs to be turned into something that can be tested and, if successful, integrated into the rest of what a company does, makes or sells."

## 7.2.8 Collecting Ideas

There are several ways to collect the ideas that are spun during creative sessions. These ideas can take place at three levels: during the session as a group, individually all the time, and in your company's "idea warehouse."

Note that many of these modes of idea collecting need to be taken into consideration even when preparing for the actual idea generation process. There should be a standard way of gathering the outputs created during the creative quests for new ideas. A company should also have its own in-house program and database system and strongly encourage all its members to keep track of their ideas, proposals, and visions and share them with the rest of the value-creating system.

The *voice recorder*, which can record the creativity-session dialogue, is a very useful way of collecting ideas because it allows everyone to engage in the process and to get it all recorded without an intermediary, such as a person taking notes. The disadvantage is the fact that we rarely dedicate time to play back the ideas.

The *video camera* has the same advantages the recorder has, but on top of it, it allows you to capture and see a number of features, clues, and reactions of the nonverbal communication cues. The disadvantage in this case is requires it takes a person to deal with the shooting.

The *computer* provides a considerable range of possibilities, a wide-span mnemonic to organize and classify ideas. With the latest technology, it is possible to integrate speech technology and dictate ideas that come to one's mind. The disadvantages are the costs, being tied to a physical space (except for portable computers, for which the problem is the battery life) and the fact that it may require fast typing. The big advantage is having voice-activated programs that allow the simultaneous transcription of verbal exchanges.

The *notebook* or *Post-it* is quite an old-school tool, but is still very effective. Using blocks of paper is a useful technique that allows you to record your ideas in the span of a moment without losing accuracy and allowing the creative session to proceed. The disadvantage is the fact that they can get lost and/or mixed up. One must always have something to write on at hand to jot down any thoughts that come to mind, whenever and wherever, not only during creative sessions.

### 7.2.8.1 The "Ideary" (and the Idea Warehouse for the Company)

We believe the "ideary" is key to being a good creator of ideas and innovations.

P. Kotler believes that no idea should ever be discarded. He suggested, from his book "Kotler on Marketing"[222], from his book that there are three fundamental reasons for companies to save and manage discarded ideas:

1. It allows you to apply other techniques, or find a different focus. It gives you the possibility to extract all its potential.
2. It makes you avoid any attempt already experienced of failing applications. It helps you save time and be more productive.
3. The marketing or company positioning could change over time, and a different marketing staff or team may find valid applications.

He strongly believes that discarded ideas can be "recycled." It is about collecting all generated ideas, solutions, and concepts into broader ones for present and future use.

P. Kotler made a company classification based on "idea harvesting system" and determined that there are four categories :

1. Poor - there is absolutely no organized way to stimulate and collect ideas
2. Fairly good - the company relies on salespeople and R&D to get new ideas
3. Good - there is a person appointed to stimulate and collect ideas, but the system needs further development

---
222 Kotler P., *Kotler on Marketing: how to Create, win and Dominate Markets*,1999 (Free Press, 1999)

# CHAPTER 7 — MARKETHINK

4. Excellent - the company has a well working idea management system that produces many useful ideas (Kotler 2001, p. 53)

The benefit of harvesting, collecting, and recording all creative inputs/outputs - ideas, solutions, etc. - is that it allows them to be taken into consideration at any point in time. Content and concepts generated and tested in the past are readily available. You can actualize them, and they will give you additional insight from which you can develop a new approach to your problem and a different way to develop your idea. It avoids the waste of time and resources of rethinking the same things, especially if they failed.

The "ideary" is the physical tool for collecting all the individual inputs and ideas proposed, exposed, and/or shared during creativity sessions. This tool is very similar to a small notebook or laptop. It needs to be incorporated into a system and available and accessible to everyone for consultation and also for contributions.

The ideary concept is not an original one; it had a distinguished user, and his name is Leonardo da Vinci. He once said, "My secret is very simple, during the day I write down all the ideas that come to my mind on a notebook, then in the evening I jot down ideas on different notebooks that are divided by subjects and categories. This is how I find a series of reflections on different topics that I can deal with individually and develop them."

The purpose is simple: make sure you harvest all your ideas, all the time, no matter what. "Verba volant, scripta manent," meaning "spoken words fly away, written words remain." Therefore, avoid losing the coup of brilliance, and record exactly what you mean, without losing any particular detail. By doing this, you will liberate your mind from trying not to forget it. Writing ideas down allows you to move on to the next thing, since you will no longer need to make an effort recalling them.

An ideary is a tool that assures that you don't lose one single detail of your illumination, giving way to a new thought process and to the ability to take the time to deal with ideas separately.

If, "genius is 1 percent inspiration, 99 percent perspiration," as T. Edison put it, then the ideary can have two main functions: didactic and creative.

Didactic - It's a perspiration, from an academic, trial-and-error point of view. It's a tool for learning. From an educational point of view, having an instrument for daily application allows you to practice and nurture your creativity and thinking skills as well as reach always higher levels of creation. It's a tool from which to get input from which to learn and gain insight, ultimately leading to new ideas, opportunities, and possibilities.

Creative: it comes from the portfolio of "ideas side of things" - the inspiration side - to collect all your brains production. It's the diary of everything that happens in your mind and imagination; it allows you to record your ideas and thoughts straightaway as they come to you so you don't lose or forget any detail.

An ideary should be made of loose sheets of paper that you can write on and move around, from one ideary to another, from one place to another, from one source to another. We advise you to have more than one; you should have a collection of idearies, carefully organized (by category, subject, etc.), managed and updated regularly. An ideary is a great source of inspiration and a valuable work tool. The main advantages of your ideary are as follows:

At a topics level, you can leave space inside the ideary and introduce new ideas, even after some time. A basic ideary can be carried around always, allowing you to collect everything that comes to mind in every situation. Once you are back in the office you can simply remove the pages and insert them in a more specific ideary.

At the *organizational* level an ideary gives the same focus, direction, and knowledge to employees, enabling them to carry out their own thought process, idea creation and collection, analysis, and evaluation, increasing the amount of qualitative ideas that can be put into practice.

## 7.2.9  Evaluation and Selection

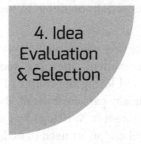

Figure 123: Idea Evaluation and Selection - The Fourth Step

> *"It is not enough to know that values are important. We need better ways of perceiving values, talking about them and assessing them. That is the best basis for action of any sort."* - E. de Bono

The biggest and most frequent mistake of the creativity process is to mix the idea-generating process with the evaluating and selection phase, because it applies negative pressure and blocks one's train of thoughts. To be able to truly assess the value of an idea is hard, but it is key to the success of the creative thinking process.

If the value of an idea is not appropriately determined, you might discard potentially successful ideas and stick with the not-so-successful one, or you might simply erroneously choose the wrong ones to develop, losing precious resources. To properly evaluate and attribute the right value, there are five techniques:

- Evaluate the *"plus, minus, interesting."* Evaluate an idea by stating and outlining the positive aspects: opportunities, benefits, and value. Then define the negative

# CHAPTER 7 — MARKETHINK

aspects: risks, difficulties, and potential problems.
- Make an *idea assessment*. This is a way of determining the feasibility of ideas quickly and properly. In this approach a series of questions are posed to see how well an idea can do by assigning a score for each one of the critical elements of the idea. The higher the score, the better the idea is, and the more potential there is for success.
- *Simulate* the idea in question one step at a time. See where it works and where it doesn't, and see if it can be accomplished and with what corrections. Is it worth it?
- Make a *pros and cons list*; point out the useful and positive aspects.
- Create *different potential scenarios* and figure out how to counteract the problems that might emerge from them and determine which one is best.

## 7.2.9.1 Idea Screening Process

The main purpose of the idea screening process, designed by P. Kotler, is to drop ideas that have little potential of success as soon as possible. It involves assessing whether the ideas match creative thinking goals, the organizational objectives, and organizational resources, in order to avoid investing precious resources in vain that could be allocated on more profitable ideas - ideas that have a higher chance of success. The idea screening process takes into consideration all the elements of the idea and states all its details: the target, the barriers and/or competition, and cost and rate-of-return estimates.

P. Kotler warns us about the two types of errors that must be avoided when screening an idea :

The first is the "drop error," which is when a company dismisses the good ideas. Give people's ideas credit, especially if the results of the idea evaluation process are positive. Give creativity a chance. Go for it!

The second is the "go-error." This is the opposite; it's about going forward with poor ideas. If the evaluating results are poor, it usually means that it's not such a good idea to develop. (2009, pp. 619–620)

P. Kotler wrote: "as the idea moves through development, the company will need to constantly revise its estimate of the product's overall probability of success." He proposes using the following formula to determine whether to proceed or not with an idea:

Figure 124: The Idea Screening Formula to Estimate the Overall Probability of Success (Kotler 2009, p. 620)

This framework allows you to uncover hidden value and strengthens your decisions. It gives you the possibility to make a go / no-go decision based on the balance of "your needs across six different categories of value - not just price."[223]

### 7.2.9.2. Six Value Medals

To fully grasp the relevance of this model, it is important to understand that we are not speaking of the value in terms of perceived or actual worth. We are talking about values that shape our behaviors and decision-making process; they are personal and deeply held beliefs and perceptions that strongly influence our attitudes and behaviors and cannot be changed.

For the purpose of a thorough evaluation phase and process, we believe it is important to mention yet again a great framework developed by E. de Bono: The Six Value Medals,[224] which allows you evaluate an idea's value based, not on the monetized and tangible, but on those values that are more intimate and that can influence our emotions.

It is a collection of thinking tools "to help people quickly but thoroughly scan for values, prioritize which values are the most important to pursue, and then ensure that top values are addressed and maximized every step of the way."[225]

The Six Value Medals and Their Specific Roles[226]

With the Six Value Medals framework, an idea is evaluated through the eyes of each one of our top values to find out its true value. Note that this means the value should be reflected on by all stakeholders.

1. The gold medal deals with human values that affect people. Gold is a superior material, and human values are the most important values of all, in the end. What are the human values here?
2. The silver medal focuses directly on organizational values - values related to the purpose of the organization (in business this would be profitability). Silver is associated with money. There are also the values involved in the actual running of the organization, such as cost control.
3. The steel medal represents the quality values. Steel should be strong. Its values go in this direction. What are the values of the product, service, or function in terms of what it is trying to do? If it is tea, is it good quality tea?
4. The glass medal covers a number of associated values: innovation, simplicity, and creativity. Glass is a very simple material originating from sand. But with

---

223 de Bono for Business at *http://www.debonoforbusiness.com/asp/six_value_medals.asp*
224 He introduced this framework in 2005 with his book, with the name,"Six Value Medals."
225 Definition found on the de Bono Thinking Systems website *http://www.debonothinkingsystems.com/tools/valuemedals.htm*
226 Retrieved from Edward de Bono's website, *http://www.edwarddebono.com/index.php/six-value-medals*

glass you can use your creativity to do a lot of things.
5. The wood medal concerns the environmental values in the broadest sense. What are the impact values on the environment, on the community, on others? The values relate to those things and people not directly involved.
6. The brass medal deals explicitly with perceptual values. How does this appear? How might it be seen? Perception is real even if it doesn't coincide with the reality. Brass looks like gold.

### 7.2.9.3 Evaluation Checklist

1. The evaluation checklist stage is where ideas need to be evaluated, taking into consideration the value-added proposition of the new idea in relation to the company's business objectives, resources, and capabilities. Below is an excellent criteria checklist developed by the Princeton Creative Research Department to evaluate ideas. It is a list of questions that need to be answered.[227]
2. Have you considered all the advantages or benefits of the idea? Is there a real need for it?
3. Have you pinpointed the exact problems or difficulties your idea is expected to solve?
4. Is your idea an original, new concept, or is it a new combination or adaptation?
5. What immediate or short-range gains or results can be anticipated? Are the projected returns adequate? Are the risk factors acceptable?
6. What long-range benefits can be anticipated?
7. Have you checked the idea for faults or limitations?
8. Are there any problems the idea might create? What are the changes involved?
9. How simple or complex will the idea's execution or implementation be?
10. Could you work out several variations of the idea? Could you offer alternative ideas?
11. Does your idea have a natural sales appeal? Is the market ready for it? Can customers afford it? Will they buy it? Is there a timing factor?
12. What, if anything, is your competition doing in this area? Can your company be competitive?
13. Have you considered the possibility of user resistance or difficulties?
14. Does your idea fill a real need, or does the need have to be created through promotional and advertising efforts?
15. How soon could the idea be put into operation?

Answering these questions will give you a clear view of the idea's potential and value for the company as well as for the consumers. This will enable you to make the best choice of ideas and solutions to bring forth, invest in, and above all believe in.

---
[227] The "Evaluation Check List" according to the Princeton Creative Research Department, retrieved from Entrepreneur, the website at http://www.entrepreneur.com/encyclopedia/checklists/article81940.html

## Criteria example

| | Idea | Speed | Cost | Value Impact | Resources | Total |
|---|---|---|---|---|---|---|
| 1 | Increase the number of cash registers open during peak hours. | 5 | 3 | 2 | 4 | 14 |
| 2 | Develop and build a shopping cart that has an RFID device that scans every item you put in the cart and automatically adds it to your bill; when you reach the checkout point of the supermarket the bill is ready. The cart is also fitted with an automatic mechanism that bags the goods, and with a credit card payment device that allows the customer to pay the supermarket and allows the supermarket or marketers to profile and gather customer information for creating future valuable marketing actions. | 2 | 1 | 5 | 2 | 10 |

Figure 125: Criteria evaluation

A very simple and powerful way for evaluating a marketing idea that we have seen work is to classify it on the basis of criteria defined a priori. For example, we can grade an idea on a scale from one to five, on four different criteria (or ten):

**Speed** = speediness in implementing the idea
**Cost** = cost of going forward with the new solution
**Value impact** = potential value of the idea and its impact, both in solving the problem and creating new opportunities
**Resources** = presence of the necessary resources available in the company to realize the idea

## Ideas to Decrease Customers' Waiting Time In Line at the Supermarket Cash Registers

In the example presented above, if the marketing manager should use the criteria: cost-resources-speed, would win the first idea, but if the policy chosen instead was connected with the potential value on the impact of the idea, would win the second one. The criteria are important because over time and with different conditions, ideas rejected in the past could be recovered for the future based on the changes of context (and Criteria too).

If you have twenty ideas, you can classify them based on what you believe are the most important criteria.

# CHAPTER 7 — MARKETHINK

## 7.3 Marketing: The Implementation

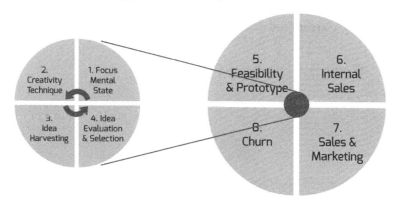

Figure 126: Marketing: The Implementation

*"We have to understand that the world can only be grasped by action, not by contemplation. The hand is more important than the eye... The hand is the cutting edge of the mind."* - J. Bronowski

*"The value of an idea lies in the using of it."* - T. Edison

*"The profit of great ideas comes when you turn them into reality."* - T. Hopkins

There are four phases of marketing implementation: the feasibility, internal sales, external sales and marketing, and "churn". But before we consider these, it is essential that you sell your idea internally, throughout the whole process of marketing.

Once you have decided on which idea to work, you should do a feasibility study of the idea - can you do it? Once the feasibility has been determined, the prototype needs to be developed; that is the tangible side of the idea. When the prototype has been developed, it is time to move to selling the idea to the market. The final and crucial step of the MarkeThink process is the "churn," the implementation, verification, control, and corrective actions that lead back to the first step - finding the focus.

At this stage, we find linear thinking to be a very useful approach in the sense that we need to use much of the usual logic and a rational point of view, keeping an open mind toward alternatives, opportunities, and possibilities. Always remember to use your creative abilities and stimulate your creative thought process in each phase of the MarkeThink process. The linearity of thinking helps you keep focus, methodology and coherency allowing you to stay on track. The creative thinking approach makes this phase even more valuable, with better probabilities of success, since creativity here can enrich the idea exponentially.

The marketing phase of our MarkeThink process is the key to the success of generated ideas. Here we will cover the four steps (steps five through eight in our process) of implementing ideas: executing them in terms of marketability, putting them into action to create and deliver value, and ultimately gaining profits.

## 7.3.1 Feasibility and Prototype

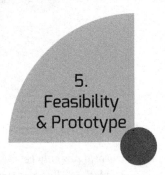

Figure 127: Feasibility and Prototype - The fifth Step

Once you have decided to move an idea from the "think" (creative) phase to the "market" (execution) phase, you must address the characteristics of its feasibility: can you do it? These characteristics can be of various types: economic, political, or social for example. You decide which are relevant. But one thing is for sure - it's fundamental to evaluate the degree of "feasibility" of an idea.

### Feasibility

Studying the idea's feasibility means analyzing its viability and procuring the necessary proof and material concerning the organization's capacity to bring an idea to life. It investigates various alternatives and helps in answering the fundamental question: Should you proceed with the proposed idea? It's the step that allows management to determine the real value of an idea before proceeding with the project development and investing valuable resources.

Studying feasibility is a controlled process to identify problems, constraints, dangers, further solutions, or opportunities of proceeding with the development of the idea, from concept to reality. It's a process whose purpose is to rationally and objectively bring forth the strengths, weaknesses, threats, and opportunities associated with the project's pursuit. It supports as well determines the necessary resources - type, amount, availability - and emphasizes the existing dependence that exists within and between the organization and its resources.

It's a well-designed analysis of the company's ability to successfully develop the idea and deliver added value. It should always provide a solid company, business,

# CHAPTER 7 — MARKETHINK

and project background, a concrete description of the idea - its purpose, expected results, benefits, etc., and how these fit together. It's all about determining if one possesses the ability and capacities to complete the project successfully through the analysis of your company: infrastructure, operations, organization, and resources. For investigating what you have to predict, the potential outcome of a specific decision, or of the future course of action undertaken.

"Conduct a feasibility study to start your course of action. It will provide you with objective information to evaluate existing services and strengths. You will gain an understanding of the competition and marketplace indicators that affect your business. This is the best way for you to grasp the impact of future decisions you may be considering. The feasibility study will help you accurately anticipate what will and will not work in different situations. You will be able to determine what resources are essential to complete varied situations and gain an understanding of how to draw on your strengths."[228]

## Feasibility versus Business Plan

People often are unaware of the difference between a feasibility study and a business plan.

The feasibility study investigates the possibility of proceeding with the idea - is the idea viable? It outlines, analyzes, and tests various alternatives, scenarios, and methods to reach the best results and achieve high levels of performance. The outcome of the analysis produces the information necessary for the development of the business plan.

The business plan organizes the development process; it outlines the actions required to pass from the "idea" to "reality." It deals with only one alternative, and provides the blueprint, a road map for executing and implementing the ideas. It uses the findings and recommendations drawn from the feasibility analysis as an important source of information.

Why Study Your Idea's Feasibility?

In broad terms, you should study your idea's feasibility to determine whether the organization has the sufficient management and technical expertise, organizational competences, and resources to successfully develop it. But there are many more reasons:

- To support management and decision makers with enough information to decide on the following:
    - Considers all variables whether the project can be done at a profit,: cost, returns, required resources, expertise, infrastructure, and so on
    - Establish a set of alternatives and the preferred course of action, whether the

---

[228] J. Capko and R. Anwar in "Feasibility Studies Can Help You Control Your Destiny," *American Medical News*, September 23, 1996.

realization of the idea will benefit and satisfy its intended users
- Provides a rough draft of the work and resources needed to get the project done
- Gives assistance in the process of identifying obstacles, downfalls, and dangers of an idea concept, as well as possible solution and alternatives not seen before
- Makes sure no one is penalized by proceeding with the ideas development To allocate resources coherently
- Helps identify extra opportunities and possibilities and also uncovers potential dangers and downfalls through thorough investigation of influential factors and the organization's capabilities
- Increases the odds of success by dealing with and mitigating information and influential factors that can shape the success of your idea early on in the process
- Catalogues the current and available resources and estimating additional ones for the assessment of your resources -
- Provides quality information and documentation on the project's feasibility and benefits to support decision making and helps establish the future steps, the business plan, and the marketing plan
- Assure funds and/or attract equity investment, find partners, collaborators, etc, it is a valuable source and baseline.
- Defines successful outcomes and assesses the costs and benefits associated with each alternative, as well as the risks and barriers to overcome

## Feasibility Factors

We will address the essential feasibility factors, bearing in mind, however, that even a small characteristic or element not taken into consideration may bias the outcome of your analysis, leading to the idea being dropped or pursued for the wrong reasons. The key concept here is that now you no longer question which ideas are valuable, but you must probe them to decide which one you can develop best based on a number of operational assumptions. We will consider three types of feasibility characteristics: technical and technological, economic, and human resources–related.

## Technical and Technological Feasibility

Technical feasibility is the assessment "based on an outline design of the system requirements, in terms of input, processes, output, fields, programs, and procedures. Technological feasibility is carried out to determine whether the company has the capability, in terms of software, hardware, personnel and expertise, to handle the completion of the project."[229]

It is determining whether or not an idea is feasible within the limits of the current technology available, within your organization as well as outside it - in your

---

[229] Retrieved from Wikipedia at http://en.wikipedia.org/wiki/Feasibility_study

# CHAPTER 7 — MARKETHINK

industry or not. It determines what type of equipment and technology is necessary to produce the idea.

The key technical questions to find answers to before deciding on whether to proceed or not are as follows:

- Is the technology or solution practical, and is it the best and highest performing one?
- Do you possess the necessary technology? If not, can you acquire it? At what cost and with what implications?
- Do you possess the required technical expertise? Can you gain it? Where, how, and at what cost? And with what risks?
- Is the technology you have ready to be applied? Does it need further development? With what resources and level of difficulty?
- Do you have the required production capabilities? If not, how will you find or acquire them?

If Leonardo da Vinci had the technical expertise and technology to realize his plans for the construction of airplanes, we could have had them many centuries sooner. The development of personal computers was made possible by the transition from thermionic valves to the silicon chip. The development of the phone was born only after the development of technologies for remote transmission. These are just some examples to show how technological constraints determine whether an idea can be achieved or not. We don't care whether the service or product is expensive; here we work on the possibility of putting it in place and making it a functional reality.

*Economic Feasibility - Cost/Benefit Analysis*

Once you have ascertained the technical feasibility of the idea, it is time to look at the economic feasibility. The economic logic is a very important criterion for evaluating an idea's overall feasibility and is usually a very difficult aspect to evaluate, especially if you don't speak the specific economic language, with its rules and jargon. If we go to a country whose language we don't know, the help of an interpreter is essential to move around (but don't forget that this will still lead to the loss of particular language subtleties). The same goes for the economic component. Once you have determined the cost/benefit ratio with a detailed analysis of an idea, you can create a variety of scenarios.

This is usually the bottom line for proceeding with an idea or dropping it because it determines the return on investment (ROI), assesses the risks, and weights the costs against the benefits of proceeding with an idea's implementation. The cost/benefit analysis gives answers to questions such as the following:

- Is the project justified, and do the benefits that derive from it outweigh the costs incurred?
- Can it be effectively and efficiently done within the cost constraints and budgets?
- What are the maximum and minimum costs associated with reaching the desired result?

It is determining the cost of proceeding with the idea's development: project related costs - development, purchasing, installations, infrastructure, conversion and training, and ongoing operational costs - personnel, maintenance, and procurement.

Makes a checklist, for assure you that is possible to develop an idea given the economic constraints:

- Makes the cost versus benefit analysis of going forward with the idea
  - Estimate the total cost of the project: development, operations, and maintenance.
  - Estimate the total earnings and the demand forecast.
- Analyze the economic patterns, trends, and drivers of demand.
- Assess the risk factors:
  - Underestimating the costs
  - Unexpected events leading to unexpected costs
  - Delays, detours, possible failures
- What will be the economic savings and earnings: monetary, tangible, and intangible?
- What will be the manufacturing costs for setting up, for the machinery, and for material procurement? And what about the cost per unit?
- Include the comprehensive analysis of competition: who and what are their capabilities, competitive advantages, and strategies?

Assessing and identifying the costs and benefits is a difficult task because they can be hidden or unclear, hard to estimate, tangible and intangible, and quantified or calculated or neither. It requires considering and ranking multicriteria alternatives and scenarios.

## Human Resources Feasibility

Another important factor is having adequate people to bring the project forth, or finding the right people to fill a competencies gap for the implementation of the idea. Do you have people who can deal with this new idea? Or are people inadequately prepared or in need of training? If so, who do you need, what capabilities should they have, what training program should you use, and can you outsource? Is the organizational structure right for carrying out the project? Also consider doing the following:

- Sketching the personnel required: who do you need now and in the long and short term? With what skills, qualifications, and expertise?
- Defining key positions: skills, experience, and qualifications, and associated responsibilities and costs. Where will you find the necessary expertise and qualifications? Do you have potential candidates or do you have to attract them? How will you retain them?
- Determining the HR plan. Do you have an HR plan (retribution, benefits…), or do you have to develop it?

Having large disposable cash flow doesn't automatically mean that you will find the right people or get what you need from them, so you also need to consider how their attitudes, behaviors, and beliefs fit with the company, how you can motivate them and get the best from them, what it is they value, and how to satisfy their needs to increase their performance and productivity.

## Other Things to Consider

*Operational Feasibility* describes how and where production will take place and how sourcing and delivery will be done. What are the physical premise requirements: location, size, production capacity, warehousing, logistics, etc.? Consider internal factors such as conflicts, employees' resistance, value chains and links, management's support, stakeholders' benefits, processes and procedures, and quality specifications. It investigates and analyzes internal operations: how specific processes/ideas will work and be implemented and how they will affect other ongoing operations. It also attempts to find ways to manage resistance to change and the level of internal acceptance.

*Organizational feasibility* determines whether the proposed business has sufficient management expertise, organizational competence, and resources to be successful.

- Evaluate management expertise that is the ability of the entrepreneur and management team
- Designate responsibilities - Determine whether the responsibilities are too great or too small for the entrepreneur. Do any of the duties need to be outsourced?
- Evaluate nonfinancial resources - Is there a sufficient labor pool (quality and quantity), available office space, protection for property, patents, etc.?

*Financial Feasibility* establishes the cash flow and capital requirements, projections, and the overall attractiveness of the investment. It examines the organization's inflows and outflows, as well as the project's, and how it affects the overall financials - can you afford it? Can you sustain your cash flow levels and financial stability considering the following key points:

- When are returns expected? And the estimated ROI?
- When are the expenses taking place?
- Is there a need to look for financing and funding? If so, how, where, with what conditions and implications on the project and organization's financial health?
- Estimate the break-even point and costs - fixed and variable.

*Legal feasibility* is concerned with identifying traps and constraints, and determining the potential conflicts with laws and regulations: contracts, liabilities, patents, etc.

*Schedule feasibility* concerns how long it will take to deliver the finished product/solution and involves establishing a time line and important deadlines, determining whether it can be done in the assigned period of time, and setting the possible time drawbacks.

It is important to note that feasibility analysis is a cycle and that each step and the decisions you make can influence the previous and following step. For example, the selection of a material - type A, which is less expensive but delicate, or type B, which is more expensive but less delicate - will not only automatically influence the economic needs and results, but require different competences and/or technical skills. Whatever decision you make has an impact on all the feasibility assumptions and choices you have made.

## 7.3.2 Prototyping

In this phase of our MarkeThink process, the "think" cycle is important and useful, because creativity plays an important role in the prototyping step. Prototyping is the visual creation or the tangible representation of your idea. Make sure you work with people who share your vision, speak your language, and believe in the idea's potential. But you must also have outside-the-box and open-minded thinkers to reach the best creative physical representation of your idea - its design, features, how it works, its various tasks, its requirements, and so on.

At this point, exploring all the possibilities and digging deeper in your creative ability can produce very positive results and allow you to catch new and better opportunities and/or solutions. Allow yourself to experiment with different things by getting out of your preconceived notions; don't limit yourself to the standard ways of doing things. Keep an open mind and try out as many alternatives you can think of when you give life to your product. Don't let yourself be brought back into your narrow thinking patterns. Prototyping is an opportunity for you to go deeper into finding true innovation, new ideas, and real value.

### Some Definitions

A prototype is "an early sample or model built to test a concept or processes."[230]

The *American Heritage Dictionary* defines a prototype as "an original, full-scale, and usually working model of a new product or new version of an existing product."[231]

The prototype is the original model of your product; it can be a basic mock-up or a fully functional sample. This is where the idea becomes tangible (or in some cases virtual - computer based*),* "reducing the invention to practice" to see and show how it works. How you do your prototype doesn't matter; what matters is that it represents your idea and its value. As long as you gave life to your idea, it is of no importance.

It is also important to consider the looks, functionality, and costs of a prototype.

---

[230] Retrieved from *http://en.wiktionary.org/wiki/prototype*
[231] *American Heritage Dictionary of the English Language*, 4th Ed. 2009. *Houghton Mifflin Company*

A good approach is to develop more than one prototype using different materials, designs, etc., to see which functional solution and which combinations work best.

It is important to keep in mind that the prototyping process is not achieved in one shot and it is not a one-step process, but rather it is an evolutionary process, where the prototype faces modifications, and alterations, until, ultimately, you have a refined enough product that you can market.

We mentioned that internal sales should be activated during the whole process; the prototype is a great means to support all your selling efforts, especially at the top level.

## 7.3.3 Internal Sales

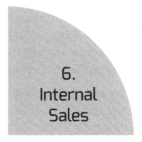

Figure 128: Internal Sales - The Sixth Step

Internal sales are fundamental to your idea's success. The fact that your business idea is technically sound and that the overall feasibility has been ascertained will not be important if it is not correctly promoted and sold within the organization and its constituencies. It is no longer the validity of your idea that matters, but your ability to sell it to top management, functional and operational areas, employees, and shareholders that will bring you glory and positive returns. You have to have the whole company buy it!

### Personal Sales

The first person to whom you must sell your idea is yourself and your team. If you are not convinced about it, it will be very difficult to sell it to others. In the end, those who have to buy your idea will have to buy it based on your enthusiasm and your selling approach, without having concrete proof on which to base their position.

Be careful though - once you are convinced by the idea, there is the risk of being so completely in love with it that you don't see potential dangers or better solutions. If you are too emotionally involved, there is a big possibility that your vision will be constricted, blocking your creative thought process.

### Internal Sales

> *"In large organizations the dilution of information as it passes up and down the hierarchy, and horizontally across departments, an undermine the effort to focus on common goals." - M. Csikszentmihalyi*

After you sell the idea to yourself...then comes the big challenge: selling the idea to the whole organization while maintaining a high level of creativity. Internal sales refers to selling your idea to your organization, top-down. The fear of being mowed down by others if you take a different stand from the company's standards and what is generally accepted is one of the worst deterrents of creativity. The internal sale is not an easy thing to accomplish, especially if you want to keep the creative touch.

At the corporate level, unless you are the president or owner, you have to convince more than one person at different levels to adopt your idea and believe in it. This is one of the reasons for which organizations with many hierarchical levels are "little" creative. The fact that decision making requires various steps through different levels takes away all the creativity from the proposal. Once it reaches the highest and final decision making level it is no longer a creative idea or solution.

Don't forget that organizations and people are driven by power, within hierarchies that influence and have great impact on what goes forth and what does not. At the highest levels there is rarely a true conviction that creative ideas lead to good returns. Selling your idea at this level is an arduous task that requires you to surpass all internal barriers. To make matters easier, when you are selling your idea internally, try to keep the creativity factor alive.

## 7.3.4 Become a Lidear

> *"I don't care if it's a white cat or a black cat. It's a good cat so long as it catches mice." - Deng XiaoPing*

"L*idear*ship" is a different approach, a new type of leadership that we have developed and wish to introduce. The "lidear" is a person who is able to successfully combine two fundamental functions:

1. Lead - the person is recognized throughout the organization as the leader.
2. Sell the idea - the person is capable to sell the idea to the whole organization and get the green light from decision makers.

With passion for the idea and an ability to persuade and engage others, the lidear can and will make sure that the new marketing idea manages to get approval. Through the use of appropriate direct and indirect persuasion strategies, he or she is able to influence key decisional people at every level of the organization.

## 7.3.5 Sales and Marketing

Figure 129: Sales and Marketing - The Seventh Step

The fact that your business idea is technically sound, that it is feasible, and that the prototype is valid won't mean anything if it is not properly launched, introduced and promoted in the marketplace, and sold to your target market. It is not the "brilliance" or validity of your idea but your ability to sell it to your customers - to penetrate the market - that matters: this is what will bring glory and returns. External sales is communicating your product and what it stands for to the consumer market, the ability to create desire and satisfy it, deliver true value, and establish contact. Ultimately making the sale and establishing a relationship that lasts with consumers.

At this level, the person responsible for marketing the idea to the market must have the dual ability to understand the creativity of a product and the value of it, and know how to sell that whole package to its target. He or she has to have an acute sensibility toward creativity and also numbers, as well as the ability to understand the consumers' needs and what drives them.

Now that you have defined your product, resulting from the previous MarkeThink steps, it's time to put it on the market: sell it to consumers. This is the ultimate goal; it's all about making the sale. To achieve this, an integrated and creative marketing strategy needs to be put in place. For this you can start the process again from the top: from establishing a focus, to generating ideas, to testing their feasibility and making the prototype:

- Define and describe the target market - its size, characteristics, attitudes, behaviors, etc. Plan the product's positioning strategy and estimate the product sales, market share, and profit for the first year.
- Lay out your standard marketing and sales practices and strategies, as well as your competitors'. Do the same for the "unconventional" approaches and see if there are other opportunities and different ways to market your product, from product launch, to promotions, to price, to distribution, etc.
- Define the marketing strategy: the price (how much will the customer pay?), the distribution (where and how will they get it?), and the marketing mix (how will

they hear about and get to know your product, and what message will you be delivering?).
- Discuss the possibility of establishing strategic partnerships for distribution, promotions, and marketing activities. What would be the advantages and disadvantages, costs, and returns? How will the risks be shared? Do potential partners give access to critical markets or other key resources?
- Decide when, where, and how to introduce the product and keep it in the mind of the consumer.
- Develop a potential marketing plan for the following years and, if possible, a contingency plan.
- Analyze all available data and dig deeper to try seeing beyond the obvious for hidden patterns, opportunities, and possibilities.
- Describe your distribution strategy: direct, web, or retail? With what profit margin projections, commissions, etc.? Establish your distribution channel partnerships and your trade marketing strategy.
- Describe your payment terms, warranties, customer service, etc.

Consider that within this phase it is very useful to restart and follow the steps of the MarkeThink process. This will give you the ability to duplicate your chances of success by doubling the amount of creativity involved in the whole project, from its creation to its execution. This will lead you to get the best innovative and creative commercial and communication formulas.

## Due Diligence Revisited

The external sales step of the marketing execution phase refers to all efforts you put into selling your new idea and product, your vision, and the process of giving it its true value in the eyes of the consumer. Selling your idea is not only selling it to consumers and your target market but also retailers and the media

Before attempting to penetrate the market with your new product or service, it is time to take due diligence a little further by conducting more in-depth market research and environmental scanning, because going to the market implies large financial expenditures and involves some risks. You want to make sure that you control all the controllable variables that can negatively influence your results. The research concerns retail price, unit cost, competition, market potential, demand and opportunities, manufacturing capabilities, the actual sales projections, and all legal, safety, and other issues.

The results from your creativity sessions and the research you have gathered (through experience, market research, and due diligence) provide a solid marketing and commercial evaluation to make the final decisions regarding the product's introduction to the market, while being in control of key elements and influential factors.

These are key questions you have to answer as best as you can before deciding to sell your product:

# CHAPTER 7 — MARKETHINK

- Is there really a profitable market for your product? What size? With what potential? Who is you target market?
- What is the level of demand - estimated, actual, and potential - or your product? Does it exist or do you need to create and develop it?
- Who will use your product, and what are their requirements regarding the product's function and performance, its look and feel?
- Do you have the necessary distribution capabilities or do you need a new distribution strategy? Which one?
- Are you really offering advanced attributes and features? What are the distinctions and improvements you have to offer?
- Is your pricing strategy valid for your selected market, consumers, and distributors? Is it a competitive advantage or not?
- Do you offer higher performance levels, features, or attributes? Which ones? Are they of value?
- Is there a particular time required to produce and market the new product? Is it time and/or seasonally sensitive?
- What are the market barriers you have to face? Will it be easy to enter and penetrate your target market?
- Are you in line with all the regulations' requirements? And what about the special and specific laws that concern your industry?
- How do you plan to market your product - its presentation, packaging, design, colors, graphics, etc.?
- How do you intend to get your target market's attention and interest, create awareness, and position yourself in the market? What are you going to do to influence their behavior and make them buy your new product or service? How do you intend to reach them?

## 7.3.6 Churn

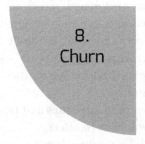

Figure 130: Churn - The Eighth Step

*"Best strategy used to be ready, aim, fire. Now the best strategy is ready, fire, steer. Put supplies where you might need them on the journey. Just get into the right neighborhood and you will find the address. 'Test fast, fail fast, adjust fast.'"* - T. Peters

This step is very important; it reminds us that we are all human, that we don't necessarily always get it right, and that we always have to work on things. We have borrowed this concept from Guy Kawasaki, former evangelist of Apple and now venture capitalist. G. Kawasaki presented this important concept of "churn" in his book *Rules for Revolutionaries: The Capitalist Manifesto for Creating and Marketing New Products and Services*<?>, in which he says, in essence, that the idea from which one starts is not necessarily as important as the winning ability to know when and how to improve quickly - simply put, to churn!

We all know that every choice, every decision we make, has consequences. Therefore, when you have implemented your idea and put it on the market, you have to pay attention to the implications of your actions and choices - cause and effect! If it's positive, great! Stay on track, but keep looking for ways to improve. If it's negative, well, then you have to reconsider everything and adapt to the marketplace and its reality. No prediction is ever right on. But you may face one of various scenarios: You are close to achieving the goal, in the best or worst ways, maybe you're reaching a goal other than what you were set or you are completely wrong. The point is that you will always need to make some kind of adjustment. It is a never-ending cycle! The ability to capture these threats, make the necessary changes, and adapt accordingly is critical for success. Being able to be proactive instead of just being reactive to events is a must!

How the market reacts is not under your total control; you can move things around to attempt to control their reactions, but you will never be able to do it completely. It reacts in different uncontrollable, unpredictable, and unforeseeable forces; it evolves and modifies behaviors. Your product might be fantastic - but for another market or for some other use you haven't yet thought of, or it may

# CHAPTER 7　　　　　　　　　　　　　　　　　　　MARKETHINK

even have real potential and value for another purpose or function. To find out if you are truly on the right track for success, you need to constantly keep up, monitor, control, adapt, change, and reconsider your actions and decisions - what you are doing and how you are doing it. It's a never-ending, back-and-forth process between you, your target market, the marketplace, your product, and its results. You must know how you are doing on the market and with your audience, your customers.

To find out how you are doing on the market, it is important to get feedback. We are not talking about the simple sales results or customers' feedback; we are talking about getting real, immediate feedback from as many different sources as possible: different opinions and points of views from people in different industries and professions and social backgrounds and with different demographics. Considering different approaches and getting inputs from various sources are essential to really see the pluses and minuses of the product, the opportunities and threats, and so on. You should consider developing research and communication plans that do the following:

- Incentivize objective feedback and advice from consumers, customers, and the field-sales people.
- Target marketing professionals from all areas, and also experts from your field and other relevant ones; consider the ones who have the same target market but are not competitors, or manufacturers with whom you may have commonalities.
- Get input from everyone, absolutely everyone! From your customer, employees, the manufacturing department, the distribution center, and your entourage. Also get input on everything, from features to price, benefits to packaging, etc. Find out what they would change or improve, and why and how they would do it.

Gathering all this information will allow you to take the necessary measures and corrective actions to stay on track and be successful with your creative and innovative product on the long run. It is an ongoing process that aims at delivering the most satisfying product or service, with the best benefits and most gratifying experience. You have to carry out this step on a constant basis not to trick ever. Note that at this stage of the process, even though it's the final one of our process, if you need to take corrective measures or if you are not entirely satisfied with the outcome, you should simply start the process again, with the recently acquired information and experience, in a way that satisfies your present situation or dilemma.

# MARKETHINK — CHAPTER 7

## The Post-it Case

Figure 131: Post-it Notes (3M)

Dr. Spencer Silver, a 3M scientist, discovered the formula for the sticky stuff back in 1968. But it was Silver's colleague, Art Fry, who finally came up with a practical use for it. The idea for repositionable notes struck Fry while singing in the church choir. His bookmark kept falling out of his hymnal, causing him to lose his page. So, taking advantage of a 3M policy known as the "bootlegging" policy, Fry used a portion of his working hours to develop a solution to his problem. Now the world is singing the praises of his pet project: Post-it Notes.

After years of product development, 3M introduced the concept of Post-it Notes in four major markets in 1977. But, without actual samples in hand to ry, consumers didn't catch on. A year later, 3M blanketed the Boise, Idaho, market with samples upon samples of Post-it Notes. After trying the notes, more than 90 percent of users said they'd buy the product themselves. The test was a success! By 1980, Post-it Notes were being sold nationally. Today, they're used and enjoyed throughout the world.

Source: www.3m.com

# MarkeThink Tools

PART FOUR

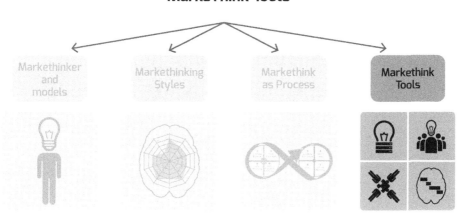

# Chapter 8
# MarkeThink Tools

## 8.1 The MarkeThink Tools and the Ideabase

> *"A vision is the art of seeing things invisible." - J. Swift*

> *"Vision without action is a daydream.
> Action without vision is a nightmare." - Japanese Proverb*

### 8.1.1 MarkeThink Tools

> *"Creativity is thinking up new things.
> Innovation is doing new things." - Theodore Levitt*

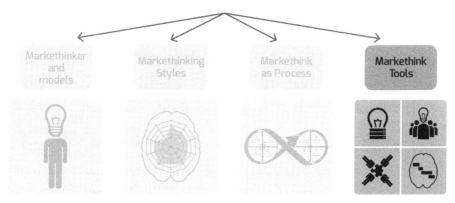

Figure 132: MarkeThink Tools

Once you know the theoretical model (the MarkeThink metamodel), the most valuable contribution is the ad hoc set of tools that we have developed. In fact, it is thanks to the application of the model and its principles that you can reach concrete, valuable achievements. To help you carry out our MarkeThink model, thee are a number of transversal and practical tools.

Below you can find the platform of tools developed. We are well aware that we are only at the beginning and that in the coming years we will continue to develop a whole series of complementary and specific tools that we are currently unable to predict; for this reason we invite you to try these here showed and eventually in the future, please, give us your feedback so that we can improve them and develop new ones.

Specifically, the tools we developed can be used for all of the five major players in the MarkeThink world:
1. Entrepreneurs
2. Managers
3. Operators and front office staff
4. Consultants
5. Professors and lecturers

## 8.2 Learning from the best MarkeThinkers

Figure 133: MarkeThinkers

Learning from the best MarkeThinkers is the best way to learn how to create something original. In essence, in this first block, there are essentially two tools that we offer:
1. MarkeThinker database

The MarkeThinker database is "an open platform where, we invite you to enter and point out marketing authors and key players' contributions around the world; here you will find entrepreneurs (Steve Jobs), and consultants or trainers (Edward de Bono and Tom Peters), as well as managers (Jack Welch) and professors (Theodore Levitt and Philip Kotler), and even some who are more than one, such as Seth Godin, who has been a consultant, an entepreneur, and a trainer. We remind you that MarkeThink is a metamodel and that our goal is to create a common language for sharing and exchange so that the professional community can grow and reach higher levels of achievements.

For each player, we would like you to indicate their books or articles they have written, and a summary of the main concepts they have developed. We also ask students to enter university professors and researchers from nations around the world; in fact, it is absolutely not assumed that the most interesting and valuable innovations come from only the usual top-ranking universities from around the world.

2. The MarkeThink "University," from gurus directly to you through YouTube and otheronline media.

The MarkeThink "University" is the YouTube University where the various gurus of thought have publicly shared their thoughts and ideas online. On this website, www.MarkeThink.guru, we have selected the most stimulating videos to increase your creative or thinking baggage and know-how. Here you will have direct access to their thinking and teaching, with no filters, the most essential part of their thinking. In fact, hearing Steve Jobs giving his famous speech at Stanford University is worth in itself an entire book; and directly hearing the words the founder of Swatch, Mr. Hayek, on how he has created a successful company, is material of immense value.

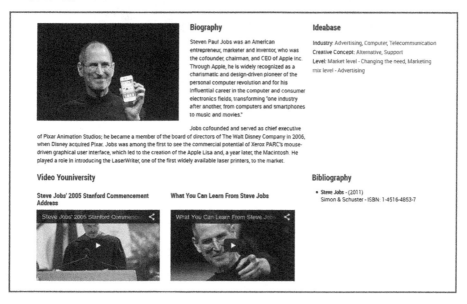

Figure 134: MarkeThinkers (www.markethink.guru)

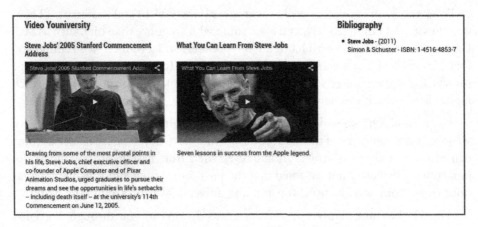

Figure 135: www.markethink.guru

Figure 136: www.markethink.guru

We invite you to come and see the videos of your favorite inspiring figures.

# CHAPTER 8 — MARKETHINK

## 8.2.1 Tools to enhance your thinking styles - The Ten CommandMents

Figure 137

There are already various tools available regarding the enhancement of thinking styles. It is true that in our book we state that every person has preferred thinking styles, but through various tools we can enrich our overall thinking style and approach and make it more flexible. In fact, to gain knowledge and increase our competence in the use of thinking styles, we can take into account three different levels of knowledge:

1. Acquisition of knowledge
2. Development or strengthening of thinking styles
3. Mastery

### 1. Acquisition of Knowledge: Knowing Oneself

The knowledge acquisition level can be developed through two main routes:
a. Testing
   We have developed a test that will allow you to assess from our point of view what your preferred thinking styles are. Through the test you will identify your strengths and your areas for improvement.
b. A 360-degree assessment
   The 360-degree assessment is a set of instruments designed for you to gain a broader knowledge and understanding of your approach to thinking. It is composed of:
   a. Test
   b. Ability tests
   c. Group dynamics
   d. Interview
   e. Feedback from employees/collaborators
   f. Feedback from leaders/bosses
   g. Feedback from peers
   h. Feedback from customers

In fact, we know that the use of predictive tools increases the percentage of accuracy to develop the actual presence of a thinking style. This plurality of tools and perspectives (boss-employee) also gives us the important keys for development.

At the present we have, on quite a few thinking styles, effective and proven tools such as the ones in the context of creativity, learning, and communication; for the other thinking styles, it will be interesting, instead, to strengthen and develop ad hoc tools in the future as we push the boundaries of our project further. This is the case for the motivation thinking style and how to increase motivation and emotional involvement of employees to make them more creative.

## 2. Development or Strengthening of Thinking Styles

To enhance a thinking style there are many macromethodologies that can be used to activate change:

1. Training
   a. Classroom training
   b. Outside the classroom
2. Online Coaching
3. Individual coaching
4. Group coaching
5. Consulting
6. Project learning

Of the ten thinking styles, we will present the ones that have solutions that have a proven effectiveness. For reasons of space, we present only the development solution of the learning thinking style; for the other nine development paths we invite you to visit our website: www.MarkeThink.guru.

# CHAPTER 8      MARKETHINK

## Learning Thinking Style Development

> *"The only sustainable competitive advantage is an organization's ability to learn faster than the competition."* - Peter Senge

One of the most important books of marketing is definitely *Marketing Management* by Philip Kotler, the latest edition, written with Keller. A well-trained university student, according to the statistics we have, reads about two hundred words per minute with an average of 30 percent of comprehension (this means that to fully understand the book he should read it three times). A book as important as *Marketing Management* can be divided into two learning objectives:

a. Understanding
b. Memory

Figure 138: Marketing Management Kotler-Keller

## a. Understanding

The time, in hours, for the complete understanding of the book *Marketing Management* is calculated as follows (the calculation is rounded down):
850 pages x 500 words per page = 425,000 words total / 200 average words per minute = 2,125 minutes = 35,41 hours (for the first reading with 30 percent of understanding/comprehension) x 3 = 100 hours, approximately, to read and fully understand the book.
Therefore, it would take at least one hundred hours to comprehensively read and gain from P. Kotler's valuable book *Marketing Management*.

## b. Memory

The strong mnemonic decay (unless you use specific techniques and apply what you read) means that within one month of having read something, you will have forgotten more than 90–95 percent of what you have read.

So it takes one hundred hours to read the book, and after one month you only remember 5 to 10 percent.

With the tool developed by Massimo Soriani Bellavista, "Read like Leonardo" (mentioned earlier on), you can enhance your reading skills and memory in a considerable manner:

Read like Leonardo for MarkeThinkers:
1. Doubled or trpled the speed of reading
2. Doubled the level of understanding
3. Improved, two- or threefold, memory/recall
4. Improved reprocessing of read material read

In this way, by increasing speed, comprehension, memory, and creative processing, you can improve your learning ability by five to ten times. Each and every MarkeThinker will gain great benefits by enhancing his ability of self-teaching.

### 3. Mastery

*"Marketing takes a day to learn. Unfortunately, it takes a lifetime to master." - Philip Kotler*

Mastery of a thinking style is when one has reached a level so high that they are able to teach it. A lot of practice and great successes are the secrets to becoming a good teacher.

## 8.2.2 Thinking Style Preference Test

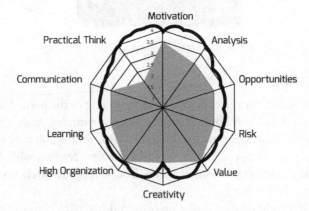

Figure 139: spider radar

After the "dominance of thought" test, which determines one's style of thinking, we will define a professional development plan to articulate over time. The test will determine your MarkeThinker profile and characteristics that serve as the foundation for the career-counseling phase.

# CHAPTER 8 — MARKETHINK

Tools applied to business-related matters

Figure 140: MarkheThink Tools (www.markethink.guru)

## 8.2.3 Meethink: The Tools for Successful and Efficient Meetings

Figure 141:
http://www.inc.com/laura-montini/infographic/the-ugly-truth-about-meetings.html

In the United States alone, companies spend $37 billion per year in unproductive meetings. The reasons are many - from poor planning to faulty management to uncreative meetings (if the group is not well trained, it kills creativity) to the mediocre organizations of the output at the end of the meeting.

Since meetings are important moments for the MarkeThinker, we developed a tool that allows you to have meetings where you maximize the potential contributions of all the participants. We have developed the Meethink, which is the set of tools developed to maximize any meeting's output.

## MeeThink Framework

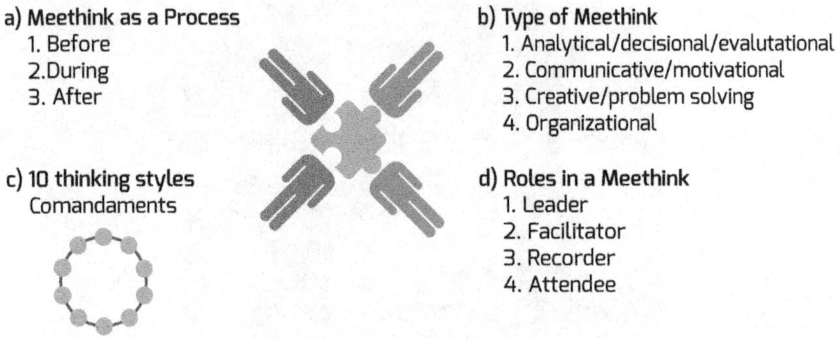

a) Meethink as a Process
  1. Before
  2. During
  3. After

b) Type of Meethink
  1. Analytical/decisional/evalutational
  2. Communicative/motivational
  3. Creative/problem solving
  4. Organizational

c) 10 thinking styles
  Comandaments

d) Roles in a Meethink
  1. Leader
  2. Facilitator
  3. Recorder
  4. Attendee

Figure 142: MeeThink Framework

Thanks to the set of tools that we developed, we are able to help you save up to 50 percent of the time spent in a meeting and increase the creative efficiency by at least 100 percent.

You may wonder how we can achieve such performance results in such a short period of time. We do this essentially through four paths:

a. The Meethink as a process
b. The types of Meethink
c. The thinking styles associated to the types of Meethink
d. The roles in Meethink

## a. The Meethink as a process essentially divides the meeting into its three basic stages: before, during, and after.

## b. The Types of Meethink

In a company, thousands of meetings take place during the year with diverse purposes such as brainstorming, coming up with new product ideas, training, managing change, exchanging information, analyzing the strategy or budget, and so on. Although there are a thousand different meeting classifications, there are basically only four main types of Meethink:

# CHAPTER 8 — MARKETHINK

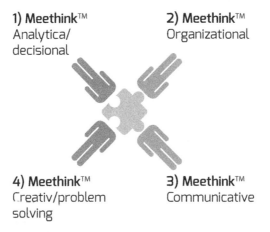

Figure 143: four types of MeeThink

### 1. The Analysis/Evaluation Meethink

During the Meethink the analysis of all the variables will be analyzed and it will be made a global picture of the business. Here we will analyze data (information), the positive aspects (value), and opportunities as well as the risks and motivations related to the business. We will then proceed with the definition of different creative focus points that will be the starting point of the creative Meethink phase.

### 2. Organizactional Meethink

The organizactional step is composed of two core phases. First we have the organizational and planning phase, where the marketing plan is defined, establishing a time line and the operational phases to be implemented. The second phase is putting the plan into action; here is where "practical thinking" comes into play and where the implementation of the plan takes place. The Organizactional Meethink is when everything is put into motion.

### 3. Communicational and Motivational Meethink

Communication is a fundamental element in the context of meetings. Communication can be of two types: informative or persuasive. In this context you also find the Meethink of a motivational type.

### 4. Creative Meethink

This is when the generation of ideas, in considerable quantities, takes place. We will use the various creativity techniques to increase the quality and quantity of ideas generated. Here we will strongly rely on the Ideabase as a stimulus for the selection of creative concepts that are most suitable for the case at hand.

There is a fifth type of Meethink that we will not explore but that is nonetheless important: the training/learning Meethink. In fact, when we are in a training/learning situations, we're in a kind of Meethink in itself, where the dominant thinking commandment is learning.

## c. The Meethink and the Thinking Styles

For each macro area of typology of Meethink, there is more than one functional thinking style. Below you will see an application of the four main types of Meethink:

### 1. Analytical-Decisional Meethink

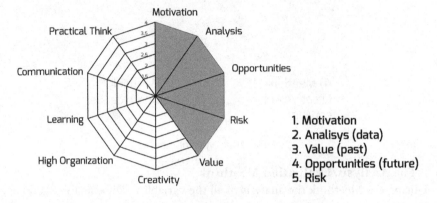

1. Motivation
2. Analisys (data)
3. Value (past)
4. Opportunities (future)
5. Risk

Figure 144

### 2. Organizational Meethink

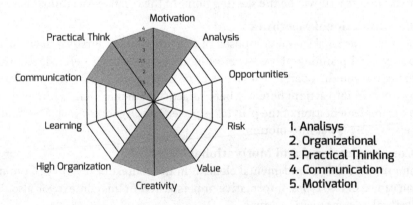

1. Analisys
2. Organizational
3. Practical Thinking
4. Communication
5. Motivation

Figure 145

## 3. Communicative/Informative Meethink

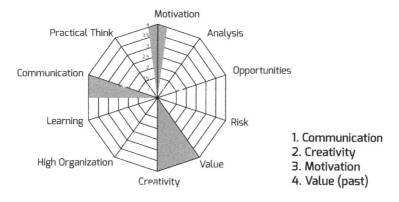

1. Communication
2. Creativity
3. Motivation
4. Value (past)

Figure 146

## 4. Creative/Problem Solving Meethink

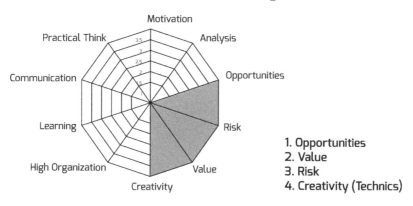

1. Opportunities
2. Value
3. Risk
4. Creativity (Technics)

Figure 147

### d. The Roles in a Meethink

Within a Meethink there are many roles that are performed; in the following lines we will present the four most important ones:

**1. The Leader**

The leader is one who will be the main beneficiary of the output of a Meethink. It can be the one who called for a meeting or the boss or whomever else.

**2. The Facilitator**

The facilitator is who controls and conducts the meeting; he or she is responsible for the lineup of the meeting (both in terms of planning and managing it) and is responsible for making sure that all the participants are focused on the thinking style and the purpose of the Meethink.

### 3. The Recorder

In Latin, they say "verba volant, scripta manent" ("spoken words fly away, written words remain"). We know that human memory has severe limitations; in fact, within twenty days of a meeting more than 90 percent of what has been said is forgotten. Precisely for this reason there has to be a person who transcribes/records all the activities that are important (today with the many technological tools it has become really easy to record/transcribe all contributions).

### 4. The Participants

The role of a participant is not simply to be a passive actor. In fact, many careers are put in play in the context of meetings; they are important moments of professional visibility. It is therefore fundamental to contribute in a meeting.

Clearly, there may be situations in which a person holds all four roles.

## 8.2.4 The Ideabase: A MarkeThink Tool

*"The secret to creativity is knowing how to hide your sources."* - A. Einstein

*"Picasso had a saying - 'good artists copy, great artists steal' - and we have always been shameless about stealing great ideas."* - Steve Jobs

For reasons of space, we will only briefly present the Ideabase; it is the most innovative tool that gives extra value to the MarkeThink process.

Our main objective is to find what the best marketing innovations available are in all industries and to extract the key creative concepts that lie behind them. The true value and the creative element appear as one uses and applies the concept behind any idea or innovation. With our MarkeThink Ideabase, we have collected the best marketing innovations and extracted the key creative concepts.

## 8.2.5 Benchmarking, "BenchMarkeThink," and the Ideabase

The concept of benchmarking is of interest to us because it is a powerful source of information, inspiration, and ideas, but above all because it enables learning and opens the door to new possibilities and opportunities. The act of tailoring, adapting, modifying, incorporating, and implementing the existing best practices, products, services, and creative concepts by innovating them rather than merely copying and/or imitating them is what we are aiming at with our "BenchMarkeThink" concept and the Ideabase of marketing.

Benchmarking is a management tool for comparing one's product, process, or service against the best practice. It's the systemic and continuous process of identifying, sharing, importing, and using the best-practices knowledge and know-how. But, it is also a structured and analytical approach to understanding and adapting these outstanding practices, ideas, and innovations to be competitive and improve performance and results.

In other words it is an improvement tool to discover what works best and how it is being achieved, even if it is taking place in a completely unrelated industry; it is a process that allows you to learn and improve, but also to find new ideas and opportunities, inspire and facilitate the realization of a vision, and to create global progress.

Benchmarking is part of an organization's learning strategies and practices, where the term "learning" is the antithesis of the term creativity - simply taking ideas from others usually reflects an uncreative behavior. But, as we have seen and will continue to see, it is not only about the ability to have good original ideas, but also about having the ability to adapt and implement them that actually leads to significant results and benefits (not only for the company but for industries, areas, etc.).

At the organizational level, benchmarking can be of three types:

1. Internal benchmarking means the best ideas that are within an organization are studied and disseminated to all internal contexts of the organization.
2. Competitive benchmarking focuses on the study and analysis of direct competitors' ideas and organizational processes.
3. Functional benchmarking provides the possibility of analyzing and copying the excellent ideas and processes that already exist in sectors and industries other than your own - ideas and processes that, with the appropriate adjustments and the correct adaptations, give way to the transfer of very valuable innovations and ideas that generate progress.

### 8.2.5.1 Benchmarking: Rearview Mirror Creativity

E. de Bono said: "The problem with the consultants is that they are best at analyzing but not on thinking or in constructing processes. In term of analysis they act as a mirror. If the mirror is a grand mirror and a good mirror and shows you things you are not aware of, it can help you very much to improve and filter the danger in term of benchmarking with other companies for instance. But that mirror cannot help you making something new. And as all consultants act as an identical mirror they propose the same thinking."[232]

Basd on this statement, consider the following from Benchmarking to Futuremarking: A significant Italian exponent of Senge's model of the study of the learning organization, V. D'amato (former president of AIADS[233]) says: "I think that the challenge of the future will not be to benchmark, but to 'futuremark': because the future cannot be predicted, there is only one way to foresee the future and that is to learn how to create it." The following defines what it is a business needs today: "Once it was enough to work hard on continuous improvement for 10, 20, 30 years and every 50 it was necessary to have a brilliant new innovative idea! That today is no longer possible! Now brilliant ideas are required every 6 to 12 months."[234]

Just like E. de Bono, we believe that benchmarking is a management practice

---

[232] Part of E. de Bono's answer to a question during an interview by Bertrand Villeret, editor in chief of Consulting NewsLine, for *Interview International*, May, 2006, during the AMCF meeting in Paris. You can read the full article at http://www.consultingnewsline.com/Info/Actu/International/Interview%20Edward%20de%20Bono%20(English).html.

[233] AIADS - Associazione Italiana di Analisi Dinamica dei Sistemi

[234] Translated from "Passione e Valori per l'Innovazione," an article by L. Angelini that appeared on *Espansione Magazine*, January, 2006. You can read the full article at http://www.thetis.it/images/stories/rassegnastampa/espansione-01-06.pdf.

that looks at and analyzes a company's past successes and therefore lacks creativity. By contrast, M. Soriani Bellavista has had the opportunity to investigate and use benchmarking methodology creatively, and this is what we are going to look at. In our case we are interested in all the advantages we can gain from the study of existing successes in other fields, sectors, and/or industries: by doing a systemic analysis of the best activities, practices, or products, we fully enter into the field of benchmarking.

The "functional" approach to benchmarking creates, in our opinion, an important link between creativity and learning. In fact, we could say that functional benchmarking is the type of benchmarking that requires the most creativity; this is the only type of benchmarking that gives way to innovation leaps that lead to significant competitive advantages. Therefore the creative use of benchmarking helps you avoid the serious risks of using this method as a lever for innovation: simply copying what worked in the past may not be effective enough to ensure future innovation. We could define benchmarking, with the exception of the functional approach, as "rearview" creativity.

The use of functional benchmarking combined with our MarkeThink process becomes a powerful tool for innovation. This is the concept that lies behind our Ideabase of marketing innovations.

In our process, after defining the focus, the 'Ideabase will be a source of inspiration to create new solutions and ideas. The Ideabase, for us, is a starting point for creating something new.

## 8.2.5.2 The MarkeThink Ideabase Explained

The Ideabase is a database of the best innovations in the field of marketing, and it is intended to be seen as an operative tool for marketing managers and entrepreneurs. In fact, most market innovations are born in other markets or businesses. The Ideabase's purpose is to catalog the best existing ideas from around the world and from any industry or market. The use of this tool, composed of our MarkeThink model and the Ideabase, it will be possible to accelerate and facilitate their application in business.

The Ideabase is inspired by models of lateral thinking "concept extraction" by Edward de Bono, the matrix of creative concepts of "TRIZ by Altshuller, the model of "lateral marketing" of Kotler / de Bes and the model of "CreActvity" by Massimo Soriani Bellavista.

We have developed (and are continuously updating) a website that makes it possible to navigate through the most important marketing innovations; you can find it at www.Markethink.guru. It's a website that focuses on our *MarkeThink* book, a project that consists of two main parts: the digital content of this book and the "Ideabase of Marketing." You can search through this database's four key areas, which can easily be cross-refereced and played around with. These are industry, creative concept, type of innovation, and marketing level.

These innovations are based on six different dimensions:

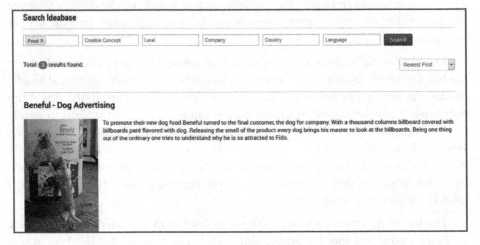

Figure 148: Six Dimensions of Ideabase (markethink.guru)

Figure 149: Ideabase by Creative Concept

### Marketing Level

Marketing level innovations are the result of altering the essential components that make up the market for a given product; they occur outside a given market. The basic product varies as well as the nature of the product or service needs creating a new market, instead of just capturing a part of it, by satisfying different needs, people, and/or situations. These innovations take place in the different levels of marketing: market, product, and mix. (We also consider price, place, and positioning.)

# CHAPTER 8 — MARKETHINK

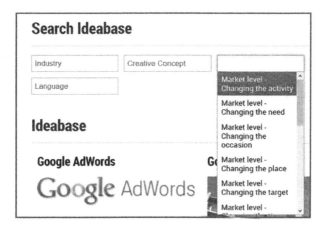

Figure 150: Ideabase by Marketing Level

1. The market level is about changing the following:
   a. Need - to cover another utility
   b. Target - going after a nonpotential target
   c. Time - finding new moments for buying, usage, or consumption of an offering
   d. Place - moving the product into new settings where the product cannot be present now
   e. Occasion - linking a product to an event where it is not considered now
   f. Activity - placing a product into experiences where there is no consideration for it but where other products are strongly positioned
2. The product level is about changing one of the main levels of a product: tangible product, packaging, brand attributes and usage, or purchase - removing or changing some of the elements or pieces.
3. The marketing mix level is about finding new marketing mix strategies for a product or finding new formulas; it concerns advertising, sales promotions, PR, personal selling, and direct marketing.

## How Does It Work?

To use the Ideabase, begin by selecting any of the dimensions of our Ideabase to launch a search; then a list of results containing them will appear (note that you can select more than one and cross-reference them as you please). Once you select the one that most interests you, you will find a brief description of the innovation with the key Ideabase information concerning the other three dimensions. Here is a visual example:

I selected Food Industry and this is the result found

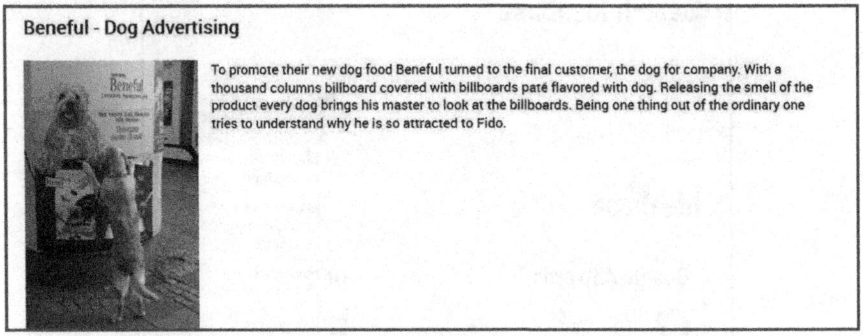

Beneful - Dog Advertising
To promote their new dog food Beneful turned to the final customer, the dog for company. With a thousand columns billboard covered with billboards paté flavored with dog. Releasing the smell of the product every dog brings his master to look at the billboards. Being one thing out of the ordinary one tries to understand why he is so attracted to Fido.

Figure 151: The Ideabase Search Result Page

Search
Italiano
English
French
Multilanguage
Newest First

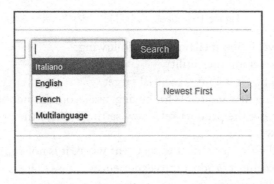

Figure 152: The Ideabase Language

You can see the product's description together with the industry it belongs to, the various creative concepts associated with it, the type of innovations it uses, and the marketing levels that are concerned wihtit. You can then click on any of them to find what other products fit this dimension of the Ideabase.

The website also provides a tag cloud, which allows you to search directly by the key word of your interest, or you can simply navigate the Ideabase by following and satisfying your curiosity.

A tag cloud is a stylized visual representation of the word content of a website; it shows the prominent key words used throughout the site. Visitors using the tag cloud can easily identify the most important key words and content, getting a general overview of the topics covered with one quick look. These terms are shown using font sizes and colors based on their importance and are hyperlinked to items associated with them.

# CHAPTER 8

## 8.3 Applications

We have developed a series of applications and solutions for our MarkeThink process and Ideabase and classified them along four main lenses.

### Lens One - Industry

| Industry - Application and Solutions | | |
|---|---|---|
| Advertising | Education | Music |
| Architecture | Energy | No Profit |
| Automotive | Fashion | Other |
| Banking | Finance | Public |
| Beauty | Food | Real Estate |
| Beverage | Food | Retail |
| Chemical | Government | Telecommunication |
| Cinema | Insurance | Television |
| Computer | Legal | Travel |
| Consulting | Literature | Utilities |
| Distribution | Manufacturing | Videogame |

Figure 153: MarkeThink Industry Application and Solutions

### Lens Two - Organizational Areas and Functions

| Organizational Function - Application and Solutions | |
|---|---|
| Marketing | Direct marketing |
| Sales | Retail marketing |
| Digital marketing | Social marketing |
| E-Learning | Green marketing |
| Media and technologies | Operations |
| Web marketing | ... |

Figure 154: MarkeThink Organizational Function Application and Solutions

## Lens Three - Mature Markets and Sectors

The third axis along which we are moving is concerned with the reconfiguration of mature sectors, such as the world of telecommunications, or the ones that are going through a reconfiguration caused by the introduction of new technologies.

## Lens Four - Public Sector and Governments

The fourth and last axis of specific applications focuses on the use of the MarkeThink strategies in the public sector and/or government. Here are a few examples, to be seen as guidelines:

Redesigning the future of a nation from a strategic entrepreneurial and managerial point of view. Specific places that could make good use of our solutions are those countries that based their successon a single resource (oil for example) and are looking to shape their future in a more creative and diverse way. Consider the cost associated with a strategic error such as the government's huge real estate investment in Dubai, which has cost more than $100 billion. We would design a master plan for the next twenty to thirty years that contains both creative aspects and practical for the nation that will develop and implement them. MarkeThink innovations have important functions for a Government, such as the tourism industry, and to consolidate and renew it.

Now all that is left for you to do is come visit us at www.Markethink.guru, let yourself be inspired, and get ready to innovate!

### The MarkeThinker Network Community

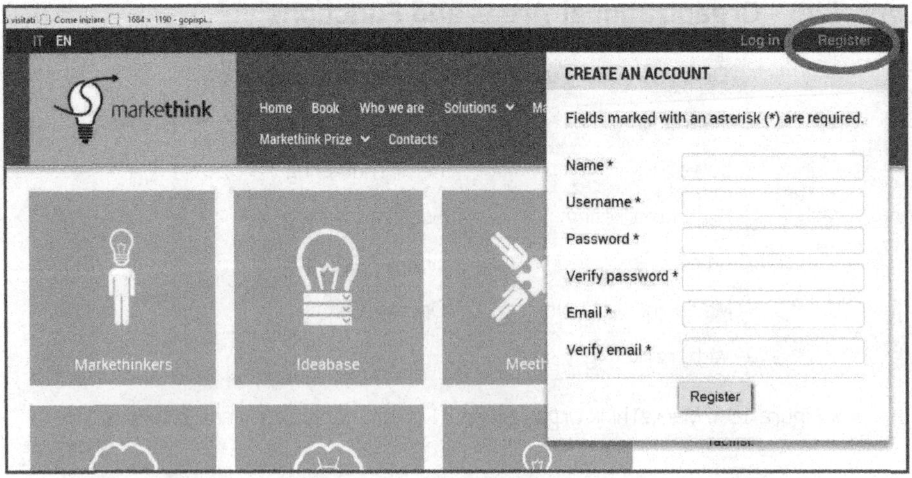

Figure 155

# CHAPTER 8 — MARKETHINK

As we have already explained in the book, MarkeThink is not a model but a metamodel. The richness of the metamodel is based on the multiplicity of models on which it is based and the contributions of great minds. In the pursuit of future enrichment we ask you to participate and contribute to it actively in order to learn by interacting with other MarkeThinkers and develop better know-how. Anyone pursuing a degree or master's thesis will be most welcome, and for those who want to report "best cases" for the Ideabase, we invite you to write a description of the case, support it with photos, videos, and links, and submit it to ideabase@MarkeThink.guru.

If you create a profile on www.MarkeThink.guru, you will gain access to a part of the additional material, audio/video, research, and creative minds. You will also be updated on the latest creativity news linked on the Ideabase.

The MarkeThink project, despite having had a maturation period of six years, is just at its beginning; we, the authors, are very excited and curious to see what will happen and how it will evolve over the next ten to twenty years…

If you want to send a suggestion or any ideas, please get in contact with me directly at : max@markethink.guru.

**Massimo Soriani Bellavista**

# Bibliography

Abbate, G. 2012: *Mind marketing: la dimensione invisibile del marketing*, Scuola di Palo Alto

Altshuller, G. 1997: *40 Principles: TRIZ Keys to Technical Innovation*, edited by Shulyak, L. and Rodman, S., Technical Innovation Center Publishers

Altshuller, G. 1997: *40 Principles: TRIZ Keys to Technical Innovation*, edited by Shulyak, L. and Rodman, S., Technical Innovation Center Publishers

Altshuller, G. 1999: *The Innovation Algorithm: TRIZ, Systematic Innovation and Technical Creativity*, translated and edited by Shulyak, L. and Rodman, S., Technical Innovation Center Publishers

Altshuller, G. 1999: *The Innovation Algorithm: TRIZ, Systematic Innovation and Technical Creativity*, translated and edited by Shulyak, L. and Rodman, S., Technical Innovation Center Publishers

Anderson, C. 2008: *The Long Tail: Why the Future of Business is Selling Less of More*, Hyperion Books

Andreini, P. 2004: *Qualità certificazione competitività: La norma ISO 9001 (Vision 2000) e la guida ISO 9004: la nuova frontiera della qualità*, Hoepli Milano, p. 1

Ashok, J. 2009–2010: *Principles of Marketing*, V. K. Global Publications, p. 89

Barron, F. 1988: *Putting Creativity to Work*, in Sternberg, R. J. (ed.): *The Nature of Creativity: Contemporary Psychological Perspectives*, Cambridge University Press

Blackshaw, P. 2008: *Satisfied Customers Tell Three Friends, Angry Customers Tell 3,000: Running a Business in Today's Consumer-Driven World*, Doubleday

Bloom, B. 1995: *Planned Short-Term Therapy*, Allyn & Bacon

Boatwright, P. and Cagan, J. 2010: *Built to Love: Creating Products That Captivate Customers*, Berrett-Koehler Publishers

Bornstein, D. 2004: *How to Change the World: Social Entrepreneurs and the Power of New Ideas*, Oxford University Press

Bucklin, L. P. 1966: *A Theory of Distribution Channel Structure*, Institute of Business and Economic Research, University of California

Buzan, T. 1974: *Use Your Head*, BBC Active - Pearson Education

Cade, B. and O'Hanlon, W. H. 1993: *A Brief Guide to Brief Therapy*, W. W. Norton & Company

Cant, M. C.; Strydom, J. W.; and Jooste, C.J. 2009: *Marketing Management*, 5th Ed., Juta and Co. Ltd.

Chandler, A. D. 1977: *The Visible Hand: The Managerial Revolution in American Business*, Belknap Press

Chandler, A. D. 1990: *Scale and Scope: The Dynamics of Industrial Capitalism*, Belknap Press

Chua, C. K.; Leong, K. F; and Lim, C. S. 2003: *Rapid Prototyping Principles and Applications,* 2nd ed., World Scientific Publisher

Davidson, H.; Keegan, W. J.; and Brill, E. A. 2004: *Offensive Marketing: An Action Guide to Gaining Competitive Advantage,* Elsevier Butterworth-Heinemann

de Bono, E. 1969: *The Mechanism of Mind,* Simon & Schuster

de Bono, E. 1985: *Six Hats: An Essential Approach to Business Management,* Little, Brown and Company

de Bono, E. 1990: *Lateral Thinking: A Textbook of Creativity,* Penguin Books, London

de Bono, E. 1990: *Lateral Thinking: A Textbook of Creativity,* Penguin Books, London

de Bono, E. 1992: *Serious Creativity: Using the Power of Lateral Thinking to Create New Ideas,* Harper Business

de Bono, E. 1993: *Surpetition Creating Value Monopolies When Everyone Else Is Merely Competing,* Harper Business

de Bono, E. 2005: *The Six Value Medals,* Random House UK

de Bono, E. 2005: *The Six Value Medals,* Random House UK

de Bono, E. 2009: *Think! Before It's Too Late,* Vermillon - Random House Group, London

De Shazer, S. 1982: *Patterns of Brief Family Therapy: An Ecosystemic Approach,* The Guilford Press

De Shazer, S. 1982: *Some Conceptual Distinctions Are More Useful than Others.* Family Process, 21

De Shazer, S. 1984: *The Death of Resistance,* Family Process 23

De Shazer, S. 1985: *Keys to Solution in Brief Therapy,* W. W. Norton & Company

De Shazer, S. 1988: *Clues: Investigating Solutions in Brief Therapy,* W. W. Norton & Company

De Shazer, S. 1988: *Utilization: The Foundation of Solutions,* in Zeig, J. K. and Lankton, S. R. (eds.) *Developing Ericksonian Therapy: State of the Art,* Brunner/Mazel

Downes, L. and Chunka, M. 1998: *Unleashing the Killer App: Digital Strategies for Market Dominance,* Harvard Business School Press

Dru, J. M. 1997: *Disruption: Overturning Conventions and Shaking up the Marketplace,* Wiley

Drucker, P. 1999: *Management Challenges for the 21st Century,* Butterworth-Heinemann

Drucker, P. 2003: *The New Realities in Government and Politics, in Economics and Business, in Society and World View,* Transaction Publishers

Drucker, P. 2007: *Essential Drucker,* revised ed., A Classic Drucker Collection, Butterworth Heinemann - Eslevier

Drucker, P. 2007: *Innovation and Entrepreneurship: Practice and Principles*, revised ed. A Classic Drucker Collection, Butterworth Heinemann - Eslevier

Drucker, P. 2007: *The Practice of Management*, Butterworth-Heinemann

Drucker, P. 2008: *The 5 Most Important Questions You Will Ever Ask About Your Organization*, Wiley

Drucker, P. F. and Beatty, J. 1998: *The World According to Peter Drucker*, Free Press - Simon & Schuster

Dunphy, D. and Benveniste, J. 2000: *Sustainability: The Corporate Challenge of the 21st Century*, Allen & Unwin, for M. Diesendorf: *Sustainability and Sustainable Development*

Fisk, P. 2012: *Marketing Genius*, Capstone

Ford, H. 1922: *My Life and Work*, Doubleday-Page and Co., Chapter IV pp. 71–72

Fourastié, J. 1979 : *Les Trente Glorieuses, ou la révolution invisible de 1946 à 1975 (The Glorious Thirty, or the Invisible Revolution from 1946–1975)*, Fayard Paris

Frisk, P. 2006: *Marketing Genius*, Capstone Publishing, a John Wiley & Sons Company

Galbraith, J. K. 1958: *The Affluent Society*, Houghton Mifflin

Galbraith, J. K. 1979: *The Nature of Mass Poverty*, Harvard University Press

Godin, S. 2000: *Unleashing the Ideavirus: Stop Marketing AT People! Turn Your Ideas into Epidemics by Helping Your Customers Do the Marketing for You*, DoYouZoom (e-book and print)

Godin, S. 2002: *Survival Is Not Enough: Zooming, Evolution, and the Future of Your Company*, Free Press

Godin, S. 2004: *Free Prize Inside! The Next Big Marketing Idea*, Portfolio

Godin, S. 2005: *All Marketers Are Liars: The Power of Telling Authentic Stories in a Low-Trust World*, Portfolio

Godin, S. 2005: *Purple Cow: Transform Your Business by Being Remarkable*, Penguin Books, London

Godin, S. 2005: *Purple Cow: Transform Your Business by Being Remarkable*, Penguin Books, London

Godin, S. 2006: *Small Is the New Big: and 193 Other Riffs, Rants, and Remarkable Business Ideas*, Portfolio Hardcover

Godin, S. 2007: *Permission Marketing: Turning Strangers into Friends and Friends into Customers*, 3rd ed., Pocket Books - Simon & Schuster, London

Godin, S. 2007: *Permission Marketing: Turning Strangers into Friends and Friends into Customers*, 3rd ed., Pocket Books - Simon & Schuster, London

Godin, S. 2007: *Permission Marketing: Turning Strangers into Friends and Friends into Customers*, 3rd ed., Pocket Books - Simon & Schuster, London

Godin, S. 2008: *Meatball Sundae: Is Your Marketing out of Sync?* Portfolio Hardcover

# BIBLIOGRAPHY — MARKETHINK

Godin, S. 2008: *Tribes: We Need You to Lead Us*, Portfolio Hardcover

Godin, S. 2010: *Linchpin: Are You Indispensable?* Penguin Group US

Godin, S. 2011: *Poke the Box*, the Domino Project

Godin, S. 2011: *We Are All Weird*, the Domino Project

Godin, S. 2012: *The Icarus Deception: How High Will You Fly?* Portfolio Hardcover

Godin, S. 2012: *Whatcha Gonna Do with That Duck? And Other Provocations*, Portfolio Hardcover

Goldsmith, R. 2002: *Viral Marketing: Get Your Audience to Do Your Marketing for You*, Pearson Education - Prentice Hall Business

Guilford, J. P. 1967: *The Nature of Human Intelligence*, McGraw Hill

Haley, J. 1963: *Strategies of Psychotherapy*, Grune and Stratton

Hamel, G. and Breen, B. 2007: *The Future of Management*, Harvard Business Press

Hamel, G. and Prahalad, C. K. 1996: *Competing for the Future*, Harvard Business School Press, Boston

Hart, S. L. 2005: *Capitalism at the Crossroads: Aligning Business, Earth, and Humanity*, Wharton School Publishers-Pearson Prentice Hall, for C. K. Prahalad

Henderson, D. R. 1993: *The Fortune Encyclopedia of Economics*, Time Warner Books, for P. Romer, *Economic Growth*

Hermann Simon, Danilo Zatta 2006: *Strategie di pricing. Come migliorare la redditività aziendale*, Hoepli, Italia

Heskett, J. L.; Sasser, W. E. Jr.; and Schlesinger, L. A. 1997: *The Service Profit Chain: How Leading Companies Link Profit and Growth to Loyalty, Satisfaction, and Value*, Simon & Schuster, New York

Hill, N. 2013: *Think and Grow Rich*, Tribeca Books - Secrets to Success

Kahneman, D. 2011: *Thinking, Fast and Slow*, Farrar Straus and Giroux, New York

Kaplan, R. S. and Norton, D. P. 1996: *The Balanced Scorecard: Translating Strategy into Action*, Harvard Business Press

Karni, R. and Kaner, M.: *An Engineering Tool for Conceptual Design of Service Systems*, in Spath, D. and Fähnrich, K. P. 2006: *Advances in Service Innovation*, Springer, p. 22

Kawasaki, G. and Moreno, M. 1999: *Rules for Revolutionaries: The Capitalist Manifesto for Creating New Products and Services*, HarperCollins

Kelly, K. 1995: *Out of Control: The New Biology of Machines, Social Systems, and the Economic World*, Perseus Books

Kelly, K. 1999: *New Rules for the New Economy: 10 Radical Strategies for a Connected World*, Penguin

Khatena, J. 1978: *The Creatively Gifted Child: Suggestions for Parents and Teachers*, Vantage Press

Koberg, D. and Bagnall, J. 1981: *The Universal Traveler: A Soft-Systems Guide to Creativity, Problem-Solving, and the Process of Reaching Goals*, William Kaufman

Kotler P.,; Lilien, G.; and Moorthy, K. S. 1992: *Marketing Models*, revised ed., Prentice-Hall

Kotler, P. 1972: *Marketing Decision Making: A Model-Building Approach*, Prentice-Hall

Kotler, P. 1972: *Marketing Management: Analysis, Planning, and Control*, 2nd ed., Prentice Hall

Kotler, P. 2001: *Kotler on Marketing: How to Create, Win and Dominate Markets*, Free Press - Simon & Schuster, Great Britain

Kotler, P. 2001: *Kotler on Marketing: How to Create, Win and Dominate Markets*, Free Press - Simon & Schuster, Great Britain

Kotler, P. 2003: *Marketing Insights from A to Z: 80 Concepts Every Manager Needs to Know*, Wiley - John Wiley & Sons, New Jersey

Kotler, P. 2003: *Marketing Insights from A to Z: 80 Concepts Every Manager Needs to Know*, Wiley - John Wiley & Sons, New Jersey

Kotler, P. 2003: *Marketing Insights from A to Z: 80 Concepts Every Manager Needs to Know*, Wiley - John Wiley & Sons, New Jersey

Kotler, P. 2004: *Ten Deadly Marketing Sins: Signs and Solutions*, Wiley

Kotler, P. 2005: *According to Kotler: The World's Foremost Authority on Marketing Answers Your Questions*, AMACOM

Kotler, P. 2008: *FAQ's on Marketing Answered by the Guru of Marketing Philip Kotler*, European ed., Marshall Cavendish, London

Kotler, P. 2008: *FAQ's on Marketing Answered by the Guru of Marketing Philip Kotler*, European ed., Marshall Cavendish, London

Kotler, P. 2009: *A Framework for Marketing Management*, Prentice-Hall

Kotler, P. and Caslione, J. A. 2009: *Chaotics: The Business of Managing and Marketing in the Age of Turbulence*, AMACOM Publishing

Kotler, P. and Keller, K. 2009: *Marketing Management*, 13th ed., Prentice Hall - Pearson International

Kotler, P. and Keller, K. 2009: *Marketing Management*, 13th ed., Prentice Hall - Pearson International

Kotler, P. and Keller, K. 2009: *Marketing Management*, 13th ed., Prentice Hall - Pearson International

Kotler, P. and Lee, N. 2005: *Corporate Social Responsibility: Doing the Most Good for Your Company and Your Cause*, Wiley

Kotler, P. and Trias de Bes, F. 2003: *Lateral Marketing: New Techniques for Finding Breakthrough Ideas*, Wiley - John Wiley & Sons, New Jersey

## BIBLIOGRAPHY — MARKETHINK

Kotler, P. and Trias de Bes, F. 2003: *Lateral Marketing: New Techniques for Finding Breakthrough Ideas*, Wiley - John Wiley & Sons, New Jersey

Kotler, P. and Trias de Bes, F. 2011: *Winning at Innovation: The A-to-F Model*, Palgrave Macmillan

Kotler, P.; Berger, R.; and Bickhoff, N. 2010: *The Quintessence of Strategic Management*, Springer

Kotler, P.; Jain, D.; and Maesincee, S. 2002: *Marketing Moves: A New Approach to Profits, Growth, and Renewal*, Harvard Business School

Kotler, P.; Kartajaya, H.; and Setiawan, I. 2010: *Marketing 3.0: From Products to Customers to the Human Spirit*, John Wiley and Sons, Inc., New Jersey

Kotler, P.; Lilien, G.; and Moorthy K. S. 1992: *Marketing Models*, revised ed., Prentice-Hall

Kuhn, T. S. 1996: *The Structure of Scientific Revolutions*, University of Chicago Press

Lauterborn, R. F.; Schultz, D. E.; and Tannenbaum, S. I. 1993: *Integrated Marketing Communication: Putting It Together and Making It Work*, McGraw Hill Professional

Levine, R.; Locke, C.; Searls, D.; and Weinberger, D. 2000: *The Cluetrain Manifesto: The End of Business as Usual*, Perseus Books Group

Levinson, J. C. 2010: *Guerrilla Marketing: Easy and Inexpensive Strategies for Making Big Profits from Your Small Business*, Piatkus, London

Lindstrom, M. 2009: *Buyology: How Everything We Believe about Why We Buy Is Wrong*, RH Business Books - Random House, London

Madanes, C. 1990: *Sex, Love, and Violence: Strategies for Transformation*, W. W. Norton & Company

Madanes, C. with Keim, J. and Smelser, D. 1995: *The Violence of Men: New Techniques for Working with Abusive Families*, Jossey-Bass

Malhotra, N. K. 2004: *Marketing Research: An Applied Orientation*, 4th ed., Prentice-Hall International

Mandell, M. I. and Rosenberg, L. J. 1981: *Marketing*, 2nd Ed., Prentice-Hall India

McCarthy, E. J. 1960: *Basic Marketing: A Managerial Approach*, Richard D. Irwin

McDonald, M. 2007: *Marketing Plans: How to Prepare Them, How to Use Them*, 6th ed., Butterworth-Heinemann

McDonough, W. and Braungart, M. 2002: *Cradle to Cradle: Remaking the Way We Make Things*, North Point Press

McQuarrie, E. 2005: *The Market Research Toolbox: A Concise Guide for Beginners*, 2nd ed., Sage Publications

Meadows, D. H.; Meadows, D. L.; Randers, J.; and Behrens III, W. W. 1972: *The Limits to Growth*, University Books

Moss, L. T. and Atre, S. 2003: *Business Intelligence Roadmap: The Complete Project Lifecycle for Decision-Support Applications*, Addison-Wesley Professional

Nanus, B. 1992: *Visionary Leadership: Creating a Compelling Sense of Direction for Your Organization*, Jossey-Bass Publishers

Nardone G. *1995: Brief Strategic Therapy of Phobic Disorders - A Model of Therapy and Evaluation Research in Propagations, J. H. Weakland - W. A. Ray,* The Haworth Press Inc., New York

Nardone, G. 1991: *Suggestione + Ristrutturazione = Cambiamento. L'approccio strategico e costruttivista alla terapia breve*, Giuffre Milano

Nardone, G. 1993: *Paura, Panico, Fobie*, Ponte alle Grazie Firenze

Nardone, G. 1995: *Brief Strategic Therapy of Phobic Disorders: A Model of Therapy and Evaluation Research*, in Weakland, J. H. and Ray, W. A. (eds.) op. cit., cap. 4

Nardone, G. 1996: *Brief Strategic Solution-Oriented-Therapy of Phobic and Obsessive Disorders*, Aronson, New Jersey, USA

Nardone, G. 2003: *Advanced Brief Strategic Therapy - Knowing by Changing*, Brief Strategic and Systemic Therapy European Review

Nardone, G. 2003: *Cavalcare la propria tigre (To Ride One's Inner Tiger)*, Ponte alle Grazie

Nardone, G. 2003: *Historic Notes on Brief Strategic Therapy*, Brief Strategic and Systemic Therapy European Review

Nardone, G. 2004: *Ethical Highlight: Constructive Ethical Principles.* In J. Sommers-Flanagan & R. Sommers Flanagan, *Theories of Counseling and Psychotherapy: A Practical Approach*, John Wiley & Sons

Nardone, G. and Fiorenza, A. 1995: *L'intervento strategico nei contesti educativi. Comunicazione e problem-solving per i problemi scolastici*, Giuffrè Milano

Nardone, G. and Portelli, C. 2005: *Knowing through Changing - The Evolution of Brief Strategic Therapy*, Crown House Publishing, Carmarthen, UK

Nardone, G. and Portelli, C. 2005: *When the Diagnosis "Invents" the Illness*, Emerald Group Publishing Limited

Nardone, G. and Portelli, C. 2007: *Caught in the Middle of a Double-Bind: The Application of Nonordinary Logic to Therapy*, Emerald Group Publishing Limited

Nardone, G. and Salvini, A. 2007: *The Strategic Dialogue: Rendering the Diagnostic Interview a Real Therapeutic Intervention*, Karnac London

Nardone, G. and Watzlawick, P. 1990: *L'arte del cambiamento: manuale di terapia strategica e ipnoterapia senza trance*, Ponte alle Grazie Firenze (En. Tr. The Art of Change: Strategic Therapy and Hypnotherapy without Trance, Jossey-Bass, San Francisco)

Nardone, G. and Watzlawick, P. 1990: *The Art of Change: Strategic Therapy and Hypnotherapy without Trance*, Jossey - Bass, San Francisco, CA, USA

Nardone, G. and Watzlawick, P. 1997: *Terapia breve strategica,* Raffaello Cortina Milano

Nardone, G. and Watzlawick, P. 2005: *Brief Strategic Therapy - Philosophy, Techniques, and Research,* Jason Aronson, a division of Rowman & Littlefield Publishers Inc., MD, USA

Nardone, G.; Loriedo, C. and Zeig, J. 2011: *Transforming Ericksonian - Methods 21st Century Visions,* The Milton H. Erickson Foundation Press, Phoenix

Nardone, G.; Milanese, R.; Mariotti, R.; and Fiorenza, A. 2000: *La terapia dell'azienda malata,* Ponte alle Grazie Milano

Nardone, G.; Verbitz, T.; and Milanese, R. 1999; *Le prigioni del cibo - Vomiting Anoressia Bulimia: la terapia in tempi brevi,* Ponte alle Grazie Milano

Normann, R. 2001: *Service Management: Strategy and Leadership in Service Business,* 3rd ed., Wiley

Norris, B. 2008: *The Creative Sales and Marketing Manual,* B. Norris Books - 53 Year Publishing (e-Book)

Omer, H. 1992: *From the One True to the Infinity of Constructed Ones,* Psychotherapy, 29

Omer, H. 1994: *Critical Interventions in Psychotherapy,* Norton

Osborn, A. 1953: *Applied Imagination: Principles and Procedures of Creative Problem Solving,* Charles Scribner's Sons

Osborn, A. F. 1942: *How to "Think Up,"* McGraw Hill, New York-London

Osborn, A. F. 1963: *Applied Imagination: Principles and Procedures of Creative Problem Solving,* 3rd ed., Charles Scribner's Son

Pearl, J. 1983: *Heuristics: Intelligent Search Strategies for Computer Problem Solving,* Addison-Wesley

Peppers, D. and Rogers, M. 1993: *The One to One Future: Building Relationships One Customer at a Time,* Doubleday Currency Books, New York

Peppers, D. and Rogers, M. 1993: *The One to One Future: Building Relationships One Customer at a Time,* Doubleday Currency Books

Perkins, D. 1981: *The Mind's Best Work,* Harvard University Press

Prahalad, C. K. 2005: *The Fortune at the Bottom of the Pyramid,* Wharton School Publishing

Prahalad, C. K. and Ramaswamy, V. 2004: *The Future of Competition: Co-creating Unique Value with Customers,* Harvard Business School

Prato Previde, R.; Milanese, R.; and Nardone, M. C. 2012: *L'azienda vincente: Migliorare il presente, inventare il futuro: problem solving per le organizzazioni,* Ponte alle Grazie Milano

Prestowitz, C. V. 2005: *Three Billion New Capitalists: The Great Shift of Wealth and Power to the East,* Basic Books

R. J. Sternberg, *Successful Intelligence: How Practical and Creative Intelligence Determine Success in Life*, Plume Book, 1996

Ries, A. and Trout, J. 2005: *Marketing Warfare*, McGraw Hill Professional, p. 2

Roberts, K. 2004: *Lovemarks: The Future Beyond Brands*, PowerHouse Books

Roberts, K. 2006: *The Lovemarks Effect: Winning in the Consumer Revolution*, PowerHouse Books

Rossman, J. 1931: *The Psychology of the Inventor: A Study of the Patentee*, Inventors Publishing Company

Sachs, J. D. 2005: *The End of Poverty: Economic Possibilities for Our Time*, Penguin Press

Schmitt, B. H. 1999: *Experiential Marketing: How to Get Customers to Sense, Feel, Think, Act, and Relate to Your Company and Brands*, Free Press

Schmitt, B. H. 2003: *Customer Experience Management: A Revolutionary Approach to Connecting with Your Customers*, John Wiley & Sons

Schumpeter, J. 1942: *Capitalism, Socialism and Democracy*, Harper and Brothers, New York

Schumpeter, J. 1952: *Can Capitalism Survive?*, Harper and Row

Schumpeter, J. 1954: *History of Economic Analysis*, Oxford University Press

Scott, W. G. 1991: *Innovazione e mercato nell'industria automobilistica*, Isedi Milano

Scott, W. G. 1997: *Marketing e Competizione*, Vita e Pensiero Milano

Stanton, W. J. 1983: *Fundamentals of Marketing*, 6th ed., McGraw Hill, p. 4, p. 66

Steinhoff, B. 1979: *The World of Business*, McGraw Hill, p. 113

Sternberg, R. J. 1984: *Beyond IQ: A Triarchic Theory of Human Intelligence*, Cambridge University Press

Sullivan, G. R. and Harper, M. V. 1996: *Hope Is Not a Method: What Business Leaders Can Learn from America's Army*, Times Books-Random House

The Report of Brundtland Commission (World Commission on Environment and Development (WCED)), 1987, Oxford University Press

Trout, J. and Ries, A. 1981: *Positioning: The Battle for Your Mind*, McGraw Hill

Tucker, R. B. 2008: *Driving Growth through Innovation: How Leading Firms Are Transforming Their Futures*, 2nd ed., Berrett-Koehler

Unknown, *The 36 Chinese Stratagems: The Secret Art of War*

Von Oech, R. 1990: *A Whack on the Side of the Head: How You Can Be More Creative*, Grand Central Publishing

Wallas, G. 1926: *The Art of Thought*, Harcourt Brace

Watzlawick, P. 2009: *Insight May Cause Blindness - And Other Essays*, Zeig, Tucker & Theisen, Inc., Phoenix, AZ, USA

Watzlawick, P. and Nardone, G. 2000: *Le strategie de La Terapia Breve*, Edition du Seuil

# BIBLIOGRAPHY

Watzlawick, P.; Weakland, J. H.; and Fisch, R. 1974; *Change: Principles of Problem Formation and Problem Resolution,* W.W. Norton & Company

Weakland, J. H.; Fisch, R.; Watzlawick, P.; and Bodin, A. M.: *Brief Therapy: Focused Problem Resolution,* Family Process, 13 (2)

Wilhelm, R. and Baynes, C. F. 1967: *I Ching or Book of Changes,* 3rd ed., Princeton University Press

Wycoff, J. 1991: *Mindmapping: Your Personal Guide to Exploring Creativity and Problem-Solving,* Brekley Books

---

[1] Oliviero Toscani was a creative director with "carte blanche" for Benetton from 1982 to 2000. During his time he created much controversy because he was shocking and blunt; these advertising campaigns were also institutional rather than on product; they were more of a brand statement.

[2] Alexander Reidl is the former marketing director of Volvo Cars Middle East found at http://www.guerrillaonline.com/cs/Guerrilla-Marketing-Principles-54.htm

[3] Retrieved from the Oxford Dictionary online http://www.oxforddictionaries.com/view/entry/m_en_gb0243670#m_en_gb0243670

Made in the USA
Columbia, SC
07 October 2023